CRAFTING STRATEGY

The rationalist approach to strategizing emphasizes analytical and convergent thinking. Without denying the importance of this approach, this book argues that strategists must learn to complement it with a more creative approach to strategizing that emphasizes synthetic and divergent ways of thinking. The theoretical underpinnings of this approach include embodied realism, interpretivism, practice theory, theory of play, design thinking, as well as discursive approaches such as metaphorical analysis, narrative analysis, dialogical analysis and hermeneutics. The book includes in-depth discussions of these theories and shows how they can be put into practice by presenting detailed analyses of embodied metaphors built by groups of agents with step-by-step explanations of how this process can be implemented and facilitated. The link between theory and practice is further supported by the inclusion of several vignettes that describe how this approach has been successfully employed in a number of organizations, including BASF and UNICEF.

LOIZOS HERACLEOUS is Professor of Strategy and Organization and head of the Strategy Group at Warwick Business School. He is also an associate fellow of Green Templeton College and the Saïd Business School at Oxford University.

CLAUS D. JACOBS is Swiss National Science Foundation Professor of Strategy at the Institute of Management, University of St. Gallen, Switzerland. He is also a visiting fellow of Saïd Business School at Oxford University and a fellow of the Daimler Benz Foundation.

Crafting Strategy

Embodied Metaphors In Practice

Loizos Heracleous
and
Claus D. Jacobs

CAMBRIDGE
UNIVERSITY PRESS

CAMBRIDGE UNIVERSITY PRESS
Cambridge, New York, Melbourne, Madrid, Cape Town,
Singapore, São Paulo, Delhi, Mexico City

Cambridge University Press
The Edinburgh Building, Cambridge CB2 8RU, UK

Published in the United States of America by Cambridge University Press, New York

www.cambridge.org
Information on this title: www.cambridge.org/9780521116558

First published 2011
Reprinted 2012

Printed at Print on Demand, World Wide, UK

A catalogue record for this publication is available from the British Library

Library of Congress Cataloguing in Publication data
Heracleous, Loizos Th.
Crafting strategy : embodied metaphors in practice / Loizos Heracleous
and Claus D. Jacobs.
p.   cm.
Includes bibliographical references and index.
ISBN 978-0-521-11655-8 (hardback)
1.   Strategic planning.   2.   Metaphor – Social aspects.   3.   Creative thinking.
4.   Organizational behavior.   I. Jacobs, Claus D.   II. Title.
HD30.28.H4767   2011
658.4′092–dc22
2011014107

ISBN 978-0-521-11655-8 Hardback

To everyone who took the journey of ideas with me
Loizos Heracleous

To Manuela, Lili & Oscar
Claus Jacobs

Contents

List of figures	*page* ix	
List of tables	xi	
Preface	xv	
Acknowledgments	xxi	
Vignette A: BASF PerForm	1	
1 Strategizing out of the box	4	
Vignette B: UNICEF	17	
2 Metaphor and embodied realism	21	
3 Analyzing embodied metaphors as an interpretive, hermeneutic endeavor	42	
Vignette C: Project Voltigo	61	
4 Crafting strategy as a practice of embodied recursive enactment	65	
5 Play, analogical reasoning and dialogue in the crafting of strategy	90	
Vignette D: Hephata Foundation	115	
6 Understanding organizations through embodied metaphors	121	

7   Sensemaking through embodied metaphors in
     organization development   156

Vignette E: Privatbank IHAG Zürich AG   173
8   Strategy as a crafting practice   177

Vignette F: World Vision New Zealand   204
9   The process of strategizing through crafting embodied
     metaphors   209

Glossary   225
Index   233

Figures

1   Outline of the structure of the book   *page* xiii
A.1 Embodied metaphor of BASF   2
B.1 An embodied metaphor of UNICEF Germany's head office
    organizational structure   18
C.1 Embodied metaphor from Voltigo workshop   63
C.2 Embodied metaphor and context from Voltigo workshop   63
4.1 The concept of crafting as strategic practice   82
4.2 Crafting strategy in Orange – synopsis of case episodes   85
5.1 Process model of analogical reasoning   98
5.2 Crafting strategy at PackCo   101
5.3 Analogical reasoning at PackCo   102
5.4 Diagnostic and generative moments of dialogue   106
5.5 Diagnostic and generative moments at SwissBank   110
D.1 Embodied metaphor 1 from Hephata   116
D.2 Embodied metaphor 2 from Hephata   117
D.3 Embodied metaphor 3 from Hephata   118
D.4 Embodied metaphor 4 from Hephata   119
7.1 Metaphors in OD   160
7.2 Example 1 of embodied metaphor of "I know my
    banker" concept   162

7.3 Example 2 of embodied metaphor "I know my
banker" concept   163

E.1 Embodied metaphors of private bankers at
Privatbank IHAG Zürich   174

8.1 Grand metaphor overview: strategy-making as
a journey   189

8.2 Constituent metaphors 1 and 2: troop of disoriented
animals and combustion engine   190

8.3 Constituent metaphors 3 and 4: gearing wheels and
safari park   191

F.1 Embodied metaphors at World Vision New Zealand   205

9.1 Strategic thinking and strategic planning as
complementary processes   211

Tables

1.1	Two modes of strategizing juxtaposed in terms of key stages of design thinking	page 10
2.1	Three perspectives on metaphor	36
3.1	Interpretive theory and hermeneutics	57
5.1	Concepts and practices of crafting strategy	91
5.2	Technologies of reason and foolishness	93
6.1	Process steps of embodied metaphorical mappings	129
6.2	Examples of initial mappings	131
6.3	Examples of relational mappings	132
6.4	Examples of integrative mappings	134
6.5	Outline of three analytical moments	136
6.6	Outline of source domains, target domains and emergent meaning in grand and constituent metaphors	143
6.7	Organizational dimensions manifested in embodied metaphors	149
7.1	Two perspectives on metaphors in OD	160
7.2	Embodied metaphors in OD: The SwissBank case	166
8.1	Target domains, source domains and emergent meanings in the metaphors of the strategy development team	187

9.1 Occasions and examples for using embodied
    metaphorical mapping   212
9.2 Guiding principles for designing embodied metaphor
    interventions   220

Preparing the ground	Theoretical antecedents	Applications
	Metaphor and embodied realism (chapter 2)	Understanding organizations through embodied metaphors (chapter 6)
Strategizing out of the box (chapter 1)	Analyzing embodied metaphors as an interpretive, hermeneutic endeavor (chapter 3)	Sensemaking through embodied metaphors in OD (chapter 7)
	Crafting strategy as a practice of embodied recursive enactment (chapter 4)	Strategy as a crafting practice (chapter 8)
	Play, analogical reasoning and dialogue in the crafting of strategy (chapter 5)	On the process of strategizing through crafting embodied metaphors (chapter 9)

FIGURE 1 *Outline of the structure of the book.*

Preface

Over the years, we have felt that whereas the technologies and analytical frameworks of strategic *planning* have been highly developed and refined over time, the complementary, creative, exploratory processes of strategic *thinking* remain fragmented, under-specified and under-employed by organizations. Strategic planning, through its employment of matrices, frameworks, graphs, numbers, and other complexity-reducing devices, engages a rational, objective, structured, analytical, convergent mindset and associated practices that many organizational members consider abstract and distant from their daily work. Further, strategy development in most organizations has been dominated by routinized processes of strategic planning as well as structured, functionally oriented managerial debates without an obvious or explicit component of creative strategizing.

Strategic thinking on the other hand, through its engagement of art, the body, role-playing, and reflective dialogue that seek to surface and explore systemic and holistic perspectives on management challenges, engages a creative, divergent, and synthetic mindset. In our experience this type of strategizing is often a useful way to achieve direct involvement in, and engagement with, strategizing processes as well as highlighting sensitive organizational and strategic issues that conventional planning may not readily be able to. Strategizing processes here are energizing, memorable, and colorful. Practices of synthetic, divergent thinking however have largely remained the domain of creativity gurus without a sound theoretical basis, and no credible linkages with organizational strategizing processes. Both conceptually and empirically, few scholars have aimed to explore the potential of doing justice to the creative act of strategizing.

We have therefore two main purposes in writing this book. First, we aim to fill the gap of a sound conceptual basis for strategic thinking through crafting embodied metaphors, drawing on such theoretical antecedents as social constructionism, metaphorical analysis, anthropological discussions of play, and the philosophy of embodied realism. We address one mode of creative strategizing practice, the playful process and intervention technology of crafting embodied metaphors. This practice usefully and productively complements typically dry, conventional strategic planning processes in order to provide a space for reflective dialogue about an organization's particular strategic challenges. Chapters 2 to 5 focus on theoretical antecedents.

Our second purpose is to provide applied illustrations and guidelines for putting these ideas into practice through in-depth analysis of actual workshops where the process of crafting strategy through embodied metaphors has been employed, and discussion of how it was employed. Chapters 6 to 9 focus on applications of this process. We address such issues as the use of embodied metaphors in organizational diagnosis, organization development, creative strategizing, as well as principles for effective play, how to design such interventions, the role of leaders and facilitators, and benefits and limitations of the process.

We also provide several vignettes of actual application of the embodied metaphors approach, to provide further examples of the types of objectives that may be pursued in a variety of contexts, of the embodied metaphors that may be constructed, and of the insights that may be gained through this approach.

This is the first book to develop a robust theoretical basis for embodied metaphors as related to organizational processes such as organizational diagnosis, strategizing and organization development; as well as an elaborate discussion of principles guiding the application of these frameworks. Through this book we aim to extend the field from a domain dominated by rationalist, convergent and conservative thinking towards a complementary domain of strategizing as a creative, divergent, synthetic process, and help legitimize robust study of such processes. Further, despite the integration of the fields of strategy and organization already well under way, there remains a lot to be done. This book draws on both scholarly traditions of strategy and organization, and integrates them in its conceptual approach in extending the strategy field towards the study of more synthetic, exploratory processes.

The first four chapters of the book give an introduction to the crafting of strategy through embodied metaphors, and outline the main theoretical antecedents of this process. In Chapter 1, entitled "Strategizing out of the box," we suggest that to develop and sustain competitive advantage, strategists need to have ways to help them see things anew; to move beyond rationalist, analytical and convergent thinking and to engage in creative, synthetic and divergent thinking, through processes such as the playful crafting of embodied metaphors. We discuss how this strategizing process differs from conventional strategizing by employing the key stages of design thinking as a way to juxtapose the two modes of strategizing practices. We then briefly outline the process of crafting embodied metaphors as a playful practice, a discussion we extend in the very final chapter, where we discuss ways that this strategizing process can be effectively implemented.

In Chapter 2, entitled "Metaphor and embodied realism," we move to discuss the key theoretical antecedents of the process of crafting embodied metaphors, primarily in terms of the two domains of metaphor and embodied realism. We address metaphor as a creative force, in the context of an evolution from the cognitive/semantic dimension, to the spatial dimension and finally the embodied dimension. Given that crafting strategy through embodied metaphors has in practice taken place in the context of organization development interventions, we then discuss the theoretical development of metaphor in this context. We finally address the paradigm of embodied realism in relation to social constructionism, in order to more clearly position embodied realism in prevailing literature and to highlight its potential contributions.

In Chapter 3, entitled "Analyzing embodied metaphors as an interpretive, hermeneutic endeavor," we continue discussing the theoretical antecedents of our approach, by outlining some basic conceptual orientations and analytical directions suggested by interpretive theory and hermeneutics which have informed how we conceptualize and analyze embodied metaphors in our work. These orientations include the concern with *verstehen*, the inseparability of action and structure, and the multiplicity, contextuality and historicity of meaning. We address and expand on these and other considerations and how they relate to the interpretation of embodied metaphors.

These theoretical antecedents form the backdrop for subsequent discussion in Chapter 4, entitled "Crafting strategy as a practice of embodied recursive enactment." By exploring Henry Mintzberg's famous "crafting strategy" metaphor literally, we highlight here the relevance of the hand–mind connection for epistemic developments and achievements. Situating the discussion within the practice turn in strategy, we discuss how integrating three foundational perspectives, namely physiological, psychological and social constructionist ones, lead us to conceptualize crafting strategy as embodied recursive enactment.

In Chapter 5, entitled "Play, analogical reasoning and dialogue in the crafting of strategy," we build on earlier discussions and contextualize the concept of crafting strategy further by exploring three social practices that are crucial to crafting strategy as embodied recursive enactment. We first explore the concept of play as a human capacity that in our context consists mainly in a relaxation of rational intentionality and the manipulation of objects in order to discover new insights. Secondly, and in terms of the cognitive/psychological dimension, we explore the human capacity of analogical reasoning, in our case through physical analogs. Thirdly, and in terms of the communicative dimension, we discuss the concept of dialogue as a specific communicative mode that allows for reflective as well as generative meaning negotiation. We illustrate each of these practices with brief applied examples. We then move to the latter part of the book (Chapters 6 to 9), which addresses applications of the concept of crafting strategy through embodied metaphors.

In Chapter 6, entitled "Understanding organizations through embodied metaphors," we operationalize the embodied metaphor approach in a study of three organization development workshops where groups of actors were engaged in constructing embodied metaphors, physical entities whose target domains were a participant's task, their organization in its business landscape, and the identity of their division. Participants drew on a variety of source domains, and the resulting metaphors produced insights for them in terms of developing shared views of their target domains, as well as for us as researchers through a three-stage analytical process involving contextual understanding, within-case analysis and cross-case analysis. We show in this chapter that analysis of embodied metaphors can afford access to actors' first-order conceptions of organizational dimensions, can reveal alternative qualities and interrelations among them, and in so doing poses substantial challenges to established conceptions of ontology and method in organization theory.

In Chapter 7, entitled "Sensemaking through embodied metaphors in organization development," we suggest that an embodied metaphor approach complements and extends traditional deductively oriented approaches to employing metaphor in organization development by emphasizing induced rather than naturally occurring metaphors, building on a developed base of diagnostic technologies, enabling a collaborative effort of metaphorical selection and diagnosis, and enabling the employment of embodied metaphors to address specific, targeted issues of consequence to participants. We illustrate these elements by discussing the case of a management retreat of a Swiss bank.

In Chapter 8, entitled "Strategy as a crafting practice," we view strategy as a practice of crafting, where actors both metaphorically as well as literally construct their perceptions of strategic issues through and into embodied metaphors within facilitated workshops. We illustrate this view by analyzing an episode of a strategy team constructing an embodied metaphor of their ideal strategizing process. In this context we suggest that the process of constructing and interpreting embodied metaphors is an effective means of intervention that can help managers debate specific strategic challenges in a generative fashion; and can also enable deeper understanding of organizational, divisional or task identities. We then address other important benefits of the process, such as the potential for shifts in the mindsets of strategists and the ability to engage actors not ordinarily involved in strategizing, and conclude by offering some suggestions on how to foster a productive process of crafting embodied metaphors.

We end the book with Chapter 9, entitled "The process of strategizing through crafting embodied metaphors," which is to a large extent a chapter concerned with application, and particularly how actors such as managers or organization development practitioners can implement these ideas in organizations. Here we summarize the benefits of the process of strategizing through embodied metaphors, and outline a detailed roadmap for how to implement it effectively. In this context, we also discuss in what situations it is more appropriate to use this process, and finally outline some enabling contextual conditions that enhance its employment.

Acknowledgments

I would like to thank all my research collaborators for taking the journey of ideas with me. Most relevant to this book, I thank my collaborators over the years on various projects related to discourse theory and analysis, including Bob Marshak, Michael Barrett, John Hendry, Sotirios Paroutis, as well as Claus Jacobs, who invited me to the Imagination Lab and to the world of tangible, three-dimensional metaphors in 2003. Given my interest in organization development, strategic thinking as well as social construction, I found that world and the access it could provide to agents' ideational domains rich and fascinating. This book is the product of our attempts to read these embodied metaphors, to try and understand what the agents had to say or portray through them (consciously or not), and to ponder the implications for organizational analysis and strategy.

Loizos Heracleous

For nearly three years, I worked as a research fellow in strategy and organization at Imagination Lab Foundation in Lausanne, Switzerland. An IMD spin-off in spirit and founding staff, the non-profit foundation was endowed with a generous sponsorship by a large construction toy manufacturer from Denmark and aimed at exploring unconventional materials, modalities and approaches for strategy work. At the time, the team experimented a good bit with the Lego Serious Play technique and adjacent approaches and materials. In turn, these learning experiences prepared the ground for shaping and contouring the embodied metaphor approach as an adjacent, yet distinct perspective presented in this book. I very much appreciated the transdisciplinary collaboration with my then colleagues Peter Buergi, Mark Marotto, David Oliver, Richard Randell, Matt Statler and Johan Roos, the foundation's entrepreneurial director. I gratefully acknowledge their conceptual contributions – often leading to co-authored work – as well as their empirical contributions in terms of excellent workshop facilitation and related data gathering.

I would like to thank our research partner organizations that kindly permitted usage of data and pictures. Lastly, I gratefully acknowledge funding by the Swiss National Science Foundation (Grant No. PP001-119062).

Claus Jacobs

BASF PerForm

Post-acquisition positioning of a divisional training and development team

Context and goal

In September 2009, the head of PerForm Academy, the training and qualification unit of BASF Performance Chemicals division, invited her team of three to explore the relevance and consequences of the recent major acquisition project by BASF for PerForm's strategic positioning in the division. A lot of the acquired operations were to be integrated into BASF Performance Chemicals division. Consequently, all parts – including HR and training functions – of the former and old organization were concerned with the organizational implications of the acquisition. The explicit goal of the intervention was to specify and shape PerForm Academy's strategic profile in terms of key clients and main offerings in this post-acquistion context.

Embodied metaphors

Participants portrayed their team as an office space on a blue platform with a variety of connections. For example, a ladder oriented to a boatful of person figures – representing future internal clients – on a green platform was meant to invite them to increase their skills

FIGURE A.1 *Embodied metaphor of BASF.*

and competences, the obvious and ultimate goal of a training function. The highest element on the platform is a wooden clown face,
representing the enjoyment, commitment and dedication that team
members experience in working in this team. A yellow car delivering a set of bricks to the entrance represents the head of the team,
always on the road to find new ideas and concepts for training. A
black-hatted man behind a fence symbolizes some of the skepticism
and ignorance of other parts of the organization vis-à-vis PerForm.
The green and red platform represent the interface with other parts
of the organization and the division's HR team, represented by two
rather remotely positioned towers overseeing but not fully understanding PerForm's activities. After completion of the model, the
team realized that no physical representation of the newly acquired
firm was included in the model. The absence thereof triggered a
most lively debate that revealed that at this stage and despite best
intentions from all parties, the new organizational structure and
culture did not yet provide sufficient common ground to engage in

detailed service offerings until legal, financial and organizational issues were settled.

Mode of interaction and role of leaders

The process of crafting these embodied metaphors was carried out in a very active and positive spirit. The team leader and team members exchanged their models and narratives in an egalitarian mode – without neglecting hierarchical and functional differences. The workshop itself was evidence of the team's self-image as having fun when working together. Yet, the seriousness of the intervention was apparent in the critical reflection on several core insights outlined below.

Insights gained: how was this session strategically consequential for the organization/the team?

The intervention confirmed the team's commitment and fun of working in the current environment. Yet, it also raised some important questions regarding the strategic profile of this function. First, the team realized that its own direction hinged crucially on the overall direction of the division. Therefore, a high level of flexibility is needed to cope with short-term adjustments in planning and designing training and events within the organization. Secondly, participants realized and acknowledged that their role and offerings in the organization and division were far from clear and were perceived by others as being rather opaque. Lastly, and in exploring the absence of a physical representation of the acquired firm, participants realized that despite the post-acquisition activities, the ground had not yet been prepared for them to meaningfully offer their services to the newly acquired firm.

CHAPTER ONE

Strategizing out of the box

Strategy is regarded as serious business. The very origin of the term "strategy," as the task of ancient Greek army generals, or *strategoi* (leaders of the army), underlies a view of strategy as rational, analytical, objective and top-down, involving extensive analysis and planning. Further, it privileges a top-down view of strategy as positioning in the battlefield, rather than organizing internally to deliver the competencies needed to effectively deliver a strategy. This emphasis on left-brain type activities and ways of thinking, as well as external positioning rather than internal organization, has hindered the development and widespread adoption of right-brain, creative, emergent ways of strategizing. These ways are more relevant to a processual, practice-oriented view of organizations, and an emphasis on actors, rather than a more static, industrial organization-inspired view of organizations concerned with external positioning. This book, based on our research and engagement with strategizing processes over the last decade, is an effort to redress the balance.

This chapter draws from Jacobs and Heracleous (2007) and from Heracleous and Jacobs (2008).

We begin this chapter by suggesting that to develop and sustain competitive advantage, strategists need to engage in practices that help them see things anew; to move beyond rationalist, analytical and convergent thinking and to engage in creative, synthetic and divergent thinking, through processes such as the playful crafting of embodied metaphors. Such a strategizing process differs markedly from conventional, analytical strategizing processes, and we employ the key stages of design thinking to highlight these differences. We finally outline the process of crafting embodied metaphors as a playful practice.

Sustaining competitive advantage requires synthetic and divergent strategic thinking

Strategic *planning* has been associated with a rational, objective, structured, analytical, convergent mindset and associated practices that most organizational members consider abstract and distant from their daily work. Strategic *thinking* on the other hand, involves a creative, divergent and synthetic mindset and associated practices (Heracleous, 1998) often seen as a useful way to achieve direct involvement in strategizing processes as well as highlighting sensitive organizational and strategic issues that conventional planning may not readily be able to. While the technologies and frameworks of strategic planning have been highly developed and refined over time (e.g. Ansoff, Declerck and Hayes, 1976), despite its shortcomings (Mintzberg, 1993), the creative processes of strategic thinking remain a fragmented, underspecified group of approaches with no clear connections to strategizing processes.

Sustainability of competitive advantage seems to be an unattainable ideal for most organizations, where any uniqueness achieved is likely to be transitory because of aggressive imitation (Frery, 2006). Strategic innovation, as a strategy of breaking the rules of an industry by redefining basic dimensions of strategy (Markides, 1997) becomes necessary for sustained advantage. Several ways have been proposed to foster strategic innovation: the monitoring their strategic (as opposed to simply financial) health; creation of "positive crises" to overcome inertia and motivate employees to embrace a new strategic direction (Markides, 1998); Abell's (1999) suggestions for the development of "dual strategies" that address both the present as well as the future of the business (how the business should be proactively redefined, and new competencies built, for future success); and March's (1991) calls for balancing exploration and exploitation.

Simply put, while focusing on better execution (exploitation) is important for efficiency reasons, without seeing things in new ways, gaining new insights and experimenting (exploration), an organization would gradually atrophy; it would be perfectly executing the wrong things. Several scholars have noted that a key enabling factor for fundamental strategic innovation is to be able to view the industry and the company in a new light, to challenge existing mental models and form new understandings (Jacobs and Heracleous, 2005). Baden Fuller and Stopford (1994: 53) for example suggested that strategic innovation as the "creation of actions hitherto deemed impossible" requires "a change in the mental models held by managers," and Markides (1998) noted that companies should attempt to institutionalize a climate of questioning and challenging current operating norms and viewing issues in new ways. Indeed, even though more than three-quarters of executives surveyed by McKinsey said their company had a formal strategic planning process, less than one quarter said that this process was instrumental in making important strategic decisions, which were led instead by the CEO and the senior team (McKinsey & Co, 2006).

Strategizing through embodied metaphors
as a practice of exploration

Since strategic decisions are driven not by strategic planning but by actors, how these actors see things (their mental maps and assumptions regarding the industry, the company and its strategic challenges) shape the decisions they make. If fundamental strategic innovation as well as the development of creative strategies can be fostered by shifts in managers' mental models, how can such shifts be facilitated so that the conditions for innovation are put in place? We propose that strategizing through embodied metaphors enables reflective dialogue which can engender shifts in mental models and potentially be a catalyst for strategic innovation.

Of course such a strategizing process focusing on strategic thinking does not replace traditional strategizing focusing on strategic planning (Heracleous, 1998), but can effectively complement it, adding much needed diversity and out-of-the-box thinking in the process. In the next section we employ design thinking to highlight how strategizing through embodied metaphors differs from conventional strategizing.

Design thinking and strategic practice

In this section we employ the categories of design thinking, to highlight how strategizing through embodied metaphors differs from conventional strategizing. Viewing strategizing as a process of design is in essence an analogical process, the use of metaphor where knowledge from the source domain (in this case, design thinking), is mapped onto the target domain (in this case the strategy process), with the aim of gaining insights that would have been difficult to gain otherwise. Viewing creative strategizing as design can shed light on how strategic thinking practices such as crafting embodied metaphors can add value to the strategy process.

According to architect Bryan Lawson (2006), there is little consensus in the design field about what the term "design" means. Both a noun and a verb, design can refer to an end product as well as to the processes involved. A variety of professions employ the term "design", each with a different interpretation of what it is. While on the one hand a structural engineer might refer to design as a systematic, quasi-scientific sequence of steps whereby the requirements and desired specifications of the end product are known, a fashion designer engaged in next season's collection can also refer to a fluid, open-ended, inspirational practice as design. Whereas these two professions exemplify extremes of a continuum of design, we will draw for our purposes on the three-dimensional design field of architecture that integrates systematic with imaginative thinking, as well as with relevant technical skills. This design domain is also most relevant to crafting embodied metaphors, themselves three-dimensional designs most often representing various types of buildings and infrastructure.

The source domain of architectural design is in itself fragmented, as witnessed by the lack of a universal design model. In spite of this, Lawson (2006) attempts to provide an integrated model of the design process that consists of six broad stages that we outline briefly below. We then discuss how these six steps relate to both conventional, analytical strategic planning, as well as creative strategic thinking processes.

Formulating: Designers must be capable of effectively identifying, stating, understanding, exploring, and providing structure to ill-structured design problems. They should also be capable of framing and examining these problems from different points of view and perspectives. In particular, the ability to generate stories to reframe issues is key.

Representing: Designers employ various techniques and materials to externalize their ideas and thoughts. This might take the form of models, sketches or prototypes. Importantly though, these are created through a variety of media, including drawings, computer models or tangible three-dimensional entities. These physical representations are not simply outcomes of an abstract thought process but are seen as essential inputs to a conversation about the representations and ideas they embody.

Moving: Designers create solution ideas, or moves, relevant to a design problem. They distinguish between lateral design moves (the extension of an existing idea or its application to a new setting), and vertical design moves (the development of a novel idea). Interestingly, and in anticipation of later stages of the process, designers also develop initial experimental ideas about solutions early on and sometimes even before they have fully understood the problem.

Bringing problems and solutions together: Designers often do not explicitly draw a hard line between problem and solution, since they consider these to be intertwined. Furthermore, in design practice, problem and solution rarely follow a clear, linear sequence. In contrast to a universal route map of design process, briefing (seen as making sense of the issues and challenges at hand) is a continuous, recurring element, rather than just the first sequential step of design. Finally, great designers are capable of developing parallel lines of thought about the problem–solution situation. This skill in particular involves maintaining a sense of ambiguity and fluidity, and not getting too concerned about the single right answer or silver bullet during the process. The narrative, storytelling capability of designers to integrate problem and solution into a relatively coherent story is important here.

Evaluating: Designers often have to judge between alternatives along dimensions where no common, universally accepted, "object-ive" metric is available. Thus, designers must be capable of integrating objective/technical as well as subjective/aesthetic judgments in making choices among competing designs. One of the key skills in this context is the ability to temporarily suspend judgment so as to maintain the creative flow. In effective design, ideas often reach a level of maturity before they are subjected to robust criticism.

Reflecting: Ideally, designers are capable of reflecting *in* action – a skill that is of course required for the above dimensions as well. But also, great designers are able to reflect *on* action – on how they go about the design process itself, on the design philosophy and guiding principles they follow; a process analogous to what Argyris (1977) referred to as double-loop learning. Skilled designers draw dramatically on episodic evidence, for example by keeping sketchbooks or collecting artifacts reflecting what they consider to be good design, and can integrate these precedents and references into their design process.

Table 1.1 provides a synopsis of these elements, and juxtaposes them with both analytical, conventional strategizing as well as creative

TABLE 1.1: *Two modes of strategizing juxtaposed in terms of key stages of design thinking*

Key stages	Design thinking	Conventional strategizing	Strategizing through embodied metaphors
Formulating	- Identifying design problem. - Naming and structuring ill-structured problems. - Framing problems from different points of view, often through storytelling.	- Preference for rationalist perspective; search for data and structured views to converge on best solutions. - Storytelling eschewed as irrelevant, subjective and non-rational.	- Fostering alternative, creative perspectives of strategic issues that diverge towards alternative futures. - Strategizing designs as metaphorical stories.
Representing	- Employing various techniques and materials to externalize ideas and thoughts. - Developing models, sketches or prototypes using a variety of media. - Discussing ideas through their physical representations.	- Employing specified range of analytical techniques such as conventional strategy frameworks. - Dominant representations are conventional 2-D media such as reports, power-points and spreadsheets. - Use of structured frameworks such as 2X2 matrices.	- Employing technologies such as projective techniques to enable subconscious understandings to manifest. - Various types of materials used, such as toy construction materials, drawings, and clay.
Moving	- Creating solution ideas, or moves. - Developing preliminary ideas about solutions very early on. - Distinguishing between lateral and vertical moves.	- Strategic frameworks used imply corresponding evaluations and solutions. - Scenario development a possibility. - Higher likelihood of lateral moves (incremental ideas) and me-too strategies emerging.	- Potential solutions emerge throughout design process. - Social processes associated with effective realization of solutions occur through design process. - Higher likelihood of vertical moves (novel ideas) emerging.

Bringing problems and solutions together	- Seeing problem and solution as interconnected and not imposing a linear order. - Briefing as a continuous element. - Developing parallel lines of thought about the problem–solution situation. - Maintaining a sense of ambiguity and not getting too concerned about the one silver bullet.	- Dominant, pre-existing understandings and rationalist frameworks foster sequential, linear, discrete-terms thinking. - Briefing occurs as initial step. - Parallel lines of thought often considered inefficient. - Ambiguity seen as barrier to effective solutions.	- Designs interweave perceptions of issues as well as potential avenues for solutions. - Briefing as making sense of the issues occurs on a continuous basis. - Process allows for maintainance of ambiguity and encourages parallel lines of thinking.
Evaluating	- Judging and selecting among alternatives where no universally accepted metrics exist. - Integrating objective/technical as well as subjective/aesthetic judgments. - Temporarily suspending judgment to maintain creative flow.	- Decisions ideally based on objective metrics (e.g. projected return on investment and profitability-mpact). - Aesthetic judgment seen as barrier to rational decision-making. - Judgment disguised as decision; deeper assumptions not externalize.	- Privileging non-metric, holistic, divergent thinking. - Encouraging aesthetic judgment. - Design process as emergent storytelling enables suspension of judgment until decoding phase.
Reflecting	- Reflecting in action. - Reflecting on action. - Collecting precedents and references to aid design process. - Developing and challenging a philosophy and guiding principles of design.	- Reflecting in action as far as allowed by strategic frameworks used. - Reflecting on action (on strategy process) unusual. - Benchmarking provides relative referencing. - Guiding principles and philosophy of strategizing taken for granted and rarely explicated.	- Reflecting in action enabled by emergent design process. - Reflecting on action enabled in decoding phase and by facilitators concerned with improving the process. - Individuals' ideas and guiding principles embodied in strategic narratives as manifested in designs.

strategizing through embodied metaphors (a mode of playful design); in this way highlighting how these strategizing modes differ.

Fostering strategizing out of the box: outlining the playful practice of crafting embodied metaphors

How can we realize the creative strategizing process outlined above? Crafting embodied metaphors is a technique that combines a facilitated playful mode of interaction with the emergent, group-oriented design of three-dimensional models for strategic sensemaking. In other words, individuals explore their strategic issues through a joint process of sensemaking that involves the design of real artifacts that are metaphors in the flesh. These designs are in effect collective narratives telling stories that become explicit when the structures are decoded and made sense of by the group that built them, through a process of facilitation.

As developmental psychologist Jean Piaget (Piaget and Inhelder, 1972) observed, human beings begin to make sense of the world by using their hands. Thus, we initially literally "grasp" the world through "manipulating" objects in the physical environment around us. While most tasks in our professional lives focus on rational, conceptual, cognitive functions, some professional disciplines still draw on this fundamental human capacity in their everyday practices. For instance, designers and architects use prototypes to externalize, represent and probe their ideas and thoughts. These three-dimensional objects are created through a variety of media including drawings, computer models or tangible three-dimensional entities, and are not simply outcomes of an abstract thought process but are seen as avenues for engaging in iterative sensemaking about the representations and ideas they embody.

In this respect, the practice of crafting embodied metaphors in strategy is reminiscent of an ancient craft of strategizing, that also drew on three-dimensional artefacts. In the eighteenth and nineteenth centuries so-called relief maps were widely used by military strategists. These maps provided a bird's-eye view of the territory – a novel and holistic perspective to strategists at that time. Embodied metaphors reintroduce this bird's-eye view to strategy by providing strategists with the opportunity to conceptually and physically construct and interrelate strategic elements deemed relevant to their situation in a synthetic, integrative manner. What distinguishes these ancient relief maps from the process of crafting embodied metaphors, though, is that in the latter practice, instead of reading a prefabricated map, participants actively and collectively create a representation of the strategic territory, that is then available for further debate, decoding, and development of action implications. As Weick (1990) observed, the strategic map as an artifact in itself may be at least as important to processes of strategizing as the actual degree of accuracy of territory representation, because it provides an interpretive hook and urges an action orientation. The process of crafting embodied metaphors provides a prime example of a strategic practice in which strategists read (interpret) a strategic map while writing (constructing) it, in the process enriching, challenging, and potentially changing their mental maps and understandings of the situations that these embodied maps represent.

Playing seriously with strategy

There is one human activity, neglected so far by most strategists, that is messy, ambiguous, subjective and not strictly rational: play. Developmental psychology and anthropology have shown that in every phase of human development, play facilitates the development of cognitive, interpretive skills and engenders an emotional sense of fulfillment (Sutton-Smith, 1997). Play is inherently group or community-oriented, contributing to the development of a shared language, identity, and social practices (Huizinga, 1950). It provides a safe and conducive environment to surface, debate, and diffuse assumptions and ideas, its potency and energy deriving from the imaginative, fresh and experimental nature of these ideas and the play context itself.

Engaging senior managers in play to develop shared views of what the company is about, what the competitors might do, how the industry is evolving, and even to spark novel strategic directions has until recently been unthinkable. Many leaders are skeptical of play as an activity that can add value to strategic thinking – therefore forfeiting the opportunity to gain from the kind of insightful nuggets, shared learning, and creative strategizing that can arise from play. Yet, enlightened organizations and strategic leaders are beginning to understand the value of playing with serious intent (Jacobs and Heracleous, 2005, 2006).

How can such play be orchestrated with maximum impact? One way that has proved fruitful is to engage senior management teams of multinational companies in using three-dimensional objects to develop shared representations of their company and its competitive landscape. The process involves inviting participants to individually, and then collectively, build representations or models of their organization, its competitive landscape including key stakeholders, and the perceived relations among these elements (Buergi, Jacobs and Roos, 2005). The results are complex and imaginative structures that are arrived at after considerable, energetic, intellectually demanding, and often heated debate.

These "embodied metaphors," as we call them, are earnestly constructed, compared, and decoded by the participants. We call these constructions embodied metaphors for two main reasons. First, they are constructed through engaging the body, our physical mode of existence, in a process that involves a very real, direct relationship between the participants and their constructions. These are not ready-made metaphors that are pre-existing in individual participants' cognitive repertoires, but metaphors that are gradually constructed in a shared, interactive, iterative fashion. Secondly, these constructions are not simply language-based metaphors, or spatially based ones such as maps or matrices, but are tangible entities extending into three-dimensional space; they are metaphors in the flesh that are simultaneously constructed and interpreted. They can be touched, moved, and examined from various angles, and are pregnant with meaning, that builds up and manifests in both the construction process and subsequent debates.

Such sessions can effectively combine the serious issue of strategizing with the highly dialogical and imagery-rich process of playful sensemaking. Almost all participants find such sessions demanding, involving, energizing, and almost invariably insightful. We observe enormous amounts of motivation and group bonding of managers whose relationships may be less than close to start with, and subsequently within the organization the use of the insights that may be emotionally, politically or cognitively uncomfortable, but usually are very valuable. While the process of these sessions is intended to be light-hearted and playful, their outcomes and consequences are both serious and relevant.

REFERENCES

Abell, D. F. 1999. Competing today while preparing for tomorrow. *Sloan Management Review*, Spring: 73–81.

Ansoff, H. I., Declerck, R. P., and Hayes, R. L. 1976. *From strategic planning to strategic management*. London: John Wiley & Sons.

Argyris, C. 1977. Double loop learning in organizations. *Harvard Business Review*, September–October: 115–25.

Baden Fuller, C. and Stopford, J. M. 1994. *Rejuvenating the mature business: The competitive challenge*. Boston, MA: Harvard Business School Press.

Buergi, P., Jacobs, C., and Roos, J. 2005. From metaphor to practice in the crafting of strategy. *Journal of Management Inquiry*, 14: 78–94.

Frery, F. 2006. The fundamental dimensions of strategy. *MIT Sloan Management Review*, Fall, 48(1): 71–5.

Heracleous, L. 1998. Strategic thinking or strategic planning? *Long Range Planning*, 31: 481–7.

Heracleous, L. and Jacobs, C. 2008. Developing strategy: The serious business of play. In Gallos, J. (ed.), *Business Leadership*, 2nd edn. San Francisco: Jossey Bass, 324–35.

Huizinga, J. 1950. *Homo ludens: A study of the play-element in culture*. London: Routledge & Kegan Paul.

Jacobs, C. and Heracleous, L. 2005. Answers for questions to come – reflective dialogue as an enabler for strategic innovation. *Journal of Organizational Change Management*, 18(4): 338–52.

2006. Constructing shared understanding – the role of embodied metaphors in organization development. *Journal of Applied Behavioral Science*, 24(2): 207–26.

2007. Strategizing through playful design. *Journal of Business Strategy*, 28(4): 75–80.

Lawson, B. 2006. *How designers think – The design process demystified*, 4th edn. Oxford: Architectural Press.

March, J. G. 1991. Exploration and exploitation in organization learning. *Organization Science*, 2: 71–87.

Markides, C. 1997. Strategic innovation. *Sloan Management Review*, Spring: 9–23.

1998. Strategic innovation in established companies. *Sloan Management Review*, Spring: 31–42.

McKinsey & Co. 2006. Improving strategic planning. *McKinsey Quarterly*, July–August: 1–11.

Mintzberg, H. 1993. The pitfalls of strategic planning. *California Management Review*, Fall, 36(1): 32–47.

Piaget, J. and Inhelder, B. 1972. *The psychology of the child*. New York: Basic Books.

Sutton-Smith, B. 1997. *The ambiguity of play*. Cambridge, MA: Harvard University Press.

Weick, K. E. 1990. Introduction: Cartographic myths in organizations. In Huff, A. S. and Jenkins, M. (eds.), *Mapping strategic thought*. Chichester: Wiley, 1–10.

UNICEF

Drafting a blueprint of an efficient organizational structure

Context and goal

In August 2009 and in the context of a newly launched strategy development process, the CEO of UNICEF Germany and her top management team of six heads of business divisions and functions gathered for a two-day management retreat to draft a more efficient organizational structure to deliver on the organization's mission. Having joined the organization only in January 2009 and with a substantial business background, the CEO invited her team to explore critically and open-mindedly potential areas for improving organizational structure and the linkages between the divisions in an open and critical way. Within the overall goal of **developing a blueprint for a revised organizational structure** ("to be"), the purpose of using embodied metaphors was to develop a joint view of the current organizational structure, in the context of what was seen as its complexity and amount of high-maintenance cross-divisional organizational interfaces.

Embodied metaphors

At the center of the model, and being the highest structure on the table, stands a tower with a blue winner's trophy on a palm

FIGURE B.1 *An embodied metaphor of UNICEF Germany's head office organizational structure.*

tree – representing the two main goals of the organization, namely to grow economically, i.e. funds raised – represented by the large blue trophy brick on top of the model, as well as to enhance UNICEF's efficacy in educating donors and the public on child rights issues – represented by the palm tree. In view of potential risk factors, e.g. with regard to public perception of professional fundraising, participants agreed to supplement this aspirational model with a safety net, so that the overall goal reads as "safe and sound growth" in the aforementioned terms.

The production process that underpins this aspiration works as an engine that transforms information about children in developing countries (represented by a filled wheelbarrow) into distinct and comprehensible messages to donors and the public (represented by a huge set of windows of different sizes). These two components form the directional metaphor of a production line (green platforms).

Feeding in and out of this production process are the head office's business divisions (fundraising, greeting card sales, communication and advocacy, volunteers) and key functions (administration and human resources), clustered as platforms around the process and goal of the organization. These functions have both robust and fragile connections to goal and process as well as amongst themselves. However, no clear structure or pattern of these connections was discerned. Most importantly, participants realized on this occasion that the various divisions and functions had different, not always synchronized, growth strategies. It also became apparent that the current organizational structure left divisions and functions unclear as to how a synchronized pursuit of the organization's goal could be orchestrated.

Mode of interaction and role of leaders

Interestingly, the leader most actively participated in the construction process without dominating it – as we have also witnessed in the past. Rather, the CEO felt the need to be extra-transparent about her view so that her team could much better assess the direction and underpinning values driving the CEO's agenda. The team engaged in a most lively debate that was characterized from the very start by a simultaneous seriousness and lightheartedness that facilitated the constructive exploration of differences.

Insights gained: how was this session strategically consequential for the organization/the team?

The intervention here not only served to develop a joint view and analysis of the "as is" status but moreover, provided tangible evidence for the complexity, interrelatedness of divisions, and relevance of acknowledging and carefully managing the multiple interfaces between divisions. Thus, participants realized that a blueprint of a revised organization structure needed to increase efficiency of cross-divisional interfaces by designing a structure that decreases the levels of bureaucratic maintenance required to manage these. The embodied metaphors intervention itself did not produce the blueprint, but by clarifying what the perceived challenges were and building consensus around them, effectively prepared the ground for a most productive second day that concluded with a blueprint of a revised organizational structure that all participants had agreed upon.

CHAPTER TWO

Metaphor and embodied realism

In this chapter we outline the key theoretical antecedents to crafting strategy through embodied metaphors, primarily in terms of two domains: metaphor and embodied realism. In particular, we discuss metaphor as a creative force, beginning from the cognitive/semantic dimension, moving to the spatial, and then the embodied dimension. Further, given that crafting strategy through embodied metaphors has in practice taken place in the context of organization development interventions, we discuss the theoretical development of metaphor in this context. We finally address the paradigm of embodied realism in relation to social constructionism, so that embodied realism can be more specifically positioned. These theoretical antecedents will form the backdrop for subsequent discussion in subsequent chapters, for example of the concept of crafting strategy as a practice of recursive embodied enactment, in Chapter 4.

Metaphor as a creative force

The linguistic turn in the social sciences has portrayed language as fundamentally constructive and constitutive of social reality, rather

This chapter is based on Heracleous and Jacobs (2008) and Jacobs and Heracleous (2006).

than merely representative and functional (Wittgenstein, 1967). In organization studies, the constructive view of language thus seeks to explore the communicative practices of organizational actors and their role in the intersubjective construction of meaning through social interaction (e.g. Alvesson and Karreman, 2000; Barry and Elmes, 1997; Ford and Ford, 1995; Gergen and Thatchenkery, 1996; Heracleous and Barrett, 2001). A conception of social reality as constructed and constituted through linguistically mediated processes, places organizational discourse at the center of investigation (e.g. Barrett, Thomas, and Hocevar, 1995; van Dijk, 1988; Heracleous, 2004; Oswick, 2000). In highlighting the context-dependent, teleological and symbolic dimensions of discursive interactions in particular, discourse can be conceptualized as situated symbolic action (Heracleous and Marshak, 2004). In this perspective, communicative actions convey actors' perceptions, values and beliefs that shape frames for interpretation and guide social reality construction. In this respect, metaphors – here conceived of as the archetype for a broader set of tropes, such as metonymy, synecdoche, simile, and analogy – play a central role (e.g. Black, 1993; Lakoff and Johnson, 1980; Lakoff, 1990).

The literal view of metaphors, aligned with objectivist approaches in social science (Tsoukas, 1993), suggests that metaphors are primarily ornamental, expendable linguistic devices that indicate similarities between a source and a target domain (Black, 1993); not only do they not lead to additional understanding, but they can distort "the facts," that should be expressed in literal language (Pinder and Bourgeois, 1982). From a constructionist viewpoint, however, this literal view of metaphors as unnecessary linguistic ornaments is rejected, and their central role in human sensemaking and understanding is emphasized (Lakoff and Johnson, 1980). Metaphors are viewed as primarily conceptual constructions that play a central role in the development of thought and intersubjective meaning-making; they can allow actors to reframe their perceptions, or "see the world anew" (Barrett and Cooperrider, 1990: 222). According to Lakoff (1993: 203), for example, "the locus of metaphor is not language at all, but in the way we conceptualize one mental domain in terms of another." In this respect, these conceptual similarities involve both ontological correspondences (target entities correspond in certain ways to source entities) as well as epistemic correspondences (knowledge of source domain is mapped on to knowledge about the target domain) (Lakoff, 1990). Social constructionists suggest that these correspondences are created, rather than just revealed by metaphor, thereby emphasizing the inherently creative dimension of metaphor rather than viewing it as something that can merely reveal an antecedently existing similarity (e.g. Black, 1993; Johnson, 1987).

Such metaphors have been described as "generative" in the sense that they can lead to novel perceptions, explanations and inventions (Schon, 1993), or "strong" by virtue of possessing a high degree of implicative elaboration (Black, 1993). In this view, metaphors are potent as creative devices if there is neither too much similarity nor too much difference between the source and target domains (Aristotle, 1991; Morgan, 1980). Morgan's work (e.g. 1980; 1983; 1986) has been seminal in helping organization theory challenge dominant mechanistic and organic metaphors that had guided theorizing within a functionalist paradigm, through a conscious understanding of the impact of such taken-for-granted metaphors on organizational theorizing. Morgan (1983) has gone as far as to suggest that seeking to minimize the influence of metaphors is not only counterproductive, but also infeasible, given their integral role to theorizing and sensemaking. According to Morgan, "the linguistic aspect is just a surface expression of a deeper process. This is why I like to describe metaphor as a primal, generative process that is fundamental to the creation of human understanding and meaning in all aspects of life" (1996: 228).

Morgan's approach (and the stream of research inspired by it) has been criticized as potentially exercising a conservative rather than enlightening influence on theorizing because of the focus of metaphor on searching for similarities between the interrelated domains, rather than highlighting differences and engendering "cognitive discomfort" (Oswick, Keenoy, and Grant, 2002). The inherent ambiguity and imprecision of metaphors (Tsoukas, 1993), in addition, entails some persistent question marks and disagreements regarding their usefulness in organizational theorizing. Pinder and Bourgeois (1982), for example, have suggested that metaphorical statements do not fulfill a critical condition of social science – falsifiability. Further, Palmer and Dunford (1996a) have raised unresolved questions such as whether a single or several metaphors should be used in interpreting a situation; the role of politics in metaphor use; the role and feasibility of "literal" language; and how to deal with incommensurable metaphors.

Morgan (1983; 1996) responds to Pinder and Bourgeois (1982) by suggesting that their approach in essence seeks to substitute the trope of metonymy for the trope of metaphor in social science theorizing. Morgan accepts many of the other critiques of his approach to metaphor, and suggests that rather than dwelling on the limitations of metaphorical thinking, we should make productive use of this avenue for understanding, bearing in mind its limitations in terms of producing "partial truths" (1996: 232) that may at times be ideologically biased or lack "rigor," as this concept is conventionally understood. Indeed, in spite of the critiques, the sheer influence of metaphorical reasoning in organization theory over the years (Oswick and Grant, 1996; Morgan, 1980; 1983) bears testament to the indispensability of metaphors as sensemaking devices that can engender or stimulate novel or at least different understandings of particular target domains through creating or eliciting correspondences with selected source domains. As Grant and Oswick (1996: 2) have put it: "there can be little dispute about the inevitability of metaphor. Nor about its having a generative quality."

Metaphor in organization development

It has long been recognized that as primarily cognitive and semantic devices, metaphors play a vital role in the discursive construction of meaning in organizational change and development processes (Cleary and Packard, 1992; Marshak, 1993: 766; Sackmann, 1989: 954). According to Burke, metaphors can be "windows into the soul, if not collective unconscious, of the social system" (Burke, 1992: 255). Metaphors are crucial dimensions of organization members' cognitive schemata, providing lenses for interpreting the world, embodying implicit evaluations, and implying "appropriate" actions based on the prevailing metaphors (Armenakis and Bedeian, 1992; Hirsch, 1986). Metaphors can help to concretize vague and abstract ideas, can holistically convey a large amount of information, and can foster new ways of looking at things (Sackmann, 1989).

While a deductive approach to metaphors attempts to apply a generic set of metaphors to organizational situations, an inductive approach operates on the assumption that organizational members already generate and use metaphors in view of their context and experience, that can be tapped on for the purposes of system diagnosis and change. Stated another way, deductive metaphorical approaches attempt to identify and suggest universal, archetypical sets of metaphors that in turn would then guide corresponding interventions (Morgan, 1986); in contrast, inductive approaches emphasize the emergent, local and contextual nature of metaphors (Palmer and Dunford, 1996b). Both the concept as well as the technology of crafting strategy through embodied metaphors operate from an inductive approach to metaphorical reasoning in organizations, since organizational metaphors are intimately related to context and experience (Heracleous and Jacobs, 2008). Embodied metaphors therefore inductively capitalize on the ultimately local, contextual and situated nature of metaphor, rather than being based on assumptions of metaphorical generality and universality.

Similarly operating from an inductive angle, Cleary and Packard (1992) suggest a two-phase process of assessment of metaphors and other symbolic aspects of the organization, and then development of change goals and planning of action steps based on that assessment. Marshak (1993), in addition, proposes that change agents can listen carefully to the metaphors used by organizational members as a means of diagnosing the organization, help them understand the implications of employing different types of metaphors by conducting relevant workshops, and try to shape the way people think about change by diffusing appropriate metaphors that align their conceptual system with the type of change that needs to be achieved.

Perhaps the potency of metaphor to effect change is related to its complexity and ambiguity that allows for multiple interpretations to coexist but at the same time can provide a shared direction. According to Pondy (1983:164), "because of its inherent ambivalence of meaning, metaphor can fulfill the dual function of enabling change and preserving continuity." This complexity and ambiguity is often downplayed in accounts of the use of metaphor in OD interventions (Inns, 2002). Despite the advantages of using metaphor for diagnostic and intervention purposes, often organization members may use mutually incompatible metaphors to describe the same organization, as Oswick and Montgomery (1999) found. In such cases, more extensive collaborative efforts need to be undertaken to explore the sources of contradiction and make further, improved diagnoses and interventions.

Toward embodied metaphors in organization development

From cognitive/semantic to spatial metaphors

Metaphors are often based on characteristics found in the physical world, as illustrated by the three generic image schemata of up/down, container, and link or connection. This suggests that sensemaking seems to emerge from the human capacity of establishing and mentally resonating with these physical relationships of and between objects (Johnson, 1987; Lakoff and Johnson, 1980). Going beyond metaphors' verbal, semantic dimension, Weick (1990) highlighted the relevance of spatial relatedness in terms of maps as two-dimensional devices of sensemaking employed in organizational practices. A map is a visual device signifying a territory that might either be spatially extended (then the map serves as a cartographic, spatial icon) or might be *conceptualized* as spatially extended (then the map is enacted as a spatial metaphor) (Robinson and Petchenik, 1976).

It is precisely due to their capacity to trigger such recursive processes of sensemaking that maps draw on the spatial dimension of metaphors by displaying relative sizes, relative locations as well as interrelations among entities. Broadening the expressive repertoire of metaphorical thinking in organizations, cognitive mapping has operationalized maps as spatial metaphors that can facilitate organizational change and development (e.g. Bougon, 1992; Brown, 1992; Calori, Johnson, and Sarnin, 1994; Clarke and Mackaness, 2001; Eden, 1992; Eden and Huxham, 1996; Hodgkinson and Johnson, 1994). Cognitive mapping involves the creation of maps as visual representations of a domain and its most relevant entities as cognitively perceived, and portrays these entities within systems of relationships (Huff, 2002). Maps can serve as triggers or focal points of reference and meaning negotiation in open-ended conversations, and it is primarily the communication around the mapping process that seems to trigger fruitful conversations and insights. Given the recursive nature of meaning-generation (Weick, 1990), a map does not solely represent but can rather construct the territory in important and consequential ways. Thus, a map does not merely reveal an antecedent order but can also instigate action that subsequently enacts a certain order; or construct a shared reality leading to corresponding actions. Extending metaphors' cognitive, verbal and semantic aspects by adding a spatial dimension can thus facilitate discursive processes of sensemaking in organizations.

Toward embodied metaphors

Phenomenology highlights the embodied nature of human experience and reasoning. In a radical rejection of the Cartesian dichotomy, the body is seen as mediating human perception and experience of the world: "I am my body" (Merleau-Ponty, 1962: 159). Human embodied existence is experienced and expressed prior to conscious processes of thinking; thus phenomena are not only purely cognitive but enacted in and through the body. Similarly, Joas (1996) reminds us of the body as the origin of pre-reflexive impetus to action. Thus, he posits, one should "challenge the presupposition that the body can be instrumentalised for the purposes of action and forces us to construe a non-instrumental relationship to the body" (Joas, 1996: 251). Thus, human knowledge and action are rooted in and emerge from bodily experience of the world.

Johnson (1987), in addition, reflects on the role of the body in human thinking from a cognitive science perspective. He views metaphorical image schemata as patterns of bodily experience that enable the structuring of bodily interactions with the world at more abstract levels. Image schemata – figurative, analogical and non-propositional in nature – emerge primarily from spatial relations, and more particularly from perceptual interactions with the manipulation of objects. Human thought is organized through metaphorical elaborations of image schemata that form and structure experience and understanding. Thus, meaning is firmly rooted in, and emerges from bodily experiences. As Johnson (1987) argues, metaphors become constitutive for structuring bodily experience and also emerge from this experience.

In what follows, we describe the relevance of embodied metaphors as sensemaking devices, as well as the different technologies through which embodied metaphors have been operationalized. We employ the term "embodied metaphor" to encompass two related ideas. First, the literal construction of a physical object as an occasion for sensemaking introduces the body in processes of creating and exploring metaphors. Primarily haptic, tactile, and kinesthetic aspects are involved in such processes extending and complementing the semantic and cognitive dimensions of metaphorical thinking. More importantly, however, the resulting physical constructions are themselves metaphors in the flesh, tangible metaphors representing organizational domains of importance to participants. Agents thus get immersed in "practicing and 'doing metaphor'," a promising avenue for innovation in the field or metaphor (Morgan, 1996: 240). Both the analogical creation process as well as the resulting physical constructions can be fruitful occasions for collective sensemaking and social reality construction, that can be immensely useful in processes of organization development and change. We offer applied examples of such processes in the second part of the book.

Sensemaking through embodied metaphors

Echoing and complementing the constitutive role of bodily experience for human thinking, Weick's (1995) concept of sensemaking refers to the ways people generate what they interpret: "What sensemaking does is address how the text is constructed as well as how it is read" (Weick, 1995: 7). Sensemaking is induced by a change in the environment that creates distortion in the routines or flow of experience engaging the people of an organization. It is these distortions, differences and discontinuities that provide the raw data from the environment that the organization and its members have to make sense of. Weick distinguishes seven properties of sensemaking: Sensemaking is grounded in the construction of individual and organizational identity, is retrospective in nature, is based on enacting "sensable" environments to deal with, is fundamentally a social, not an individual process, is ongoing, is focused on cues in the environment and focused by cues in the environment, and is driven by the plausibility of possible interpretations (Weick, 1995).

Contentious issues can induce organizational ambiguity and uncertainty as the two primary occasions for sensemaking. While uncertainty refers to issues of ignorance that can be remedied by additional information, ambiguity relates to a confusion to a situation in which several different interpretations at the same time emerge and persist so that additional information cannot resolve the confusion, i.e. imperfect understanding of the world. Multiple interpretations and meanings that create confusion call for social construction and invention in adequate conversational modes and settings (Weick, 1995: 91–4). Thus, in an organizational state of affairs where additional, more detailed information does not remedy the inherent ambiguity, a sensemaking practice such as cognitive mapping is required that allows for multiple interpretations to be voiced so as to come to a shared understanding. Thus, and in view of embodied metaphor, sensemaking could be reframed as "reading a metaphor while writing it."

Thus, the process of constructing embodied metaphors echoes Weick's properties of sensemaking (in the order discussed by Weick and as outlined above) in that it literally invites a physical construction of individual and organizational identity; it draws on past experience and learning; it encourages various perspectives to be brought to bear on collective reasoning; it is ultimately a social construction process that taps into an ongoing conversation in the organization; it facilitates the exploration of an enacted organization/environment boundary, and finally allows for a collective, social plausibility check on the various interpretations and constructions.

Technologies of embodied metaphors

In terms of sensemaking through embodied metaphors, several approaches have emerged over the last decade or so. For example, Barry (1994) draws on depth psychology and art therapy to introduce the concept of *analogically mediated inquiry*. An object or model created by participants ("the analog"), allows the process consultant and the participants to engage in a collaborative process of interpretation and sensemaking. Thus, analogically mediated inquiry engages the client actively in creating a spatial metaphor that is not only of a semantic, cognitive or graphical nature, but also importantly of a physical nature. This process allows literal, embodied engagement with otherwise elusive mental images, and the relatively safe debate of alternative perspectives. Taking a psycho-analytical view, this resembles the process of surfacing conscious as well as unconscious aspects of participants' cognition that might have been projected onto the analog, whereby the analog absorbs and encompasses these projections and serves as a "positive scapegoat" for participants (Barry, 1994: 39).

Building on Lakoff and Johnson's (1980) hypothesis that perception is bound up with figurative thinking, Doyle and Sims (2002) discuss "cognitive sculpting," the construction of three-dimensional objects in the context of conversations for change. Participants are invited, using several objects on a table, to form a sculpture of an organizational issue at hand. This process involves verbal and non-verbal meaning negotiation that has both a mnemonic as well as a constructive effect. Paralleling the "positive scapegoat" effect of objects in analogically mediated inquiry, objects in cognitive sculpting also take attention away from the speaker and allow participants to focus on the collaboratively created sculpture, which in turn enables the exploration of meanings that could be politically contentious and would otherwise be undiscussable. The primary outcome of cognitive sculpting consists of developing a shared metaphorical language within a group that can be drawn upon in subsequent strategic conversations. Finally, cognitive sculpting fosters a collaborative setting of shared sensemaking. When two or more groups work independently on the same theme, the groups can discuss the differences in features and genesis of the construction, as well as critically reflect and comment on these differences. Cognitive sculpting results in an enhanced capacity to think and reason about a constructed concrete, physical object; but more importantly, to debate and make sense of the organizational issues it represents.

Buergi and Roos (2003) in addition, have discussed *serious play* as a multimodal process of sensemaking that goes beyond metaphors as pure cognitive devices by similarly employing physical analogs. This process invites participants to configure and represent abstract organizational issues such as organizational identity or the landscape of an organization or team by means of three-dimensional metaphorical objects made of construction toys. The theoretical antecedents of this approach include both Black's (1979) discussion of the creative potential of metaphors as well as Oswick *et al.*'s (2002) proposition to consider structural dissimilarities as origins for metaphorical reasoning. Drawing on Worren, Moore, and Elliott (2002) and Gardner (1993), in addition, the relevance of visual and tactile/kinesthetic knowledge as a complement to propositional knowledge or intelligence is emphasized.

All these approaches exemplify and acknowledge the relevance of conceptual, creative metaphors, and extend the generally accepted semantic-cognitive dimension of metaphorical reasoning by viewing constructed physical objects as occasions for shared sensemaking. In this process, participants are actively involved in constructing or sculpting metaphorical symbols. Size, spatial relatedness, variety of materials, and haptic and tactile aspects of the social construction process all contribute to the recursive process of sensemaking, involving the dynamic interpretation and reading of these embodied metaphors while constructing them. Even though these approaches draw from diverse theoretical underpinnings, they all share an attempt to surface participants' pre-reflexive knowledge, assumptions and experience to develop shared sets of metaphors and shared interpretations.

In summary, we took as a starting point the cognitive and semantic aspects of metaphors in terms of their constructive role in meaning-making, and then proceeded to address two further dimensions. First, through the *spatial* dimension, operationalized in concepts such as cognitive or strategic mapping, the inherently spatial nature of metaphors (image schemata) can be brought to bear literally. Secondly, through the *bodily* dimension, exemplified in concepts such as analogically mediated inquiry, cognitive sculpting, or serious play, embodied metaphors can be brought to bear on processes of shared meaning construction and sensemaking about issues of shared concern. In the next section we present perspectives on embodiment, as well as a discussion of embodied realism in relation to social constructionism.

Embodied realism

Perspectives on embodiment

Rohrer's (2007) survey of the senses in which the term "embodied" has been employed suggests that at least four modes of usage can be identified. First, a meta-theoretical mode that sees embodiment as inherent to cognition, and which stands against a Cartesian philosophy that views knowledge and thought as distinctly and ideally separate from any bodily involvement or perspective. An aspect of this meta-theoretical mode is also inherent in the suggestion of unidirectionality in metaphor mappings from a more embodied source to a more abstract target; and in the grounding of meaning in a finite number of source domains arising from our bodily existence – what Lakoff and Johnson have initially labeled "experientialism" (1980) and subsequently "embodied realism" (1999).

Secondly, a perspective on embodiment as broadly an experiential phenomenon, relating for example to how socio-cultural aspects such as child-rearing practices can influence cognition and language, to the phenomenology of the lived experience of our bodies and its influence on our self-identities, or to our bodies as enablers of particular, subjective vantage points.

Thirdly, embodiment is often seen as the physical substrate of experience, as for example in studies of the unconscious neurophysiological processing that enables routine cognitive activities. Finally, embodiment has a temporal dimension, in that organisms go through developmental changes over time that relate to their ability to acquire certain cognitive skills, and in the context of longer time frames and as whole species, through evolutionary developments such as humans' acquired ability to use language.

From social constructionism to embodied realism

A social constructionist perspective gives primacy to actors' first-order interpretations of what are the phenomena of interest and how they should be understood; and recognizes the role of agents and theorists in constructing concepts that are in time institutionalized and established as solid truths (Astley, 1985). Even though the embodied realism view could initially be perceived as a variant of social constructionism, it has some important differences. In terms of ontology, embodied realism holds that reality neither possesses a fixed essence independent of perception as in positivism, nor fully depends on the institutionalization of interpretations and practices as in social constructionism (Berger and Luckmann, 1966). Rather, it holds that our bodily experience and ongoing patterns of interactions with the physical world are central to structuring our throughts, interpretations and actions through the transfer of conceptual correspondences from this experience to more abstract domains (Lakoff and Johnson, 1999; Lakoff, 1990). This is consistent with phenomenology's emphasis on human experience's fundamental corporeal nature where bodily experience both precedes and shapes conscious processes of thinking and interacting with the world (Merleau-Ponty, 1962).

Embodied realism holds that metaphorical image schemata (figurative, analogical, and non-propositional in nature) that enable the structuring of interactions with the world at both physical and more abstract levels, as well as meaning and interpretation, themselves arise from patterns of embodied experience, and have a neurological basis. Human thought is seen as organized through metaphorical elaborations of image schemata that form and structure experience and understanding. Thus, metaphors are constitutive of the structure of bodily experience, as well as emerging from this experience (Johnson, 1987; Lakoff and Johnson, 1999).

This constitutive image-schematic view that allows for the emergence of new knowledge and insights from metaphorical image schemata, that were not initially present in the features of the tenor or vehicle, contrasts with the traditional objectivist/comparison view of metaphor. This view holds that both the tenor and vehicle have preexisting features with some partial resemblance, that metaphors allow some features of the tenor map onto some features of the vehicle, and that these mappings are reducible to literal propositions that, to be correct, have to correspond to the objective features of the world that they represent (Cornelissen, 2004; 2006).

Further, in terms of epistemology, embodied realism rejects both rationalism (the positivist assumption of innate reason) and empiricism (the constructivist assumption of learned reason). It views the rationalist–empiricist dichotomy as too simplistic and unhelpful, refuted by the empirical evidence gathered by neuroscience showing, for example, that babies can learn even before they are born, from their stay in the womb; and therefore when they are born they have knowledge that is both innate as well as learned (Johnson and Lakoff, 2002). Embodied realism is proposed as an alternative that accepts both innate and learned aspects of conceptual systems.

Methodologies in organization theory that take embodiment seriously, in addition to highlighting the constructive role of metaphor, would also seek to gain understanding through a focus on the embodied nature of interpretation and on aspects such as space and topological interrelationships as manifested and constructed in actions, discourses and artifacts or material expressions. In this view, organizational levels of analysis as conventionally understood are explicitly regarded as dependent on the embodied, orientational nature of our existence in the world as well as the hierarchical nature

TABLE 2.1: *Three perspectives on metaphor: positivism, social constructionism and embodied realism*

Paradigmatic approaches	Ontology: nature of reality	Epistemology: theory of knowledge	Methodology: how to research reality	Role of researcher	View of metaphor
Positivist organization theory (Donaldson, 1985, 1996)	Essentialist realism; reality is rule-governed, external, fixed, independent of observers' perception and experience.	Rationalism; knowledge derives from pure reason and can be expressed and analysed in terms of formal logic or other symbolic systems. A priori knowledge is thus possible.	Nomothetic; seek to uncover universal regularities and causal laws of a rule-governed reality via survey instruments and statistical analysis so that valid predictions can be made.	Researcher is independent observer, an expert, objective scientist who can have unmediated access to universally applicable, uncontaminated knowledge.	Metaphors are merely ornamental and expendable linguistic devices. They distort analysis of the "facts" that should be stated literally, and have no place in an objective, rational science.
Social constructionism (Berger and Luckmann, 1966; Gergen, 1999)	Ideationism; social (and for some authors even material) reality is context-dependent, shifting, based on perspective, values and interests of observer. There are no fixed essences but only ephemeral social constructions.	Early philosophical empiricism; we can only know reality through our sense-perceptions or mental constructs, rather than a priori. Relativism; there are no universal laws, only contingent contexts.	Idiographic; seek to gain understanding of unique life-worlds through in-depth immersion and direct, empathetic engagement. Reflexivity is essential in this endeavor.	Researcher is part of the setting, seeking to understand actors' first-order interpretations; observations are mediated by existing interests, values and mental constructs of researcher.	Metaphors are constructive of social and organizational reality, as well as social science. Views differ as to metaphors' creative potential (e.g. comparison vs. domain-interaction views).

| Embodied realism (Johnson, 1987; Lakoff, 1990; Lakoff and Johnson, 1980, 1999) | Experientialism; we perceive and understand physical and social reality through the way our body shapes our experiences and perceptions through ongoing patterns of interactions with the world; there is no ultimate separation of mind and body. | We perceive social reality via our image-schemas, themselves both metaphorical as well as with a neurological basis, and arising from the way we exist, experience and interact with the world in and through our bodies. | Idiographic with topological emphasis; seek to gain understanding through focus on the embodied nature of interpretation, the constructive role of metaphors, and aspects such as space and interrelationships | Researcher pays close attention to the topography of image-schemas and to metaphors-in-use as evident in actions, discourses and artifacts or material expressions of actors. | Metaphors, particularly spatial and orientational ones, are fundamental to our reasoning and interpretation, and are derived from our embodied existence. We employ familiar source domains to understand complex target domains. |

(Adapted from Heracleous and Jacobs, 2008; used with permission.)

of our reasoning and mental constructs (Eysenck, 1993). Rather than an objective, inevitable representation of the "true nature" of things, they are seen to arise from the structuring of our conceptual systems. By analyzing artifacts that can be interpreted to encompass the same categories as in the dominant conception (individual, group, organization and environment), we aim to present an alternative way of understanding and researching these categories.

Table 2.1 presents central features of the paradigmatic approaches of positivism, social constructionism and embodied realism, along with associated views of metaphor.

REFERENCES

Alvesson, M. and Karreman, D. 2000. Taking the linguistic turn in organizational research. *Journal of Applied Behavioral Science*, 36: 136–58.

Aristotle. 1991. *On rhetoric* (G.A. Kennedy, transl.). New York: Oxford University Press.

Armenakis, A. and Bedeian, A. 1992. The role of metaphors in organizational change. Change agent and change target perspectives. *Group & Organization Management*, 17: 242–9.

Astley, W. G. 1985. Administrative science as socially constructed truth. *Administrative Science Quarterly*, 30: 497–513.

Barrett, F. J. and Cooperrider, D. L. 1990. Generative metaphor intervention: A new behavioral approach for working with systems divided by conflict and caught in defensive perception. *Journal of Applied Behavioral Science*, 26: 219–39.

Barrett, F. J., Thomas, G. F., and Hocevar, S. P. 1995. The central role of discourse in large-scale change: A social construction perspective. *Journal of Applied Behavioral Science*, 31: 352–72.

Barry, D. 1994. Making the invisible visible: Using analogically-based methods to surface unconscious organizational processes. *Organization Development Journal*, 12(4): 37–47.

Barry, D. and Elmes, M. 1997. Strategy retold: Toward a narrative view of strategic discourse. *Academy of Management Review*, 22: 429–52.

Berger, P. and Luckmann, T. 1966. *The social construction of reality*. London: Penguin.

Black, M. 1993. More about metaphor. In Ortony, A. (ed.), *Metaphor and thought*, 2nd edn. Cambridge: Cambridge University Press, 19–43.

Bougon, M. G. 1992. Congregate cognitive maps. *Journal of Management Studies*, 29: 369–89.

Brown, S. M. 1992. Cognitive mapping and repertory grids for qualitative survey research. *Journal of Management Studies*, 29: 287–307.

Buergi, P. and Roos, J. 2003. Images of strategy. *European Management Journal*, 21(1): 69–78.

Burke, W. W. 1992. Metaphors to consult by. *Group & Organization Management*, 17: 255–9.

Calori, R., Johnson, G., and Sarnin, P. 1994. CEOs' cognitive maps and the scope of the organization. *Strategic Management Journal*, 15: 437–57.

Clarke, I. and Mackaness, W. 2001. Management "intuition": An interpretative account of structure and content of decision schemas using cognitive maps. *Journal of Management Studies*, 38: 147–72.

Cleary, C. and Packard, T. 1992. The use of metaphors in organizational assessment and change. *Group & Organization Management*, 17: 229–41

Cornelissen, J. 2004. What are we playing at? Theatre, organization and the use of metaphor. *Organization Studies*, 25: 705–26.

2005. Beyond compare: Metaphor in organization theory. *Academy of Management Review*, 30: 751–64.

2006. Organization theory: A case study of the organizational identity metaphor. *Journal of Management Studies*, 43: 683–709.

Dijk, T. A. V. 1988. Social cognition, social power and social discourse. *Text*, 8: 129–57.

Donaldson, L. 1985. *In defence of organization theory: A reply to the critics*. Cambridge University Press.

1986. *For positivist organization theory*. London: Sage.

Doyle, J. R. and Sims, D. 2002. Enabling strategic metaphor in conversation: A technique of cognitive sculpting for explicating knowledge. In A. S. Huff and M. Jenkins (eds.), *Mapping strategic knowledge*. London: Sage, 63–85.

Eden, C. 1992. On the nature of cognitive maps, *Journal of Management Studies*, 29: 261–5.

Eden, C. and Huxham, C. 1996. Action research for management research. *British Journal of Management*, 7: 75–86.

Eysenck. M. W. 1993. *Principles of cognitive psychology*. Hove: Erlbaum.

Ford, J. D. and Ford, L. W. 1995. The role of conversations in producing intentional change in organizations. *Academy of Management Review*, 20: 541–70.

Gardner, H. 1993. *Frames of mind: the theory of multiple intelligences*. New York: Basic Books.

Gergen, K. J. 1999. *An invitation to social construction*. Beverley Hills, CA: Sage.

Gergen, K. J. and Thatchenkery, T. J. 1996. Organization science as social construction: Postmodern potentials. *Journal of Applied Behavioral Science*, 32: 356–77.

Grant, D. and Oswick, C. (eds.), 1996. *Metaphor and organizations*. London: Sage.

Heracleous, L. 2004. Interpretive approaches to organizational discourse. In Grant, D., Phillips, N., Hardy, C., Putnam, L., and Oswick, C. (eds.), *Handbook of Organizational Discourse*. Beverly Hills, CA: Sage, 175–92.

Heracleous, L. and Barrett, M. 2001. Organizational change as discourse: Communicative actions and deep structures in the context of information technology implementation. *Academy of Management Journal*, 44: 755–78.

Heracleous, L. and Jacobs, C. 2008. Understanding organizations through embodied metaphors. *Organization Studies*. 29(1): 45–78.

Heracleous, L. and Marshak, R. 2004. Conceptualizing organizational discourse as situated symbolic action. *Human Relations*, 57: 1285–1312.

Hirsch, P. M. 1986. From ambushes to golden parachutes: Corporate takeovers as an instance of cultural framing and institutional integration. *American Journal of Sociology*, 91: 800–37.

Howe, M. A. 1989. Using imagery to facilitate organizational development and change. *Group & Organization Studies*, 14: 70–82.

Hodgkinson, G. P. and Johnson, G. 1994. Exploring the mental models of competitive strategists: The case for a processual approach. *Journal of Management Studies*, 31: 525–51.

Inns, D. 2002. Metaphor in the literature of organizational analysis: A preliminary taxonomy and a glimpse at a humanities-based perspective. *Organization*, 9: 305–30.

Jacobs, C. and Heracleous, L. 2006. Constructing shared understanding – the role of embodied metaphor in organization development. *Journal of Applied Behavioral Science*, 42(2): 207–26.

Joas, H. 1996. *The creativity of action*. Cambridge: Polity.

Johnson, M. 1987. *The body in the mind : The bodily basis of meaning, imagination, and reason*. University of Chicago Press.

Johnson, M. and Lakoff, G. 2002. Why cognitive linguistics requires embodied realism. *Cognitive Linguistics*, 13: 245–63.

Lakoff, G. 1990. The invariance hypothesis: Is abstract reason based on image schemas? *Cognitive Linguistics*, 1: 39–74.

1993. The contemporary theory of metaphor. In Ortonty, A. (ed.), *Metaphor and Thought*. Cambridge University Press, 202–51.

Lakoff, G. and Johnson, M. 1980. *Metaphors we live by*. University of Chicago Press.

1999. *Philosophy in the flesh*. New York: Basic Books.

Marshak, R. 1993. Managing the metaphors of change. *Organizational Dynamics*, 22(1): 44–56.

Merleau-Ponty, M. 1962. *Phenomenology of perception*. London, New York: Routledge.

Morgan, G. 1980. Paradigms, metaphor and puzzle solving in organization theory. *Administrative Science Quarterly*, 25: 660–71.

1983. More on metaphor: Why we cannot control tropes in administrative science. *Administrative Science Quarterly*, 28: 601–7.

1986. *Images of organization*. Beverly Hills, CA: Sage.

1996. An afterword: Is there anything more to be said about metaphor? In Oswick, C. and Grant, D. (eds.), *Metaphor and organization*. London: Sage, 227–40.

Oswick, C. 1996. Insights into diagnosis: An exploration using visual metaphors. In Oswick, C. and Grant, D. (eds.), *Organisation development: metaphorical explorations*. London: Pitman. 137–51.

Oswick, C. and Grant, D. (eds.), 1996. *Organisation development: metaphorical explorations*. London: Pitman.

Oswick, C. and Montogomery, J. 1999. Images of an organization: The use of metaphor in a multinational company. *Journal of Organizational Change Management*, 12: 501–23.

Oswick, C., Keenoy, T., and Grant, D. 2002. Metaphorical and analogical reasoning in organization theory: Beyond orthodoxy. *Academy of Management Review*. 27: 294–303.

Palmer, I. and Dunford, R. 1996a. Coflicting uses of metaphors: Reconceptualizing their use in the field of organizational change. *Academy of Management Review*, 21: 691–717.

1996b. Understanding organisations through metaphor. In Oswick, C. and Grant, D. (eds.), *Organisation development: metaphorical explorations*. London: Pitman, 7–15.

Pinder, C. C. and Bourgeois, V. W. 1982. Controlling tropes in administrative science. *Administrative Science Quarterly*, 27: 641–52.

Pondy, L. R. 1983. The role of metaphors and myths in organization and in the facilitation of change. In Pondy, L. R., Frost, P.J., Morgan, G. and Dandridge, T. C. (eds.), *Organizational symbolism*. Greenwich, CT: JAI Press: 157–66.

Robinson, A. H. and Petchenik, B. B. 1976. *The nature of maps: Essays toward understanding maps and mapping*. University of Chicago Press.

Rohrer, T. 2007. The body in space: Embodiment, experientialism and linguistic conceptualization. In Ziemke, T. Zlatev, J. and Frank, R. (eds.), *Body, language and mind*, Vol. 1. Berlin: Mouton de Gruyter.

Sackmann, S. 1989. The role of metaphors in organization transformation. *Human Relations*, 42: 463–85.

Schon, D. 1993. Generative metaphor: A perspective on problem-setting in social policy. In A. Ortony (ed.), *Metaphor and thought*, 2nd edn. Cambridge University Press, 137–63.

Tsoukas, H. 1993. Analogical reasoning and knowledge generation in organization theory. *Organization Studies*, 14: 323–46.

Weick, K. E. 1990. Introduction: Cartographic myths in organizations. In A. S. Huff and M. Jenkins (eds.), *Mapping strategic thought*. Chichester: Wiley, 1–10.

1995. *Sensemaking in organizations*. Beverley Hills, CA: Sage.

Wittgenstein, L. 1967. *Philosophical investigations*, 3rd edn. Oxford: Blackwell.

Worren, N., Moore, K., and Elliott, R. 2002. When theories become tools: Toward a framework for pragmatic validity. *Human Relations*, 55: 1227–50

CHAPTER THREE

Analyzing embodied metaphors
as an interpretive, hermeneutic endeavor

In this chapter we continue discussing the theoretical antecedents of our approach, by outlining some key conceptual orientations and analytical directions suggested by interpretive theory as well as hermeneutics as a key interpretive approach, that have informed how we conceptualize and analyze embodied metaphors. We begin with the concern with *verstehen*, the effort to understand how agents see their own situation both in and through their symbolic artifacts, and in turn employ this understanding in our interpretations of the symbolic artifacts agents produce, be it texts or embodied metaphors analysed as texts, to reach explanations adequate at the level of meaning. We also address the inseparability of action and structure, where actions can inform an understanding of context, and vice versa; the constitutive role of language not just as representation but as shaper of thought; and the multiplicity of meanings where iterations between part and whole can enrich interpretation further until an acceptable saturation of meaning can be reached. Finally, we note the contextuality and historicity of meaning, not just as embedded in the text analyzed but also as encoded in the researcher's pre-understandings that inform the interpretation. We address all of these considerations and how they relate to the interpretation of embodied metaphors.

Interpretive theory

There is a variety of interpretive approaches deriving from or inspired by the German idealist tradition, beginning with Kant's emphasis on the importance of a priori knowledge of mind as logically and ontologically preceding efforts to grasp empirical experience.[1] The German idealist tradition encompassed theorists such as Dilthey, Weber, Husserl, and Schutz, and inspired severe challenges to the dominant paradigm of sociological positivism. These challenges were primarily on the grounds that science was not, and could not, be value-free and able to offer objective, unmediated access to universal truth as assumed; and secondly, that the nomothetic methods employed in the natural sciences aiming to identify general laws and causal explanation were unsuitable for the "cultural sciences," whose domain was human life, its processes and outcomes (Burrell and Morgan, 1979).

From an interpretive perspective, social life is not a predetermined, independent universe of objects that are there to be discovered and their stable interactions analyzed, but is instead an ongoing, skilled, contingent accomplishment constituted by active and reflexive agents. Agency is seen as intentional but constrained, as historically located and both bounded and enabled by broader structures. Contrary to positivist conceptions, these structures are not an overarching mass distinct from agents' everyday actions, but as structuration theory suggests, such actions and social practices are the medium of their constitution, occurring through structuration processes imbued with dimensions of meanings, norms, and power (Giddens, 1984).

Interpretive approaches have developed from a challenger position, to a well-established approach in organization theory with a rich intellectual legacy and an array of methodological options. Early work in organization theory, such as Egon Bittner's (1965) classic article on the concept of organization and David Silverman's (1970) critiques of

[1] For a more extensive discussion of interpretive theory, see Heracleous (2007a).

functionalist sociology, fostered a trend that has continued strongly to this day. Interpretively inspired approaches rooted in social theory, linguistics, and other domains, such as hermeneutics, phenomenology, symbolic interactionism, ethnomethodology, critical theory, story-telling analysis, metaphorical analysis, and rhetorical analysis have all been employed by organization theorists. While these approaches have subtle differences, they all subscribe to a voluntarist orientation with respect to agency (Astley and Van de Ven, 1983), view the social construction of reality as taking place through language and social practices, place emphasis on understanding agents' first-order realities, and emphasize the historicality and situatedness of experience (Heracleous, 2006).

Our interest in embodied metaphors as both a process or meaning negotiation, and a symbolic artifact, stems from our interpretive orientation in terms of ontology as well as method. If social life is intersubjectively constructed, if actions and outcomes, including symbols, should and could be understood at the level of meaning, then embodied metaphors can serve as rich sets of data that provide access to agents' ideational worlds with respect to a variety of domains. This access can occur in relation to not only the target domains of these embodied metaphors (the agents' organizations, their conception of group or organizational identity, their key tasks, a topical strategic challenge, or whatever else the workshops within which these meta-phors are constructed are structured to address), but also in relation to the dynamics of negotiation of meaning that could shed light on processes of social construction. Further on we discuss the methodo-logical directions for analyzing embodied metaphors implied by inter-pretive theory.

Interpretive methodology

Based on Wilhelm Dilthey's and Max Weber's imperative of *ver-stehen*, interpretively oriented approaches aim to achieve a *meaningful understanding* of the actors' frames of reference. Dilthey argued that whereas the natural sciences seek to *explain* nature, human studies should try to *understand* expressions of cultural life based on a historical consciousness of lived experience, grasped through its observable expressions. He viewed understanding as the comprehension of forms of life that can open up new possibilities for our own experience. Influenced by the earlier writings of Schleiermacher, as well as the positivist spirit of his time, Dilthey aimed to develop "objectively valid" interpretations and data, to embed in the method of *verstehen* the search for scientific objectivity (see Harrington, 2001).

Weber (1991) also held that what distinguishes the social from the natural sciences is this effort to understand the agents' own views and meanings. For him, *verstehen* was a methodological approach that could lead to knowledge that would both be "adequate at the level of meaning," as well as comparable in terms of objectivity to knowledge derived from the positivist tradition. The assumption, however, that a method could provide both empathetic access to agents' ideational world, as well as objective validity of the type sought in positivist science, has been seen as problematic. Ricoeur (1991), for example, supported the initial contrast made by Dilthey between meaningful understanding of the type sought in interpretive theory on the one hand, and explanation as the search for causal, law-like deterministic regularities based on the natural science paradigm on the other, and did not seek to integrate them.

Interpretive researchers aim to understand social life through attention to agents' first-order interpretations, and drawing on their own stocks of knowledge and pre-understandings. They often immerse themselves in other forms of life, as for example in ethnographic research, but keep in mind the danger of going fully native and thus losing the necessary critical distance from the data. Researchers' descriptions are necessarily "mediated" by the discursive categories of both language and social science, obeying a "double hermeneutic." Researchers make second-order interpretations of agents' first-order interpretations of their situation, aiming to stay as close as possible to these interpretations (Giddens, 1993).

One critique of interpretive approaches is that they are too subjective, that they lack "objectivity," affording primacy to the idiosyncratic, subjective meanings of single actors, be it researchers or those they study, with no necessary relation to a shared, inter-subjective and verifiable reality. If interpretivism was indeed fully subjective, this would imply the potential for unlimited interpretations of observations and research data, with no means of verification or validation. In line with this assumption, Denzin (1983) proposed that interpretivists reject generalization, since each observed social interaction is unique, and takes place within complex and indeterminate social contexts.

To accept this premise, however, is to misunderstand the interpretive project, where the challenge of producing valid interpretations has been long recognized and debated. Interpretive understanding does not equate with a degeneration to extreme subjectivism, unlimited interpretations and the inability to make any kind of generalization. Influenced by the positivist spirit of his time, as well as by Schleiermacher's writings before him, Dilthey proposed that the researcher's interpretive framework should be based on "objective spirit," by which he meant the "whole range of human objectifications, whether they be expressions meant to communicate or deeds meant to influence" (Makkreel, 1999: 426). This implies that a broader understanding of historical, social and cultural systems in which a text (or symbolic artifacts or action analyzed as text) is embedded, can be drawn upon to inform its interpretation. Further, Weber (1991) saw his aim of deriving objective generalizations from first-order data as both compatible with, and dependent on, meaningful understanding of social action; and his "ideal types" were based on this type of generalizing endeavor.

Eco (1990) further held that the potential for unlimited interpretations does not imply that all interpretations are equally likely or valid. As Dilthey had noted, Eco held that there are several domains that can guide textual interpretations, going beyond the semantic meaning of the words and the internal coherence of the text, and these include the cultural context, the interpreter's own frame of reference, and the interpreter's immersion into the life-worlds from which the texts, actions or artifacts arise from and refer to.

Interpretive researchers therefore do not aim for total generalizations (deterministic laws or axioms) or statistical generalizations (where the probability of a situation or feature occurring can be calculated from its instances within a sample representative of a wider population) (Williams, 2000) but for moderatum generalizations (where aspects of a situation are seen as exemplars of broader sets of features). Moderatum generalizations are subject to the limits of the inductive problem (that one cannot unproblematically generalize from a small number of known cases to a large number of unknown ones), and of the ontological problem of categorical equivalence (that generalizations within one category of experience of domain may not apply to other categories). Yin (1994) similarly proposed that interpretive work can lead to analytical generalizability, rather than statistical generalizability. Analytical generalizability can refer to principles expounding for example an understanding of how divergent deep structures of discourse can inhibit understanding and productive dialogue among stakeholders in a change process (Heracleous and Barrett, 2001); or how to appreciate the connotational aspects of an utterance and their effects on stakeholders, an understanding of nested contexts is necessary (Heracleous and Marshak, 2004).

Interpretive directions for analyzing embodied metaphors

Embodied metaphors are at a basic level collections of signs, which become symbols that acquire contingent meanings, based on how they are employed in the narrative portrayed by the embodied metaphor. The researcher's task is to understand these symbols and the narratives they are part of, so as to access the ideational world of the agents who developed those narratives through a facilitated process of meaning negotiation. This is in effect an application of the concept of *verstehen*, both as a concept as well as a methodological orientation. Further, the constructions themselves as a whole, are symbols of the interpretive position that agents are active in constructing their social reality through a negotiation process, within broader constraints (which in the construction process manifest as the structure and process of the workshop, as well as the organizational contexts in which the agents participating are embedded).

All of the construction pieces are imbued to an extent with pre-configured meanings. For example, a piece shaped like a crocodile at a basic semantic level denotes this specific animal, but then this becomes a symbol that may refer to an aggressive competitor, if it is employed as such in a narrative. A piece shaped as a round mirror may become a competitor that likes to imitate the focal organization; and a piece shaped as a sheep may refer to a non-threatening, docile competitor. Other pieces (such as simple orthogonal ones) have preconfigured meanings in terms of their potential to be parts of constructions that tell a story; as well as their specific color, which can symbolize certain qualities in the construction; based on the shared pre-understandings of the agents building the construction. Given that these constructions are collections of signs that become symbols, they can be analyzed as texts, employing several approaches that are appropriate to analyzing text, such as metaphorical analysis, narrative analysis, or hermeneutic analysis. In this book we offer several analyses of such constructions employing a variety discourse analysis approaches.

Metaphorical approaches find natural application here (Heracleous and Jacobs, 2008), since these constructions are metaphors *par excellence*. The facilitation process usually entails agents building representations of their organization and its environment, and in doing so they create structures that are in essence metaphorical, drawing from source domains they deem appropriate or enlightening to represent

target domains. Secondly, the debriefing process led by the organization development practitioners facilitating the construction process,
makes narratives, even those that may not have been explicit up to
that point, apparent and subject to examination. Temporal dimensions are introduced in the process of sensemaking, and the elements
of the construction play a role in a progression of events. The protagonists of the narratives are often the agents and their colleagues, represented either by person figures, or even by different types of animals
in the physical constructions.

The interpretation process by the researcher is underlied by the
fact that language is both constructive as well as representational
(Heracleous and Barrett, 2001). The pieces metaphorically represent
aspects of the agents' environment and organization. But at the same
time, they are a medium of constructing shared realities, through the
interactive negotiation process as well as through the subsequent uses
of what is built. These shared understandings relate for example to
the nature of the environment and the organization, and of strategic
challenges; understandings that may not have been there when the
process started. Therefore, the researcher pays attention to not only
the denotative aspect (the basic dictionary meaning of the elements
of the construction), but more importantly to the connotative aspect
(what the signs symbolize) of the construction, as implicit or explicit
in the broader narratives. Further, if the available data allows, the
researcher aims to understand not only the static outcome of the process (through for example metaphorical or narrative analysis of the
embodied metaphor), but also analysis of the process itself, which can
shed light on how shared understandings on specific issues are negotiated and crystallized.

Keeping in mind the double hermeneutic of social science (Giddens,
1984), the second-order interpretations of the researcher gain part of
their validity from closeness to the first-order interpretations of participants, as well as from robustness of method such as effective triangu-
lation and accurate coding. The extensive communication between

the participants and the researcher enhances what Sandberg (2005) refers to as "communicative validity." The relevance of the structure and aims of the facilitation process, as well as the resulting embodied metaphors of participants' strategic challenges, enhance "pragmatic validity." If we accept the agents as "authors" of the embodied metaphors, the researcher tries to understand the authors' intentions as a key input that can enhance the validity of the interpretative process, as Giddens (1979, 1987) proposed. Even if it is impossible to fully enter the authors' states of mind, as Dilthey accepted, their own intentions and interpretations of what they've built enhance the validity of the researcher's second-order interpretations. Below, after the description of hermeneutics as a type of interpretive theory, we extend the methodological discussion with reference to how hermeneutics contributes to analyzing embodied metaphors.

Hermeneutics

The Greek terms *hermeneuein* ("to interpret") and *hermeneia* ("interpretation"), from which hermeneutics derives, are associated with the god Hermes, the messenger of Zeus, god of commerce, master thief, and patron of merchants and thieves.[2] The linkage of hermeneutics with Hermes denotes a bringing forth to understanding of something previously foreign or unintelligible. The three main meanings associated with the term hermeneutics in ancient Greek usage underlie current understandings of hermeneutics: first saying or expressing something, secondly explaining or clarifying something drawing on context and pre-understanding, and thirdly translating, or mediating between two different worlds (Palmer, 1969).

Whereas the initial meaning of hermeneutics in the seventeenth century related to principles and methods of biblical interpretation,

---

[2] For a more extensive discussion of hermeneutics, see Heracleous (2007b).

it was, over time, extended to encompass general rules of philological exegesis. With Heidegger's and Gadamer's subsequent development of "philosophical hermeneutics" the reflexive concern with the nature of understanding and interpretation itself was added as a central concern. The view of language underlying hermeneutics is consistent with the critiques of logical atomism and its representational view of language, as developed by the later Wittgenstein in his *Philosophical Investigations* (1967). Wittgenstein suggested that there was no fixed essence associated with each word, as logical atomism had held, but that words acquire their meaning through use within particular language games.

An early text on hermeneutics, Friedrich Ast's *Basic Elements of Grammar, Hermeneutics and Criticism*, notes that hermeneutics aims to understand the spirit of a text through the three moments of historical understanding, grammatical understanding, and understanding the text in relation to its author and the spirit of the age in which it was written. Ast proposed in this text the principle of the hermeneutic circle: that one can only understand the spirit of an age through the individual works that exemplify it; but that these works can themselves be understood only through their interrelationship with the whole.

In order to address what he saw as the fragmentation of hermeneutics, in the early nineteenth century Schleiermacher sought to develop a "general hermeneutics" whose principles could serve as the foundation for any type of textual interpretation, viewing hermeneutics as applicable to any type of text. Schleiermacher elevated conversation to a model for hermeneutics, since every utterance in conversation expresses an aspect of the speaker's life, is linked with a wider series of utterances, and lies within a broader context of the speaker and their situation. Schleiermacher distinguished between grammatical or historical hermeneutics, concerned with analyzing the language of a text in relation to its historical context, and psychological or technical hermeneutics, concerned with the effort to understand language as an expression of the author's individuality and mental processes (Vedder, 1999).

Wilhelm Dilthey believed that hermeneutics could serve as the foundational discipline for all humanistic studies, and as an antidote to the mechanistic reductionism of the natural sciences. He viewed interpretation as "a process of coming to know" (Makkreel, 1999: 425), that led to a fuller understanding of psychic and historical life, the grasping of "lived experience" through its expressions. Understanding, for Dilthey, was not just related to what the text means generally, or to its author, but also to its implications for the reader's own experience.

Martin Heidegger, moving away from earlier concerns, was primarily interested with issues of ontology, the nature of being, rather than epistemology (developing valid rules for interpreting texts). Heidegger's view of hermeneutics, in *Being and Time*, was as the explication of human existence and as a process by which words bring forth understanding. Similarly to Heidegger, who was his teacher, Gadamer was interested in the nature of understanding itself, proposing that the hermeneutical experience is constituted by the aesthetic, the historical and the linguistic spheres. He viewed understanding as essentially historical, taking place through language (Gadamer, 2006 [1970]), and gave primacy to conversation or dialogue in achieving understanding. The central role of history and the boundedness of truth with it, meant that despite the finitude associated with claims to knowing, no absolute truth was ever possible (Schmidt, 1999). As Gadamer (2006 [1970]: 26) put it: "the meaning of a word resides not just in the language system and in the context; rather, this 'standing-in-a-context' means at the same time that the word is never completely separated from the multiple meanings it has in itself, even when the context has made clear the meaning it possesses in this particular context." Critical hermeneutics, arising from Habermas's work, and in particular his exchanges with Gadamer, brought considerations of power and ideology in hermeneutical interpretation.

Language here is seen as mirroring the interests of dominant classes, and hermeneutics as a way to decode these representations in the interests of emancipation.

Hermeneutic methodology

Methodologically, the hermeneutic circle encourages an analytical approach to textual interpretation operating as an iterative process of discovery, moving from part to the whole and vice versa, progressively reaching enriched interpretations, taking into account nested levels of context until saturation is reached, when the researcher judges that sufficient understanding of the text has been gained (Kets de Vries and Miller, 1987; Prasad, 2002; Thachankary, 1992). Saturation in hermeneutic textual interpretation is often expressed through reaching an understanding of overall narratives, central themes, how these themes relate to each other in argumentations, or other key features of the text such as root metaphors or use of a certain type of vocabulary or style; all of these being informed and related to ethnographically derived data where available and applicable (Heracleous, 2006).

Schleiermacher saw a logical contradiction in the hermeneutic circle; if the whole derives its meaning from its parts, and the parts from the whole, and in order to understand one we must first understand the other, how do we start? In this context, Schleiermacher proposed that a leap beyond logic was needed, and that "divinatory certainty," characterized by conjecture and interpretation based on the context of a text, the author's situation and the combination of words employed was applicable, rather "demonstrative certainty" based on scientific proof. This "divinatory" element assumes a shared pre-understanding within a community of meaning that enables the operation of the hermeneutical circle in the first place.

Ricoeur focused on hermeneutics as the interpretation of texts, whether spoken or written. Similarly to Gadamer, he did not accept the possibility of complete closure in interpretation, suggesting that there are hidden, indirect meanings within the apparent meanings of texts, which can be attained through hermeneutic detours in other domains. Rather than the self being master of meanings, Ricoeur saw existence itself is a mode of interpretation and the self as understanding itself through the other and through language (Kearney, 1999). Having defined hermeneutics as the "art of interpreting texts" (1997: 66), Ricoeur noted that once spoken language is inscribed as text, it becomes autonomous, divorced from its author and subject to a variety of intepretations (Ricoeur, 1991: 105–24). These interpretations of written texts however, in a variety of situations, beyond opening up new horizons for the self, and engaging the interpreter's own pre-understandings, ideally also involve a concern with the text's own historical and cultural context (1991: 1–20).

Despite post-structuralist claims about the irreducible plurality and indeterminacy of meanings, where a text "practices the infinite deferment of the signified" (Barthes, 1977: 158), or the claims of critics of interpretive methods more generally, a consistent theme in the hermeneutics of Ast, Wolf, Schleiermacher, Dilthey, and Ricoeur is that meanings, even though in theory infinite, when considered in the context of particular hermeneutic processes some meanings are more applicable than others, given a text's particular social-historical context (see, for example, Ricoeur, 1991: 144–67; cf. Phillips and Brown, 1993). Other hermeneutically oriented theorists, such as Giddens (1979, 1987), propose that interpretive validity can be improved if interpretation is informed by ethnographic inquiry in the context of a text, including an understanding of the characteristics and values of the audience and the author, as well as the author's intentions.

Hermeneutic directions for analyzing embodied metaphors

Validity concerns are crucial when interpreting embodied metaphors. The surface narrative of a construction may involve, for example, a troupe of animals facing in all directions and positioned everywhere without any obvious boundaries, then undertaking a journey which culminates in a circumscribed field where they all face in the same direction and have a better understanding of a shared destiny.

Understanding more about the context and goals of the process, helps to shed light not just on the surface story, but what it means, its connotations, the indirect meanings that Ricoeur referred to. Understanding context and interpreting the construction in this light could tell us that metaphorically speaking, the animals are the agents who created the construction, whose organization just underwent an acquisition, where their destiny and identity suffered a displacement. The explicit target domain of the construction was their strategy development process, showing a progression from current to ideal, moving from an unstructured process without a shared understanding to one with clear parameters where everyone faces in the same direction. Knowing these contextual elements informs the hermeneutic process to an extent where they reveal the indirect, connotational meanings that an interpreter without this contextual knowledge could never access.

With respect to the application of the hermeneutic circle, researchers aim to reach saturation of meaning through iterations between part and whole. Bearing in mind the general aversion to the complete closure of meaning that most hermeneutic scholars display, however, whereas context can inform meaning, it can never close it in the sense of finding transcendental truth. With data as rich as three-dimensional metaphors expressed physically (embodied metaphors), this possibility of ever-enriching interpretations is even more pronounced. Beyond the debriefing phases of the process of constructing embodied metaphors, researchers can examine for example the interplay between overall narratives and specific events or actions of protagonists, or grand metaphors and constituent metaphors. Saturation does not mean here a truth that is final, but rather that it is acceptable in terms of offering insights to the agents participating in the process, meets validity criteria, and is sufficient for the goals of the research. There is always more to be understood by returning to the text and conducting more symbolic detours (in the sense that Ricoeur used this term), exploring avenues not explored before. But bearing in mind the practicalities of conducting organizational research, for example, where organizational members need actionable insights and researchers aim for publishable outcomes, there has to be a judgment of when provisional saturation is reached (until perhaps the opportunity presents itself to return to the data from a different angle or with different concerns).

As Gadamer noted, it is the pre-understandings of the interpreter, or "prejudices", as he called them, that enable the act of interpretation itself through constituting a shared context between the text and the interpreter. Understandings are developed through a dialogue between the interpreter and the text, keeping in mind the inevitable historicality of both. Prejudices could be productive or unproductive, and as researchers we can try to understand what our prejudices are so that we can gauge their effects on our textual interpretations, and how they may change in the act of interpretation. Since such pre-understandings are constitutive of interpretation, we cannot remove or sanitize them in the search of ultimate truth and closure of meaning. Such considerations lead to the need to be reflexive in any type of interpretively oriented research.

In our case, as organization development researchers, our pre-understandings relate for example to some of the central values of organization development. These include the effort to help agents make sense of their challenges and think through potential directions not through conventional consulting where the advisor is seen as an expert who has the answers, but rather through process consultation as developed for example by Edgar Schein (1988). Further, rather than aiming to develop dependency between the organization and the expert, organization development aims to give agents the skills and frameworks to make sense of their future challenges themselves. In this light, we would provide the organization with literature outlining

TABLE 3.1: *Interpretive theory and hermeneutics: Conceptual orientations and analytical directions*

	Conceptual orientations	Analytical directions
Interpretive theory Berger and Luckmann (1967), Bittner (1965), Gergen (1999), Silverman (1970), Weber (1991)	• Social life is an ongoing skilled accomplishment, located in but not determined by broader structures. • Voluntarist rather than determinist view of agency; agents make choices, even if these choices are constrained and shaped. • Language is not merely representational, but rather constructive of social life. • Reality is socially constructed through social interaction, language use and social practices.	• Aim for *verstehen*; understanding should be adequate at the level of meaning, aiming to access agents' first-order interpretations. • Engage in longitudinal, processual analysis rather than static, cross-sectional one. • Seek to incorporate levels of context in the analysis. Some interpretations are more applicable than others, given the social and historical context of the text, the authors and the interpreters. • May make analytical or moderatum generalizations as opposed to statistical generalizations.
Hermeneutics Gadamer (1970), Giddens (1984), Palmer (1969), Ricoeur (1991, 1997).	• Hermeneutics as the art of interpreting texts, bringing forth to understanding something previously unintelligible. • Hermeneutics as concerned both with epistemology (principles of textual interpretation) as well as ontology (the nature of interpretation itself as well as the nature of being). • Inter-textuality; texts can be understood as parts of the whole and the whole as manifested in individual texts. • The surface text is not all there is; search for indirect, connotational meanings through hermeneutic detours.	• Seek to understand not only the text itself, but also the horizons this understanding opens for yourself, as well as others. • Need to be sensitive to the pre-understandings of the interpreter and how they inform interpretation (reflexivity), as well as those encoded in the text and those of the author, if accessible. • Employ the hermeneutic circle, an iterative process between text and context, part and whole, until (provisional) saturation of meaning is reached. • Seek not just surface meanings but also indirect or hidden meanings through engaging in dialogue with the text and taking into account levels of context.

the process of constructing embodied metaphors and how this process can be facilitated effectively. With respect to the specific target domains of the embodied metaphors, for example the strategy development process, our pre-understandings relate to what an effective process entails, and what the desired outcomes of such a process are, which informs how we interpret what is built by agents, in conjunction with what they tell us about what they've built.

Finally, our prior work in embodied metaphors and a knowledge of how issues of power may physically manifest in such metaphors (Heracleous and Jacobs, 2008), lead to pre-understandings which help us probe areas of the construction where we believe there is more to be learned, areas whose significance agents may not consciously recognize, for example, the use of certain colors and connections, sizes and location of elements of the construction, or person figures facing one way instead of another, or positioned higher or lower than other elements of the construction. This leads to a process of dialogue, not just between us as interpreters and the embodied metaphor as text, but between us and the authors of that text, the agents who built the embodied metaphor.

Table 3.1 outlines the conceptual orientations and analytical directions suggested by interpretive theory and hermeneutics.

REFERENCES

Astley, W. G. 1985. Administrative science as socially constructed truth. *Administrative Science Quarterly*, 30: 497–513.

Astley, W. G. and Van de Ven, A. H. 1983. Central perspectives and debates in organization theory. *Administrative Science Quarterly*, 28: 245–73.

Barthes, R. 1977. *Image, music, text*. London: Fontana.

Bittner, E. 1965. The concept of organization. *Social Research*, 32: 239–55.

Burrell, G. and Morgan, G. 1979. *Sociological paradigms and organizational analysis*. Andover: Gower.

Daft, R. L. 1983. Learning the craft of organizational research. *Academy of Management Review*, 8: 539–46.

Denzin, N. 1983. Interpretive interactionism. In Morgan, G. (ed.), *Beyond method: Strategies for social research*. Beverly Hills, CA: Sage, 129–46.

Eco, U. 1990. *The limits of interpretation.* Bloomington, IN: Indiana University Press.

Gadamer, H. G. 2006 [1970]. Language and understanding. *Theory, Culture and Society,* 23(1): 13–27.

Gergen, K. 1999. *An invitation to social construction.* Beverley Hills, CA: Sage.

Giddens, A. 1979. *Central problems in social theory.* London: Macmillan.

   1984. *The constitution of society.* Cambridge: Polity.

   1987. *Social theory and modern sociology.* Cambridge: Polity.

   1993. *New rules of sociological method.* Stanford University Press.

Harrington, A. 2001. Dilthey, empathy and verstehen: A contemporary reappraisal. *European Journal of Social Theory,* 4: 311–29.

Heracleous, L. 2006. *Discourse, interpretation, organization.* Cambridge University Press.

   2007a. Hermeneutics. In Clegg, S. R. and Bailey, J. R. (eds.), *International encyclopedia of organization studies,* Vol. 2, Beverly Hills, CA: Sage, 582–5.

   2007b. Interpretive Theory. In Clegg, S. R. and Bailey, J. R. (eds.), *International encyclopedia of organization studies,* Vol. 2, Beverly Hills, CA: Sage, 720–3.

Heracleous, L. and Barrett, M. 2001. Organizational change as discourse: Communicative actions and deep structures in the context of IT Implementation. *Academy of Management Journal,* 44: 755–78.

Heracleous, L. and Jacobs, C. 2008. Understanding organizations through embodied metaphors. *Organization Studies,* 29(1): 45–78.

Heracleous, L. and Marshak, R. 2004. Conceptualizing organizational discourse as situated symbolic action. *Human Relations,* 57: 1285–1312.

Kearney, R. 1999. Ricoeur. In Critchley, S. and Schroeder, W. R. (eds.), *A companion to continental philosophy.* Oxford: Blackwell, 443–51.

Kets de Vries, M. F. R. and Miller, D. 1987. Interpreting organizational texts. *Journal of Management Studies,* 24: 233–47.

Lee, A. S. and Baskerville, R. L. 2003. Generalizing generalizability in information systems research. *Information Systems Research,* 14: 221–43.

Makkreel, R. A, 1999. Dilthey. In Critchley, S. and Schroeder, W. R. (eds.), *A companion to continental philosophy.* Oxford: Blackwell, 425–32.

Palmer, R. E. 1969. *Hermeneutics.* Evanston, IL: Northwestern University Press.

Phillips, N. and Brown, J. L. 1993. Analyzing communication in and around organizations: A critical hermeneutic approach. *Academy of Management Journal,* 36: 1547–76.

Prasad, A. 2002. The contest over meaning: Hermeneutics as an interpretive methodology for understanding texts. *Organizational Research Methods,* 5 (1): 12–33.

Prasad, A. and Prasad, P. 2002. The coming of age of interpretive organizational research. *Organizational Research Methods,* 5: 4–11.

Ricoeur, P. 1991. *From text to action.* Evanston, IL: Northwestern University Press.

1997. Rhetoric-poetics-hermeneutics. In Jost, W. and M. J. Hyde (eds.), *Rhetoric and hermeneutics in our time: A reader.* New Haven, CT: Yale University Press, 60–72.

Sandberg, J. 2005. How do we justify knowledge produced within interpretive approaches? *Organizational Research Methods,* 8: 41–68.

Schein, E. H. 1988. *Process consultation Vol. I: Its role in organization development,* Reading, MA: Addison-Wesley.

Schmidt, D. J. 1999. Gadamer. In Critchley, S. and Schroeder, W. R. (eds.), *A companion to continental philosophy.* Oxford: Blackwell, 433–42.

Schwandt. T. A. 1994. Constructivist, interpretivist approaches to human inquiry. In Denzin, N. and Lincoln, Y. (eds.), *Handbook of qualitative research.* Beverley Hills, CA: Sage, 118–37.

Silverman, D. 1970. *The theory of organizations: a sociological framework.* London: Heinemann.

Thachankary, T. 1992. Organizations as "texts": Hermeneutics as a model for understanding organizational change. *Research in Organization Change and Development,* 6: 197–233.

Thompson, J. B. 1981. *Critical hermeneutics: A study in the thought of Paul Ricoeur and Jurgen Habermas.* Cambridge University Press.

Vedder, B. 1999. Schleiermacher. In Critchley, S. and Schroeder, W. R. (eds.), *A companion to continental philosophy.* Oxford: Blackwell, 417–24.

Yin, R. 1994. *Case study research: Design and methods,* 2nd edn. Beverley Hills, CA: Sage.

Weber, M. 1991. The nature of social action. In Runciman, W. G. (ed.), *Weber: Selections in translation.* Cambridge University Press, 7–32.

Williams, M. 2000. Interpretivism and generalization. *Sociology,* 34: 209–24.

Wittgenstein, L. 1967. *Philosophical investigations,* 3rd edn. Oxford: Blackwell.

Project Voltigo

Exploring interdisciplinary cancer care service

Context

By default, cancer care requires a multidisciplinary concept of care and treatment. Yet, few healthcare providers have successfully implemented an interdisciplinary team that comprises nurses, psychologists, social workers, and physicians. In 2010, a pilot project, called VOLTIGO, to explore such novel and interdisciplinary team work in cancer care, was initiated jointly by HFR, the association of six regional hospitals in the canton of Fribourg, and the Cancer League of Fribourg, Switzerland. The challenge in the early stages of its formation was to form and specify a clear and coherent identity of the team and its task. Thus, the goal of the workshop was to identify the status of the team's cohesion and focus, current fault lines and challenges, as well as to discuss a way forward.

Strategic goal of intervention

Only two months into the team's initial formation and within a three-hour workshop, the six members of the team gathered to explore the status of the team in terms of its cohesion and focus. The intervention aimed to provide a psychologically safe space to discuss critical issues in the early stages of interdisciplinary team formation. The actual assignment for the team was to build a joint model of how they saw the current status of the team.

Embodied metaphors

The joint model that the group built had six person figures on a platform in a circle around a table with a large person figure sitting on top – representing the project. The size of the person figure was meant to represent the huge task in front of them. However, the table was refered to several times as "being empty," indicating a lack of topical clarity and focus for the project. Thus, this element represented the sense that the group was facing a demanding project without knowing exactly what the project was about.

The six person figures were loosely and separately connected with tubes to represent the different personal relationships between some team members. This emphasized that not all members had had a chance to establish personal relationships with all team members yet. Somewhat sidelined on the model lay a person figure without a head – to represent the patient – the espoused focus of the team's task. This element showed vividly the current lack in focus of the team, and the explicit agreement was to bring the patient into the team's focus of attention. Right behind the "neglected patient" and behind a green branch stood a big black person figure "hiding behind the tree" to represent the felt and unknown threats to the project. Outside the platform of the team were a scattered set of person figures to represent the different stakeholders to the project, such as patients, and relevant professions who might join the interdisciplinary team – such as physicians who were not yet connected with, and who were placed rather remotely to the project.

FIGURE C.1 *Embodied metaphor from Voltigo workshop.*

FIGURE C.2 *Embodied metaphor and context from Voltigo workshop.*

Insights gained: how was this session strategically consequential for the team?

Acknowledging that the team was in the early stages of its formation, the workshop revealed several aspects critical to the future success of the project. First, participants agreed that not all members had established personal relationships with other team members. Secondly, the team realized that despite the overall challenge and stakeholder expectations, they were unclear about the focus of the project – which in their view should be the patient's wellbeing. Thirdly, the team realized also that not all relevant professions were part of the team, in particular the lack of a physician was noted. Within a fairly short amount of time, the team gained some fundamental insights on where action was needed, and thus provided the ground for more focused work and future development of this interdisciplinary team.

CHAPTER FOUR

Crafting strategy as a practice of embodied recursive enactment

Before elaborating our approach of crafting strategy and drawing on Sennett's (2008) recent analysis, we first reflect on the notion of craftsmanship in a socio-cultural context. Then and in extending the metaphorical view of strategy as craft, we conceptualize crafting as an actual practice of strategy. Situating our approach within the practice-based view of strategy (e.g. Jarzabkowski, 2005; Whittington, 2006), we discuss how integrating three foundational domains, namely physiological, psychological and social constructionist perspectives, lead us to conceptualize crafting strategy as embodied recursive enactment. We demonstrate this conceptualization through the case of strategy work at Orange UK in the early 2000s.

"Making is thinking" – reflections on craftsmanship from a cultural materialist perspective

Crafting as the skill of making things well

While traditionally we associate craftsmanship with a pre-industrial, manual worker involved in making singular objects, such as a

This chapter draws on Buergi, Jacobs, and Roos (2005).

medieval carpenter, Sennett refers to craftsmanship more generally as "the skill of making things well" (2008: 8).[1] In his compelling
analysis, he acknowledges the relevance of crafting technique, but
beyond this considers craftsmanship as "an enduring, basic human
impulse, the desire to do a job well for its own sake" (2008: 9). Such
an impulse is not limited to ancient manual workers but similarly
applies to such diverse occupations as contemporary artists, doctors,
laboratory technicians or computer programmers, or such different
domains as bricklaying, cooking, playing the piano or analyzing a
chemical substance. Skill, commitment and judgment of intimately
connecting hand and head are crucial to understanding craftsmanship in this broader sense. In particular, Sennett posits that "every
good craftsman conducts a dialogue between concrete practices and
thinking" (2008: 9).

However, Western civilization seems to have separated hand and
head. In particular, several fault lines seem to exist between theory
and practice, technique and expression, craftsman and artist as well
as producer and user. These socially constructed and arguably false
dichotomies have led social science and practice to privilege the mind
over the body, head over hand and subsequently, cognitive over manual work (2008: 11). Unless we understand the socially constructed
nature of these fault lines and develop a more holistic perspective, we
risk neglecting the crucial role of material objects and practices in our
daily lives.

Often, social sciences consider material objects such as cloth, cir-
cuit boards or buildings as mirrors or repositories of social norms and
economic interests. In order to counterbalance and complement
this view, Sennett proposes a "cultural-materialist" approach by asking "what the process of making concrete things reveals to us about

---

[1] As does Sennett (2008), we acknowledge the gendered nature of the term "craftsmanship". Our argument however refers to craftsmanship carried out by both
genders.

ourselves" (2008: 8). Thus, a cultural materialist approach strives to explore the minute details of making material objects well, which in turn allows us to reconstruct more broadly how these characteristics bring forth and shape religious, social or political norms, or criteria of goodness for that matter.

Sennett grounds his overall argument on two main premises. First, that "all skills, even the most abstract, begin as bodily practices" and second "that technical understanding develops through the powers of imagination" (2008: 10). While the first premise emphasizes the connection between hand and head as well as the knowledge created through touch and movement, the second premise suggests that imagination and creativity mainly develops through, and is triggered by, the use of imperfect or incomplete tools (2008: 10).

If we follow Sennett's broader notion of craftsmanship as the ethos of making things well, it not only applies to carpenters but also to a variety of other professions. In this regard, each individual's commitment and engagement with the respective task at hand is primarily or exclusively driven not through instrumental, but rather through practical reasoning – supporting the effort of making things well. Moreover, the motivation is rather intrinsic and the rewards are emotional in nature; such as anchoring in tangible reality and taking pride in one's work. Work ethics rather than extrinsic rewards drive the individual's commitment to quality and its improvement: "the aspiration for quality will drive a craftsman to improve, to get better rather than get by" (2008: 24).

Crafting as contribution to communal development

Initially, craftsmen in archaic Greece drew on their skills and tools for advancing communal progress and thereby facilitated the change from a nomadic to a more urban, or arguably civilized, culture. More than a technician, "the civilizing craftsman has used these tools for a collective good, that of ending humanity's wandering existence as hunter-gatherers or rootless warriors" (2008: 21). Through this communal contribution, craftsmen were both skilled users of their tools but equally recognized members of the community. The Greek term for craftsman, *demioergos*, is evidence of this consideration. It is a compound of "public" (*demios*) as well as "productive" (*ergos*) and referred to middle-class citizens including potters, doctors, professional singers, heralds and lower magistrates (2008: 22). The present-day meaning of "demioergos" is "creator," reflecting the ancient meaning of the person who makes things.

However, in classical Greek times, craftsmanship lost its relative societal status since the term "demioergos" was being replaced by "cheirotechnon," which simply means "manual worker." While practical skills remained at the source of societal progress, they were no longer credited at the same level as in archaic Greece (2008: 23–4).

Sennett exemplifies the community-based notion of craftsmanship, drawing on the contemporary example of the Linux open source software development. He views the Linux operating system as a public craft, and consequently its contributors as craftsmen who embody the idea of "demioergos." In this open source, grass-roots driven technology, individual, voluntary software developers collectively craft the Linux software without endorsement or contract from a firm or a central coordinating body. A strong ethos of quality, intrinsic motivation and aspiration for improvement seem to drive the community that ultimately produces a software code available for public usage. In contrast, Wikipedia, an open technology online encyclopedia which according to Sennett does not seem to operate yet on a similar level of craftsmanship (2008: 24–7), has suffered severe quality challenges in its entries.

Sennett suggests that C. Wright Mills' arguably over-idealistic criteria of craftsmanship might help in explaining such difference. For Mills, the craftsman is highly engaged with the work for its own sake; is continuously and well connected to the outcome of the work effort; can control all activities; can improve skills during the process; has the freedom to experiment; and lastly, is able to combine family, community, and politics (2008: 27). Linux community members seem to score high on most of Mills' above criteria, whereas Wikipedia contributors do not.

The intimate link between hand and head

When reflecting on the relevance of our bodily-manual experience for carrying out complex tasks, Sennett problematizes the consequences of a disconnect between hand and head by drawing on the use of computer-assisted design (CAD) in architecture. CAD allows architects to instantaneously draw and design buildings of any shape; to zoom in and out; and to rotate in 3D as well as to amend the size.

Traditionally, however, architects had sketched and drawn the design of a building, and would subsequently build a physical model. The architect learned and explored the territory and its affordances through drawing. Quoting a young architect from MIT: "When you draw a site, when you put in the counter lines and the trees, it becomes ingrained in your mind. You come to know the site in a way that is not possible with the computer … You get to know the terrain by tracing and retracing it, not by letting the computer 'regenerate' it for you" (Turkle, 1995, quoted in Sennett, 2008: 40).

On the same note, renowned architect Renzo Piano emphasizes the crucial quality of the recursive visual-manual practice: "You start sketching, then you do a drawing, then you make a model, and then you go to reality – you go to the site – and then you go back to drawing. You build a kind of circularity between drawing and making and then back again" (Robbins, 1994, in Sennett, 2008: 40). In other words, architects explore the possibilities of the territory and the building when sketching, much more effectively and closely than through software. In addition, CAD risks glossing over potential problems in the detail that the software simply cannot detect, but an experienced architect would, and to overdetermine the object in question. By doing so, it might hinder the creative exploration of alternative usage of either the territory or the building.

While CAD might enable faster virtual modeling, it cannot simulate or substitute for the tactile, manual and bodily experience of the sketching, drawing and exploration of a physical model. In acknowledging the usefulness of machines such as CAD, Sennett concludes nevertheless that if head and hand are disconnected, the head will suffer: "both understanding and expression are impaired" (Sennett, 2008: 20); and the tangible outcome may not be as inspiring or inspired as when the head and the hand are integrated.

Craftsmen as icons of Enlightenment

Despite the fact that industrial machines such as the weaving loom (or currently CAD) were often portrayed in opposition to manual labor in terms of potentially replacing it, craftsmanship nevertheless served as an icon of the Enlightenment (Sennett, 2008: 88). One of the most influential books of the Enlightenment era, Diderot's Encyclopedia (*Dictionnaire des arts et métiers*), for instance, explored "how practical things get done and the way to improve them" and celebrated "those who are committed to doing work well for its own sake" (2008: 90).

The Encyclopedia asserted craftsman labor as an icon of Enlightenment by putting manual work on an equal footing with cognitive work, and in doing so echoed archaic Greece's appreciation of manual work for the benefit of the community. Furthermore, freedom was not only or primarily suggested as the free use of reason but moreover the freedom to carry out useful work. In his capacity as editor of the Encyclopedia, Diderot faced the challenge that craftsmen were often inarticulate in terms of their activities. Diderot substituted and complemented the linguistic descriptions through the use of images that exemplified steps of crafting by reducing the act of crafting to its most crucial instances; in this way using images to partially overcome the inherent limitations of language in describing the bodily experience of movements.

The role of the hand in craftsmanship

Craftsmanship crucially relies on the intimate connection between hand and head. Kant for instance, observed that the "the hand is the window on to the mind" (Tallis, 2003, in Sennett, 2008: 149). Of all human limbs, it is the hand that possesses the largest repertoire of intentional movements. The physical structure of the human hand being a recent occurrence in evolutionary development (with respect to opposing thumbs), has more possibilities for grip and touch than the primate hand.

For instance, gripping is a voluntary action and, in contrast to involuntary ones such as eyelid movement, is based on a deliberate decision (Sennett, 2008: 150). Ethnologist Mary Marzke has distinguished three basic forms of how we grip things. First, we pinch small objects between the side of the index finger and the tip of the thumb. The second form involves cradling of objects in the palm as well as moving them by pushing and massaging actions between thumb and fingers. While advanced primates are capable of performing these grips, humans can perform them with more facility. It is the third form of grip that sets humans and primates apart. The cupping grip – "as when a ball or other biggish object is held by the rounded hand, thumb and index finger placed opposite the object – allows us to hold an object securely in one hand while we work on it with the other hand" (Sennett, 2008: 151).

An even more advanced hand technique involves also the precise knowledge when to let go. When learning the piano or the violin, such capacity is key in mastering the instrument. Cognitively, when we let go of a problem, we create a cognitive distance in order to take a fresh look. Thus, releasing is a crucial component in humans' repertoire of grip and touch. Also, it provides the basic bodily experience for "letting go" of a problem, fear or obsession at the conceptual level. We learn to release control over an object – physically or cognitively

(Sennett, 2008: 152) in the service of reasserting control at a later point.

An adjacent movement to grip and touch is grasping. When we reach out for an object, we aim to grasp it. The human sensory-motor cortex is capable of anticipating a physical movement such as grasping – a capacity referred to as prehension: "the body is ready to hold before it knows whether what it will hold is freezing cold or boiling hot". Thus, we take action although not all relevant sensory data are available in our mind; rather, based on bodily experience, our mind anticipates sensory data and acts accordingly. An intuitively compelling example for prehension is the directive hand of a conductor that always needs to be a moment ahead of the sound – with the orchestra acting accordingly. Prehension involves anticipation of the object and its characteristic as well as the relevant bodily movement in question; the actual contact that generates sensory data; linguistic cognition when naming the object one holds; and reflection on what has been done. Interestingly and similar to the speech figure of "coming to grips," the notion of "grasping" also has a cognitive meaning, namely that we understand something (Sennett, 2008: 154), symbolizing the intimate connection between the hand and the mind.

Incomplete tools and imagination

Solid command, or even virtuous use of a tool, is a key characteristic of craftsmanship. Thus, tools play a crucial role in crafting and they do so not only because of their instrumental role in working an object but because they trigger our imagination. In particular, tools that are imperfect or multi-purpose seem to induce learning: "getting better at using tools comes to us, in part, when the tools challenge us, and this challenge often occurs just because the tools are not fit-for-purpose" (Sennett, 2008: 194).

Thus, the incompleteness of a tool is actually an occasion for the craftsman to learn, since it fosters or even forces his imagination of how to better control the tool and complete the task at hand. For example while medieval doctors used cooking knives for dissection, the development of much finer scalpels challenged the hand technique of the dissector: "the very simplicity and lightness of the scalpel was a challenge" (Sennett, 2008: 198).

According to Sennett, the process of intuitive leaps of imagination involves four stages. First, intuition begins with "the sense that what isn't yet could be." The frustration with a tool's limitations, for instance, typically leads us to "break the mold of fit-for-purpose." Sennett calls this first stage reformatting, or "the willingness to see if a tool or practice can be changed in use" (Sennett, 2008: 210). The second stage involves the establishment of adjacency by bringing two yet unrelated domains close together. For instance, mobile telephony initially started through a juxtaposition of radio and fixed line telephony: "it was necessary for researchers to shove close together two quite different technologies, those of the radio and the telephone, then to think what they might, but didn't yet, share" (Sennett, 2008: 211).

The third stage involves the frustration of prejudices and expectations when actually carrying out the comparison. Simply put, surprise is experienced as "a way of telling yourself that something you know can be other than you assumed" (Sennett, 2008: 211). The final stage is to recognize that no intuitive leap actually defies gravity, that unresolved issues may remain unresolved. Such recognition teaches us humility about overambitious technology and practice transfer. Sennett's bottom line here is that the ground for surprise and intuition can actually be prepared and crafted: "tools used in certain ways organize this imaginative experience and with productive results" (Sennett, 2008: 213).

Developing crafting skills through play

In his concluding chapter, Sennett explores how crafting skills and abilities are being developed. Apart from obvious and repetitive training and refinement of routines, he suggests that the development of crafting skills relies and is fundamentally based on an early childhood experience, namely play. Play involves an exploratory, experimental dialogue with materials and rules. Rather than an escape from reality, "play teaches children how to be sociable and channels cognitive development; play instills obedience to rules but counters this discipline by allowing children to create and experiment with the rules they obey" (Sennett, 2008: 269).

He distinguishes two basic forms of play. While competitive games such as chess or sports require players to accept and obey ex ante rules, exploratory play involves experimentation not only with the objects of play but also with the rules – where appropriateness and legitimacy of the rules are both objects of exploration and playful negotiation. Sennett views this exploratory form of play as the origin of crafting skills, and concludes that crafting skills are grounded in our childhood experiences of play as the exploratory dialogue with materials and rules.

Geertz (1975, in Sennett, 2008) in particular posited that the link between the experience of childhood play and adult behavior of dealing with rules is never broken because the active exploration of materials and rules is an ongoing characteristic of human life. On a similar note, Erikson (1995, in Sennet, 2008) observed young boys building towers with wooden bricks until they collapsed. Rather than offering an obvious Freudian interpretation, he suggested that these boys tested the boundaries of the material objects and explored the rule of "how high can it go?" Similarly, he suggested that when young girls continuously dress, undress and redress their dolls, they are experimenting with the affordances and possibilities of the material objects of clothes.

Conclusion: strategy work as a form of craftsmanship

We find Sennett's cultural materialist analysis of craftsmanship inspiring for our own approach of strategy as craft. In particular,

Sennett's work raises the following set of questions that we will explore throughout the book and that provide overall guidance of our approach.

Role of bodily experience in skill development: If all skills including the most abstract are ultimately rooted in our bodily experience and in the movement of the hand, how can we honor such insight for strategy work?

Role of materiality in strategy: How does or could strategy work involve material objects? What is or could be their role and function?

Link between hand and head: Might traditional analytical, deductive strategic planning practice be susceptible to the risks of a counter-productive separation of hand and mind, in terms of limiting understanding and experience? To put this positively, might a closer linkage between hand and mind, in terms of constructing physical analogues, be productive for strategy work?

Use of hand: If the hand is a window on to the mind, how can we better involve manual practice in the development of strategy? What processes and technologies are or should be involved?

Role of tools: If incomplete tools actually spark and facilitate imagination, how can we extend the currently incomplete and mostly rationalist repertoire of strategy tools in this respect?

Imagination through reformatting tools: If imagination fundamentally relies on engagement with, and reformatting of, material objects, which material objects could be constructed, examined, and reformatted to spark the strategist's imagination?

Developing crafting skills through play: If crafting skills, imagination, and other social processes are fundamentally rooted in and inextricably linked to the social practice of play as the exploratory, experimental dialogue with materials and rules, how can play be meaningfully mobilized in strategy work?

In the following section, we propose crafting as a practice of strategy work, and outline our approach in more detail.

Strategy as social practice – the practice turn in strategy

While scholars in fields adjacent to strategy have fruitfully employed a practice-based view (e.g. Miller and Hopwood, 1994; Orlikowski, 2000; Brown and Duguid, 1991; Gherardi, 2000), strategy research has only recently begun to explore the potential of a practice perspective (Johnson *et al.*, 2003). A practice view on strategy aims to understand "the messy realities of doing strategy as a lived experience" (Jarzabkowski, 2005: 3). Within a broader practice turn in social theory, the actual, mundane activities (praxis) and institutionalized routines guiding these (practices) have become focal issues for social theorists including Bourdieu (1990), de Certeau (1984) and Giddens (1984), among others. Although differing in details, they share an interest in the concept of practice since it (re-) introduces human activities as foci of scholarly interest in social studies.

Differences in approaches notwithstanding, Schatzki (2001) identifies three common themes of a practice perspective. First, a practice view foregrounds actual human activities, and thereby highlights the potential relevance of even the most mundane ones (de Certeau, 1984). Then, any such praxis is considered to be situated in a field of practices that in turn provides the necessary communal resources of sensemaking and action (Bourdieu, 1990; Giddens, 1984). Finally, a practice view emphasizes the role of human actors, their skills and resources in carrying out their activities. In summarizing these meta-theoretical considerations, Schatzki (2001) proposes practices as "embodied, materially mediated arrays of human activity centrally organized around a shared practical understanding" (2001: 2).

Rather than conceiving of strategy as a position a firm has, the practice-based view of strategy assumes strategy as an activity, something that organizations and their members actually do (Jarzabkowski, 2005; Whittington, 2006). Thus, Jarzabkowski *et al.* (2007: 7) conceptualize strategy as a situated, socially accomplished activity that is consequential for the organization. A practice view on strategy distinguishes among strategy praxis (the local, actual activities of organizational actors in the doing of strategy), strategy practices (institutionalized regularities and idealized routines of strategic praxes such as engaging in strategic planning, using SWOT analysis, or Porter's five forces), and strategy practitioners (groups of organizational actors in organizations who draw upon such practices in their strategic activities) (Whittington, 2006). In this respect, the notion of strategizing refers to "how people go about the process of making strategy" (Johnson et al., 2007: 27).

Mapping the research domain of a practice-based view, Johnson et al. (2007) distinguish among the micro-level of analysis that focuses on actual activities (or praxis) of organizational actors; the meso-level of analysis that adheres to organizational actions (e.g. strategic change) and the macro-level of analysis that is concerned with the institutionalized field practices or routines of strategizing. So far, strategy research has predominantly focused on the organization-level of analysis. While stressing the importance of a micro-level view on strategy, a practice-based view simultaneously emphasizes the institutionalized practices that organizations and organizational (groups of) actors draw on (Molloy and Whittington, 2005).

In terms of empirical study, the practice-based view suggests several empirical units of analysis that enable us to examine the situated activities of strategy work (Jarzabkowski, 2005). For instance, rational administrative practices such as planning, budgeting, forecasting, control systems, and performance indicators populate everyday organizational strategizing activities. Episodic practices refer to the specific contextual settings and preconditions deliberately created as opportunities for strategy practitioners to interact around strategy (Hendry and Seidl, 2003). These practices involve strategy meetings, strategy workshops, and strategy retreats, among others, and pay attention to artifactual elements such as powerpoint slides, flipcharts, as well as planning techniques. Finally, communicative practices refer to the linguistic and symbolic resources employed by organizational actors

when interacting about strategy. In the following section we conceptualize and extend Mintzberg's initial metaphor of crafting strategy in
terms of a communicative practice of strategy in general and of strategic thinking in particular.

Crafting strategy as recursive embodied enactment

While Mintzberg (1987) offered initially an analogy between a potter's activity (source domain) and the strategist's task (target domain)
in order to suggest strategy as a craft (emergent meaning), we choose
to return this initial trajectory in the opposite direction, to its source
domain. That is, we take the source domain of "crafting" at face value,
namely the use of our hands in creating new artifacts and meanings,
and discuss it in terms of developing a theoretical basis for the concept of crafting as a practice of strategy. In particular, we explore how
the link between the hand and the mind might be mobilized in the
making of strategy and ground our argument in three bodies of theory, namely physiological, psychological and social constructionist
perspectives on meaning generation. We suggest that manual activity
is far from disconnected to cognitive operations, but rather, is crucial
to how human beings enact their world.

Thinking with our hands. Actual crafting activities – such as
pottering and the like – represent a basic form of human experience.
However, in a so-called knowledge-based economy, value-adding
work is typically attributed to those in white collars, in contrast to
"blue collar," "manual" work. The value system underpinning this
simplified distinction privileges and superordinates cognitive over
manual, or mind over hand, for that matter, which has led to many
people assuming manual activities to add less value than cognitive
activities do. Similar to Mintzberg, though, we aim here to foreground
the formative, developmental potential of crafting.

The hand is important not only as an instrument for manipulating
the physical world, but also as a large source of feedback and data for

the brain. The link between hand and brain is an important one in human physiology and development. Interestingly, the archaeological records of human development show that important physiological aspects co-emerge in the anatomy of human progenitors, including a five-fingered grip with opposable thumb, the increasing size of the brain, and the development of speech centers in the brain (Gibson and Ingold, 1993; Tattersall, 1998; Wilson, 1998). With these elements converging, the hand is assumed to play a central role of the developing capacity of human cognition.

Furthermore, research on the nexus between speech and gesture suggests an instrumental connection between the act of speaking and the use of the hand (Krauss, Chen, and Gottesman, 2000; Hadar et al., 1998; Krauss, 1998). Anecdotal evidence at the linguistic level is the fact that in some languages, the corresponding expressions for the English "to understand" actually make a strong reference to motor activity of the hand; for example the German "*begreifen*" or French "*comprendre*" – which can also be translated back as "*to grasp*". Thus, we not only manipulate the world with our hands, but we use feedback from this to construct our inner world with.

Appropriating the world through manipulating objects. A further, additional aspect for consideration is the relationship between action and cognition. Educational psychologist Piaget's concept of genetic epistemology is based on the assumption that human childhood offers an ontogenetic view of the evolution of human cognition (1971). His theoretical approach to human psychological development, which he called constructivism, essentially assumes that human intelligence develops through the close interaction between the outer world and the mind. For instance, when exposed to one tall glass and one wide glass of water – containing the same amount of liquid – young children often believe that the tall glass contains more water than the wide glass. Moreover, children will suggest that the amount of water changes when poured from one shape to another. This theory-in-use on the relationship between shape of glass and amount of water would only be challenged and adjusted if children practically "construct" it through their own manual activities. Even conceptual categories such as time, space or causation, he suggested, are not inherent to human nature but appear to develop through feedback between mind and world. What we call "knowledge" might actually be conceived of as active, "manual dialogue" with the world.

Based on Piaget's foundations, Papert advocates a "constructionist" approach to learning and education by ensuring that learners have appropriate materials at their disposition and are set the right tasks in accordance with the intended learning outcomes (Harel and Papert, 1991). A positive and continuous self-reinforcement kicks in, namely that the creation of new knowledge results in new means of world exploration that in turn provide the basis for new knowledge to be explored, and so on. Thus, Papert's constructionist approach advocates the active and literal manipulation of material objects in order to understand and mentally appropriate the world around us. This close interaction between action and cognition – as suggested by Piaget and Papert – demonstrate a close, recursive link between these two domains.

Generating meaning through discursive interaction. Since learning entails more than an individualistic process, we should further explore how knowledge and meaning are intersubjectively and thus socially created. A social constructionist view of knowledge and knowledge generation assumes that our social "reality" is a perceived, interpreted, and thus negotiated one (Gergen, 1999; Gherardi, 2000). Given that meaning and knowledge are closely related, they are at the center of such discursive processes of social construction. While social constructionism has primarily focused on spoken and written accounts, there are other non-linguistic aspects of human action and behavior that constitute meaning and sense. Bodily experience is central to human experience and meaning-making, as sociologists such as Bourdieu or Giddens or cognitive linguists such as Lakoff and Johnson (1980; 1999) or Gibbs (2005) would suggest. On the same note, Gergen observes that "the terms and forms by which we achieve understanding of the world and ourselves are social artifacts, products of historically and culturally situated interchanges among people" (1994: 49). Such situatedness highlights knowledge in organizations as highly context-dependent and as arising from and circulating in social networks characterized by intensive interaction among members.

Thus knowledge, as well as meaning in general, and abstract organizational concepts such as strategy, for that matter, are socially constructed. Highlighting this fundamental link, Weick (1987: 231) posits that the knowledge being created in organizational strategy implementation combines the situation with *action in the situation*: namely, the idea that "execution is analysis and implementation is formulation."

We observe a structural similarity shared by Mintzberg's (1987) crafting metaphor and the three literature streams we have discussed: namely, that the construction of physical or abstract objects occurs in a recursive process of enactment. We therefore conceptualize the interrelationship between activity and thought which characterizes all three levels of theory presented as *embodied recursive enactment*. This concept specifies and echoes Mintzberg's example of the potter, who in manipulating the clay is undergoing iterative and recursive processes of exploring the material, gaining insights, making adjustments to the material, and so forth. This close feedback loop between material experience and conceptual thinking forms the basis of our conceptual suggestion of crafting strategy as recursive embodied enactment. For our purposes, we refer to enactment to describe reciprocal dynamics of two related domains, such as hand/mind, action/cognition, speech acts/meaning – as summarized in Figure 4.1.

We demonstrate this framework by means of strategy work at Orange UK in the early 2000s.

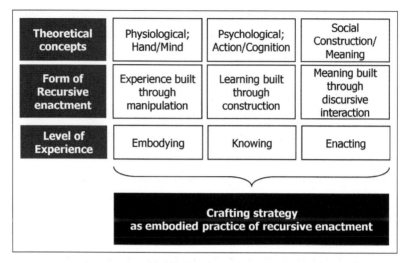

Theoretical concepts	Physiological; Hand/Mind	Psychological; Action/Cognition	Social Construction/ Meaning
Form of Recursive enactment	Experience built through manipulation	Learning built through construction	Meaning built through discursive interaction
Level of Experience	Embodying	Knowing	Enacting

Crafting strategy as embodied practice of recursive enactment

FIGURE 4.1 *The concept of crafting as strategic practice (Buergi et al., 2005: 83; used with permission).*

Crafting strategy at Orange UK

By the end of the 1990s, Orange UK – a mobile telephony provider – gained increasingly in market share due to a concert of innovative pricing approaches, non-traditional advertising, a highly responsive customer service, and avant garde lifestyle appeals. However, when Orange was acquired by a large national telecommunications provider from another EU country, one of the founders of Orange decided to leave the CEO position to an appointee from the new holding company. The change in CEO and board composition, in conjunction with organizational post-merger "traumata" of various kinds, left the organization with the challenge of how to respond to the current strategic challenges in this new organizational and strategic setup. With Orange now being part of a larger corporate structure, some corporate strategists started to become concerned about dilution of what they viewed as core elements of Orange's successful growth, namely an avantgardistic attitude to business, close attention to customer service, an entrepreneurial level of commitment to the organization, and a set of brand values. As part of their action to substantiate their concerns and to explore strategies to counter these, a two-day workshop was arranged that involved a group of senior managers (from strategy, brand management, and HR management) in the crafting of strategy by using toy construction materials. The specific goal of the workshop was to reconsider, revise, and extend the current strategy grounded in the power of the brand in view of the different challenges that the acquisition presented.

During the two-day workshop, participants constructed, deconstructed, and reconstructed – literally and figuratively – their perceptions of the firm and its competitive landscape. The first crucial element of the workshop involved building a joint model representing the firm's identity as an organization. After some serious and sometimes frustrating debates around the appropriateness of suggested elements of this model, the group seemed relieved to settle for a "flotilla of ships" of different sizes and shapes – jointly travelling to the icon of the brand representing a sort of lighthouse. Participants then explored the firm's competitive landscape, including models of its social and economic environment. For instance, one participant represented an incumbent, so far neglected competitor entering direct competition with Orange as a large, bulky figure on the bookshelf near the wall "coming in from left field". Physically positioning this competitor model outside the group's immediate focus of attention provided an eye-opener for most participants. As one participant observed: "I used to think we had maybe three or four competitors. But now the table just isn't big enough to hold all of them!"

Retrospectively, the workshop was characterized by participants as a most revealing experience. As one participant reflected: "It's like, once you get all the problems on the table, you can deal with them. And that's what we've done – we've got them all on the table!" Drawing most effectively on the power of the technique, one participant experimented with the "right" position of the brand icon. Initially, it had been placed in front of the flotilla, leading it on. Yet, this participant put the icon deliberately at the rear of the flotilla – representing the sense that the brand was somehow "behind."

In this workshop, participants explored strategic challenges for Orange and thereby developed not only a more nuanced understanding of the competitive landscape but, moreover, identified the need for critically reviewing a supposedly mystified brand. As a direct consequence of this latter insight, a large-scale executive education program – initially designed around an unproblematized concept of the brand – was put on hold until a better understanding of the Orange brand had been reached.

Based on this brief outline, we reflect on each component of our framework to see how crafting strategy as embodied recursive enactment was manifest in this strategy work at Orange UK.

Case reflection

The Orange UK case demonstrates the concept of crafting strategy as embodied in recursive enactment in terms of strategy work as a manual activity in manipulating objects; as a process of social learning as well as the social construction of meaning. Figure 4.2 provides a synopsis of these considerations.

Using hands and body. In this workshop aimed at contouring Orange's strategy, people used their hands and manipulated physical objects in their collective sensemaking of their competitive landscape – a practice that we rarely observe in managerial settings. Surely, writing text, typing numbers or designing slides with keyboard and mouse technically also qualify also as "manual" activities. Yet, the latter differ from the former insofar as building physical models and configuring them collectively and meaningfully atop a table draws on the distinct and more demanding human ability of making and using "tools," in a group setting. By assembling approximately 15 models each, every participant represented and contributed to the overall model of Orange's competitive landscape.

Strategic issue	Physiological: Experience built through manipulation	Psychological: Learning built through construction	Social: Meaning built through discursive interaction
Identity	Building & arranging different models of ships	Exploring the arrangement in terms of independent, yet related entities	Flotilla metaphor emerged as an accurate, integrative model of Orange's identity
Competition	Constructing a large, bulky figure situated on the shelf behind	Investigating this competitor's size, position and relevance	Relevance of previously underestimated competitor was acknowledged
Brand	Experimenting with the relative position of the brand icon vis-à-vis the flotilla	Inquiring the nature and role of the brand in this transition phase	Rather than drawing the organization, the brand was considered « somehow behind »

FIGURE 4.2 *Crafting strategy in Orange – synopsis of case episodes (Buergi et al., 2005: 83; used with permission).*

While some of the models are ultimately discarded, others remain objects of meaning negotiations and are thus being modified, repositioned, relabeled throughout the days and are thereby changing and gaining in meaning. Also, their positioning relative to each other, their relative height, proximity and distance are tested, adjusted and changed until no obvious disagreements are voiced. In contrast to the regular form of strategy work, participants were required to use their motor manual skills in exploring strategic issues. Their hands were crucial in accomplishing the workshop task as well as in thinking strategically.

More closely exploring the three strategic issues of the workshop, the relevance of this manual activity for strategy work in this setting becomes more pronounced. Constructing different models of ships and (re-) configuring their positioning allowed participants to explore the organization's identity in cognitive and material terms. Modeling a neglected competitor as a large, bulky figure "coming in from left field" exemplified its relative threat in a manner that was physically experienced by participants. Similarly, repositioning the brand icon from the front end of the flotilla to its rear equally demonstrated a shift in a bodily material fashion that had important implications for how the strategic role of the brand was perceived.

The reported and observed experience of participants suggests that creating and *manipulating* material objects was experienced as a cognitively stimulating, and for many even an exhausting, process. This exhaustion illustrates the physiological aspect above, namely how the use of hands in creating and manipulating physical objects induces cognitive processes and thus provides a bodily material experience of strategy work.

Manipulating objects. On a related note, the case also exemplifies the idea that manipulating objects stimulates and contributes to cognition. Providing managers with toy construction materials when reflecting on their organization and its competitive landscape seems close to a "constructionist" learning ideal both theoretically and literally in terms of providing construction materials in context. Here, nine participants used approximately 6,000 pieces of toy construction material to build nearly 80 different models of the firm, its competitors and other elements of context.

In terms of the psychological aspects of our framework, the model-constructing activity can be seen as a form of synchronizing visual, tactile and cognitive aspects of knowledge. Each newly created element becomes a component in a locally created universe to be further manipulated to generate and refine strategic knowledge.

Again, these considerations are manifest in the way the aforementioned three strategic issues were explored. The cognitive exploration of Orange's identity through a flotilla of ships shaped the idea of Orange as an organization with independent, yet related, organizational entities. Portraying the incumbent competitor invited a closer investigation of its strategic position. Lastly, experimenting with the brand icon allowed participants to speculate and challenge the nature of the brand in this phase of transition. This construction and manipulation process reduces the often suggested gap between thought and activity.

Generating and negotiating new meaning. In parallel to the physical construction of conceptual objects, participants offered, considered, rejected and confirmed different meanings attributed to these representations. By tapping into the human need for "making sense," these meaning negotiations resulted in the participants' verbal acknowledgement of the flotilla as a valid, metaphorical, integrative representation of the Orange organization; and recognized the threat of a previously underestimated competitor and the demystification of the brand through the performative act of placing the brand model behind, rather than in front of the flotilla.

The discursive social interaction of the group of participants in their collective work of building a coherent construction of their work environment created new knowledge and interpretations of their situation. Some explicit observations that indicate this include the statements about being surprised at the number of "competitors," as well as about having a more holistic vision of the strategic challenges confronting the organization. Arguably, the participants were able to construct a more comprehensive and interactive overview of the organization and its context than they had previously experienced.

Conclusion: "How can we know what we mean until we see what we build?"

Most generally, the concept of crafting strategy as embodied recursive enactment echoes what Weick (1987) calls "strategy substitutes." He views strategy neither as a retrospective rationalization of success nor as a cognitive forecasting activity, but rather as a generator of meaning arising from making sense of actions and events: "Because situations can support a variety of meanings, their actual content and meaning is dependent on the degree to which they are arranged into sensible, coherent configurations" (1987: 231).

Building on this concept of strategy as embodied recursive enactment, we explore in the next chapter the relevance of analogical reasoning to the crafting of strategy, and how this process can foster reflective dialogue as well as engender a mode of interaction known as serious play.

REFERENCES

Bourdieu, P. 1990. *The logic of practice*. Cambridge: Polity.

Brown, J.S. and Duguid, P. 1991. Organizational learning and communities of practice: Toward a unified view of working, learning and innovation. *Organization Science*, 2(1): 40–57.

Buergi, P., Jacobs, C., and Roos, J. 2005. From metaphor to practice in the crafting of strategy. *Journal of Management Inquiry*, 14 (1): 78–94.

de Certeau, M. 1984. *The practice of everyday life*. Berkeley, CA: University of California Press.

Gergen, K. 1994. *Reality and relationships: Soundings in social construction*. London: Sage.

  1999. *An invitation to social construction*. London: Sage.

Gherardi, S. 2000. Practice-based theorizing on learning and knowing in organizations. *Organization*, 7(2): 211–23.

Gibbs, R.W. 2005. *Embodiment and cognitive science*. New York: Cambridge University Press.

Gibson, K. R. and Ingold, T. (eds.), 1993. *Tools, language and cognition in human evolution*. Cambridge University Press.

Giddens, A. 1984. *The constitution of society. Outline of the theory of structuration*. Cambridge: Polity.

Hadar, U., Wenkert-Olenik, D., Krauss, R., and Soroker, N. 1998. Gesture and the processing of speech: Neuropsychological evidence. *Brain and Language*, 62, 107–26.

Harel, I. and Papert, S. (eds.), 1991. *Constructionism*. Norwood, NJ: Ablex.

Hendry, J. and Seidl, D. 2003. The structure and significance of strategic episodes: Social systems theory and the routine practices of strategic change. *Journal of Management Studies*, 40(1): 175–97.

Jarzabkowski, P. 2005. *Strategy as practice: An activity-based approach*. London: Sage.

Jarzabkowski, P., Balogun, J., and Seidl, D. 2007. Strategizing: The challenges of a practice perspective. *Human Relations*, 60(1): 5–27.

Johnson, G., Melin, L., and Whittington, R. 2003. Micro strategy and strategising: Towards an activity-based view. *Journal of Management Studies*, 40 (1): 3–22.

Johnson, G., Langley, A., Melin, L., and Whittington, R. 2007. *Strategy as practice: Research directions and resources*. Cambridge University Press.

Krauss, R. M. 1998. Why do we gesture when we speak? *Current Directions in Psychological Science*, 7, 54–9.

Krauss, R. M., Chen, Y., and Gottesman, R. F. 2000. Lexical gestures and lexical access: A process model. In D. McNeil (ed.), *Language and gesture*. New York: Cambridge University Press, 261–83.

Lakoff, G. and Johnson, M. 1980. *Metaphors we live by*. Chicago University Press. 1999. *Philosophy in the flesh*. New York: Basic Books.

Miller, P. and Hopwood, A. G. 1994 (eds.), *Accounting as social and institutional practice*. Cambridge University Press.

Mintzberg, H. 1987. Crafting strategy. *Harvard Business Review*, 65(4), 66–75.

Molloy E. and Whittington R. 2005. Organising organising: the practice inside the process, *Advances in Strategic Management*, 22: 491–515.

Orlikowski, W. J. 2000. Using technology and constituting structure: A practice lens for studying technology in organizations. *Organization Science*, 11(4): 404–28.

Piaget, J. 1971. *Biology and knowledge*. University of Chicago Press.

Schatzki, T.R. 2001. Introduction: Practice Theory. In Schatzki, T. R., Knorr Cetina, K., and von Savigny, E. (eds.), *The practice turn in contemporary theory*. New York: Routledge, 1–14.

Sennett, R. 2008. *The craftsman*. London: Allen Lane.

Tattersall, I. 1998. *Becoming human: Evolution and human uniqueness*. New York: Harcourt Brace.

Weick, K. 1987. Substitutes for strategy. In D. J. Teece (ed.), *The competitive challenge: Strategies for industrial renewal*. Cambridge, MA: Ballinger, 221–33.

Whittington R. 2006. Completing the practice turn in strategy reseach. *Organization Studies*, 26: 613–34.

Wilson, F. 1998. *The hand: How its use shapes the brain, language, and human culture*. New York: Pantheon.

CHAPTER FIVE

Play, analogical reasoning and dialogue in the crafting of strategy

In the previous chapter, we developed a concept of crafting strategy as embodied recursive enactment by drawing on theoretical/conceptual antecedents, namely physiological, psychological and communicative aspects of crafting. In this chapter, we extend and nuance this line of reasoning by exploring three social practices that are crucial to crafting strategy as embodied recursive enactment.

First and in terms of the physiological/manual dimension, we explore the concept of play as a human capacity that in our context consists mainly in the relaxation of rational intentionality and manipulation of objects in order to discover new insights. Secondly, and in terms of the cognitive/psychological dimension, we explore the human capacity of analogical reasoning, in our case through the process of constructing and interpreting physical analogs. Thirdly, and in terms of the communicative dimension, we discuss the concept of dialogue as a specific communicative mode that allows for reflective as well as generative meaning negotiation.

This chapter draws on Jacobs and Statler (2006), Jacobs and Heracleous (2005), and Statler, Jacobs, and Roos (2008).

TABLE 5.1: *Concepts and practices of crafting strategy*

Conceptual dimension	Corresponding practice	Function
Physiological	Serious play	Relaxing rational intentionality and manipulating objects to challenge existing rules and explore the possibilities of new ones.
Cognitive	Analogical reasoning	Reasoning through analogies and through the process of constructing and interpreting physical analogs.
Communicative	Dialogue	Reflective and generative meaning negotiation through dialogical interaction.

Crafting strategy draws on and mobilizes these three related, yet distinct practices in terms of embodied recursive enactment. We present each of them in a separate section and illustrate with empirical examples. Table 5.1 summarizes these considerations.

Playing seriously: relaxing rational intentionality and manipulating objects

Serious play as a technology of foolishness

Strategy formation has intentional as well as emergent aspects. Typically, intentionality in strategy research refers to actions that are deliberately directed towards the achievement of some purpose. Chandler (1962: 15), for instance, referred to strategy's generic purpose as the "determination of the basic long-term goals and objectives of an enterprise and the adoption of courses of action and the allocation of resources necessary for carrying out these goals". Furthermore, the purpose of strategy has been defined as the attempt to provide the organization with a direction (Rumelt *et al.*, 1994) and as a means for achieving sustainable competitive advantage (Hoskisson *et al.*, 1999).

Thus, strategy presupposes a notion of intentionality that involves clearly defined purposes and actions that are deliberately directed to achieving those purposes. However, the challenge of such notion of intentionality might come at the expense of strategy's inherently emergent character.

Mintzberg and Waters (1985) differentiated between deliberate and emergent strategies and called attention to the fact that strategies form not just from the directives that are issued by the leadership team, but also from ideas that emerged "during the journey," with some intended ideas never being implemented. Thus, realized strategy can be considered an emergent phenomenon because it involves a series of complex interactions between individual agents and social systems at various levels, and because it cannot be understood as simply the implementation of intended strategy. More recently, MacIntosh and Maclean (1999) refer to emergence as a property of a social system characterized by non-equilibrium conditions as well as non-linear, random developments that "create new system configurations in a way which is largely indeterminate" (1999: 301). Such a concept of emergence, however, risks leaving little room for deliberate and planned action, or intention.

Thus, we are faced with the challenge of striking a balance between the intentional and the emergent aspects of strategy formation. We propose that the technologies of reason (such as strategic planning and adjacent analytical practices) need to be supplemented with technologies of foolishness (such as play) so as to balance and account for intention as well as emergence. Playfulness appears to provide "a natural outgrowth of our standard view of reason. A strict insistence on purpose, consistency and rationality limits our ability to find new purposes. Play relaxes that insistence to allow us to act 'unintelligently' or 'irrationally', or 'foolishly' to explore alternative ideas of possible purposes and alternative concepts of behavioral consistency" (March, 1979: 77).

Technologies of reason (such as strategic planning) tend to presuppose a pre-existing purpose for action, insisting on the necessity of

TABLE 5.2: *Technologies of reason and foolishness*

	Technology of reason	Technology of foolishness
Nature of purpose	Pre-existing	Emergent.
Congruence of action	Consistency necessary	Ambiguity and fluidity allowed and desired.
Intentionality	Primacy of functional rationality	Relaxation of functional rationality and emphasis on utility of randomness and exploration.

(Jacobs and Statler, 2006:80; used with permission.)

consistency among actions, and resting on the primacy of functional rationality. By contrast, technologies of foolishness operate in a different mode, namely an emergent and transitional nature of purpose, encourage ambiguity and fluidity of action, and accept a relaxation of functionally rational imperatives. Table 5.2 juxtaposes these different technologies (March, 1979).

Although March acknowledged that the technology of reason has undoubtedly been very successful in strengthening human capabilities for effective social action, he also reminds us of its limitations. The exclusive attachment to purpose, consistency, and rationality may not be the most appropriate mode in organizational situations that would benefit from reason's "arational" cousins, including impulse, intuition, and lived bodily experience. Thus, play mobilizes an archetypical human activity of foolishness that allows for a "deliberate, temporary relaxation of rules in order to explore the possibilities of alternative rules" (1979: 77).

Furthermore in an organizational context, play allows organizational actors to see different things as well as to see things differently. Seeing and experimenting with new perspectives and novel possibilities for action are central aspects in strategy formation in general, and for fundamental strategic innovation in particular. Hence, we suggest that strategy formation that aims at strategic innovation can benefit from a relaxation of functionally rational imperatives, perhaps through the use of play as a technology of foolishness.

Play has been recognized as serving the development of cognitive skills (Piaget and Inhelder, 1958), the capacity to understand meaning in context (Vygotsky and Cole, 1978), as well as the development of social institutions (Huizinga, 1950), and forms of cultural identity (Geertz, 1973). In particular, we draw on the psychoanalytic idea of play as the primary process of meaning-generation (Winnicott, 1971). At a point in time when the concept of self is not fully developed and distinguished from the environment, the infant attaches meaning to a "transitional object" (such as a source of food). This object is core to a playful exploration of object relations through which the differentiation of self and other gradually takes shape. Over time, these object relations become ever more complex and are retained throughout life. Thus, play provides human beings with a mode of coping with ambiguity, i.e. a state of affairs that cannot be remedied by additional or perfect information, but which rather consists in a situation where too many possible interpretations exist (Weick, 1995: 95–100).

Furthermore, educational psychology frames this mode of coping with ambiguous experience in terms of human adaptive potential (Sutton-Smith, 1997). Since play "contains so much nonsense, so much replication, and is so flexible ... it is a prime domain for the actualization of whatever the brain contains," so that "[play] is typically a primary place for the expression of anything that is humanly imaginable" (1997: 226–7). Thus, play can be conceived not only as an "exemplar of cultural variability," but as providing an arena within which novelty and alternative views may legitimately be explored (Sutton-Smith, 1997: 230).

Extending this often assumed frivolous intentionality of play, Gadamer (2002: 102) points to a serious intent of play when reflecting on its qualities:

Play has a special relation to what is serious ... More important, play itself contains its own, even sacred, seriousness. Yet, in playing, all those purposive relations that determine active and caring existence have not simply disappeared, but are curiously suspended. The player himself knows that play is only play and that it exists in a world determined by the seriousness of purposes. But he does not know this in such a way that, as a player, he actually intends this relation to seriousness.

In this regard, the concept of serious play appears to preserve the intrinsic motivation of play activities while focusing intentionality not on the emergent, adaptive outcomes themselves, but rather on the conditions for their possibility (Jacobs and Statler, 2005). In other words, play may not directly lead to adaptive outcomes, but instead fosters the thought processes of seeing things differently as well as seeing different things, which in the context of crafting strategy means that new understandings and strategic directions can emerge.

Thus, processes of crafting strategy through serious play change the mode of interaction (from work to play) and the medium of communication (from verbal to object-mediated), while retaining a focus on the seriousness of the strategic issues in question. In this sense, serious play provides a technology of foolishness that can complement the technologies of reason commonly deployed in strategy work. It also reaches beyond an a priori functional rationality, encouraging ambiguity and fluidity of action, and accepting a relaxation of functionally rational imperatives. Below, we briefly exemplify these considerations by reflecting on the moments of serious play in Orange UK's strategy workshop, which we described in more detail in Chapter 4.

Beyond functional rationality: By playfully configuring and reconfiguring the elements on the table, such as the organization as a flotilla of ships in difficult waters initially oriented towards the brand icon, participants could probe further into the relevance of the brand. Subsequently, and through a playful, yet serious gesture, the brand was physically repositioned to the opposite end of the construction. This prompted a collective acknowledgement from the group that resulted in a subsequent systematic review of the brand and its taken-for-granted values in order to sustain organizational performance after the acquisition. This episode illustrates the efficacy of playful experimentation with the literal positioning of objects, which is simultaneously symbolic, which enables the challenging of taken-for-granted assumptions supported by functional rationality (in this case that a strong brand is always a positive resource rather than a restrictive constraint).

Allowing for ambiguity and fluidity: The crafting process allowed participants to mobilize their tactile and kinesthetic abilities, and to bring these to bear on strategic challenges. All of the tactile objectifications of strategic concepts – the relative size, distance and positioning of ships and the relative position of the brand – functioned as extra-verbal devices that extended the expressive repertoire of the team. The models as well as their configuration had no pre-existing, a-contextual meaning, but rather gained in meaning throughout the workshop in a non-linear fashion. Thus, the physical shift of the brand's relative position effectively shattered the consistency of the team's traditionally unquestioned brand narratives. In the transitional space of play, the team confronted an ambiguous lack of differentiation and entertained a variety of new possible, alternative meanings for the existing brand values. In other words, the "holy grail" of the brand got demystified by challenging existing brand values and entertaining alternative ones.

Toward an emergent purpose: Moving the brand icon from the front to the rear end of the model seemed at first sight a senseless gesture. And yet, this participant followed a non-rational impulse that, in his words, something about the configuration "did not feel right." This individual's impulse preceded an immediate rational purpose. Yet, and in the ambiguous domain of play, participants were willing to jointly explore the potential meaning and purpose of the gesture and in retrospect realized how meaningful this performative, playful gesture had been.

Analogical reasoning: making sense through analogies and material analogs

Crafting strategy as embodied recursive enactment involves analogical reasoning by not only using cognitive-linguistic but also material analogs. Generally, analogical reasoning refers to the cognitive process of applying knowledge from a relatively familiar domain (the source) to another less familiar domain (the target). According to cognitive science, the application of knowledge by analogy involves at least two distinct forms of relation between source and target (Gentner, Holyoak, and Kokinov, 2001; Holyoak and Thagard, 1997; Vosniadou and Ortony, 1989). At one level, there is a superficial similarity that involves a recognized correspondence between the features of the objects in the source and target domains. At another level, there is an assumed structural similarity that involves a semblance of the deep structures within the source and target domains. Because this higher-order similarity can exist irrespective of superficial similarities between the objects involved (Forbus, Gentner, and Law, 1995), structural similarities have been understood as the most essential characteristic of analogical reasoning (Gentner and Markman, 1997).

Within organizational studies, Tsoukas (1993, 1991) has demonstrated that people who engage in knowledge generation and sensemaking processes in organizations employ analogical reasoning – often involving the use of metaphors. Metaphors function by introducing an initial, superficial similarity at the object level between source and target that may then be explored and "tested" for potential structural similarities through a process of analogical reasoning in a deeper, more systematic manner (Tsoukas, 1993: 342). From a constructionist perspective, metaphors can enable actors to reframe their perceptions (Barrett and Cooperrider, 1990) in social practices of sensemaking. In this sense, the analogical similarity between source and target domain may not only be identified

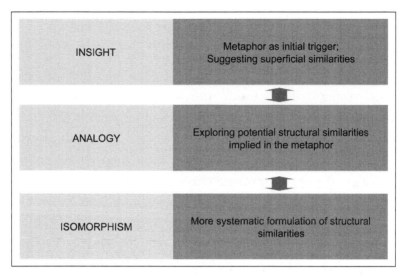

FIGURE 5.1 *Process model of analogical reasoning (Statler, Jacobs and Roos, 2008; used with permission).*

through the use of metaphor, but may additionally be created by it. Building from Tsoukas' process model (1991) (Figure 5.1) we can understand analogical reasoning through metaphors from a constructionist perspective.

First, an initial insight might be triggered by some metaphor that suggests a superficial similarity at the object level. Secondly, the implied similarity is intersubjectively explored for further structural similarities that lead to the establishment of an analogy. Through an oscillatory process of examining more thoroughly and systematically the plausibility of the suggested structural and relational similarities, a more fine-grained understanding is generated, and an isomorphism – i.e., a correspondence or identity between structural features of source and target – can be claimed (Tsoukas, 1991: 574ff.). Throughout this process "higherorder semantic relations (i.e., relations between relations) are preserved at the expense of lower order relations or mere isolated properties" (Tsoukas, 1991: 574). Through such an iterative "drilling" process, the sensemaking potential of a metaphor can be brought to bear in contexts such as strategy, organizational learning and organizational development processes.

Case example: Strategizing on after-sales services at PackCo. A global player in the consumer packaging industry with a 10 per cent share of the global market, PackCo's (pseudonym) selling proposition has been to supply systems for processing, packaging, and distribution of consumer goods. In the late 1990s though, PackCo's leadership team realized that other firms had outsourced their own after-sales service function at client sites in some small markets. PackCo's service business involved many highly qualified technical experts travelling to resolve problems with PackCo equipment as they emerged in client organizations. Although at the time a cost center, some senior managers were advocating its transformation into a profit center. While some of the executives considered this challenge strategically irrelevant, another group of executives kept emphasizing the strategic relevance of the after-sales function.

In 2001, the CEO of PackCo invited three of his fellow executives to participate in a strategic conversation to explore the status of this contentious issue in more detail. In order to facilitate strategic thinking, toy construction materials were proposed to explore this issue. The four participants were invited to build physical models of PackCo as an organization, their industry in general as well as the competitive landscape in the after-sales service business in particular. PackCo was represented as a white fortress full of chests of gold, guarded heavily with cannons pointing in all directions and a palm tree on top to indicate PackCo's attractiveness to investors. Besides two "windows of information" to the outside world, the fortress had only one connection to the model representing PackCo's customers, namely a single, large and solid monochromatic bridge equipped with a flexible and thin "line of communications," through which information was informally "pumped" in both directions.

By contrast, the physical model of PackCo's customers employed a variety of colors and was placed on four pillars, populated with person figures to represent the variety of facets in terms of products and businesses. The model also portrayed the customers' customers, i.e. the retailers using PackCo's packages. Then, the four executives connected these elements through colorful and flexible elements to represent a more flexible customer relationship than the one implied by the monochromatic, solid bridge.

While constructing these models, PackCo's sources of competitive advantage as well as the firm's core competencies were put at the center of the conversation. In an ironic performance, one participant challenged the official version, by placing a sarcophagus brick in a larger solid box built by bricks that had been placed within the center of the fortress. Opening this box slowly and blowing off imagined dust it might have collected, he said: "This is our core competency." When the other participants looked inside, they saw that the box was – empty.

Exploring the competitive landscape of after-sales services, the participants built a pirates' nest comprising of pirates armed with swords and guns, who were about to enter PackCo's market. Without any direct connections made to the customer model, potential and flexible points of connection had been prepared. The pirates' nest's agility, flexibility and connectivity was demonstrated by moving the model to every corner of the table as well as near the customer model and in this way emphasizing the various points of contact PackCo's competitors were able to mobilize vis-à-vis the customers (Figure 5.2).

The participants realized that PackCo's technical experts were mainly concerned about quality assurance and equipment support, were considered low in status and pay, and were framed as a non-value adding cost. In conclusion, participants agreed to consider new approaches to this now jointly acknowledged competitive field, as well as to systematically explore after-sales service's relevance for developing and retaining customer relationships.

Case reflection. First, we note that analogical reasoning took two distinct forms, namely a more conventional, cognitively oriented

FIGURE 5.2 *Crafting strategy at PackCo (Statler, Jacobs and Roos, 2008; used with permission).*

one in terms of using a flipchart to demonstrate how after-sales services could offer value to customers. Second, a multimodal form of analogical reasoning was employed by using toy construction materials. The latter process resulted in image-rich, nuanced physical models that induced novel meaning through the process of mapping a source to a target domain. In terms of the generic process of analogical reasoning outlined above, the metaphorical exploration involved an initial, superficial similarity between source and target domains that was inquired into by team members. Through this iterative, drilling process, the team members were able to identify not only superficial but structural similarities between the models and the organization. The organization, like the fortress, was wealthy, heavily guarded and inflexible. The competitors, like the pirates' nest, were diverse, aggressive, hostile and flexible. PackCo's customer relationships, like the fixed bridge, were unidirectional, with a single, inflexible point of contact at each end. And PackCo's

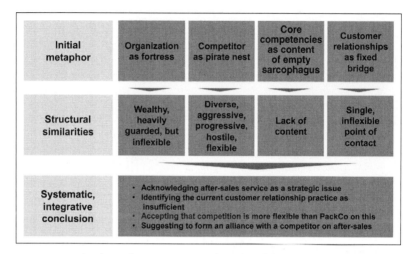

FIGURE 5.3 *Analogical reasoning at PackCo (Statler, Jacobs and Roos, 2008; used with permission).*

core competency, like the sarcophagus, appeared, to the executives' dismay, to lack content.

Through carefully exploring the organization's self-image and its competitive landscape, executives appreciated a different perspective on the contentious issue before reaching a joint view of the strategic relevance of after-sales service – what we would refer to as an isomorphic stage of the conversation. In turn, they had to realize that at the time their competitors were more flexible and agile in providing after-salesservice. Figure 5.3 represents this process of analogical reasoning.

Dialogue: reflective and generative negotiation of meaning

One key requirement for strategic innovation is to be able to view the industry and the company in a new light. Baden Fuller and Stopford (1994: 53) suggest that strategic innovation as the "creation of actions hitherto deemed impossible" requires "a change in the mental models held by managers," or as Choi and Valikangas (2001: 425) phrase it, it requires "strategy paradigm-shifts", as companies attempt to institutionalize a climate of questioning and challenging current operating norms and viewing things in new ways (Markides, 1998). One key requirement for achieving strategic innovation is, therefore, a challenge to existing mental models and the forming of new understanding.

How can such a mental shift be facilitated? Innovation per se cannot be designed, but it can be *designed for*, where the conditions fostering innovation can be put in place. We believe that crafting strategy as embodied recursive enactment can provide the conditions of possibility of a shift in mental models, since it involves a specific quality of conversation that can alter managers' mental models, this being reflective dialogue.

Mental models in communities of practice. Mental models are devices through which individuals make sense of current perceptions in the context of longer-term perceptive repertoires (Johnson-Laird, 1983; Minsky, 1986; Papert, 1980). Mental models are highly local and contextual and are developed primarily in the context of social and cultural practices, through discursive interaction (Heracleous, 2006). Mental models shape arguments, interpretation, and ultimately action. They emerge from and are enacted in what Fish (1980) has referred to as "interpretive communities," communities that share more or less the same "theory" of the world. In organization studies, this concept has been echoed by the concept of communities-of-practice (Brown and Duguid, 1991; Wenger, 1998; 2000). Competent participation in such a community involves a shared understanding of the essence of this community, its norms and relationships, as well as a common repertoire of language, routines, artifacts and narratives.

Integral to the shared repertoire of meaning-making in communities-of-practice are mental models. A management team, for example, constitutes such a community-of-practice through a shared understanding that they carry the responsibility for an entire firm or unit. A management team might establish certain norms, such as to follow a certain agenda and practice of decision-making, as well as developing a local language imbued with industry and organization-specific jargon. They might develop a shared understanding about what is to be perceived as an opportunity or threat in the business landscape, or a strength or weakness in the firm's internal processes.

Mental models have a dual, paradoxical effect. On the one hand they reduce complexity and thereby enable us to identify a particular course of action as appropriate. On the other hand, it is precisely by reducing complexity that they also lead us to downplay certain data in our search for appropriate action. Owing to their internally coherent nature, confirmatory bias and selective perception, mental models are relatively stable and persistent over time and within communities-of-practice. Disconfirming evidence is initially interpreted through the lens of the existing mental models, and ample disconfirmatory evidence or even a crisis are often required before existing mental models are challenged and critically examined (Kuhn, 1962). A necessary first step for critically reviewing mental models is to first render them visible. "Making those mental models explicit," Kim (1993: 44) suggests, "is crucial to developing new shared mental models."

Altering mental models through dialogue. A significant body of literature suggests that dialogue, as a reflective conversational mode, can enable managers to alter their mental models (Isaacs, 1999; Schein, 1999) and can transform social interactions and relations due to its diagnostic and generative potentials (Gergen *et al.*, 2001, 2004). In particular, conversations for understanding involve making claims, giving evidence, examining hypotheses, exploring beliefs and feelings, as well as maintaining contentions (Ford and Ford, 1995). By rendering visible taken-for-granted causal linkages, managers' understandings can be mapped out and made explicit in order to explore alternative perspectives, relationships, opportunities, threats and actions (Ford and Ford, 1995: 563). The opportunity for managers to see things differently, as to well as see different things by engaging in such conversations, results from these conversations' threefold potential. Conversations for understanding provide managers with the opportunity to critically examine the underlying assumptions of their thinking and their implications; to collectively develop a shared language that emerges from the social practice of inquiry; as well as to create a learning context in which reflective conversation is being practiced (Ford and Ford, 1995: 548). In contrast to conversations for understanding – or dialogue – conversations for performance and closure tend to operate in a competitive mode of "debate" or "discussion" that are more concerned with "winning" the argument and with advancing particular interests, than with self-reflection.

With regard to the diagnosis of mental models, dialogue enables inquiry into privately held assumptions of organizational participants. As Schein (1999: 209) suggests, "We have to listen to ourselves before we can really understand others." Critical reflection on one's own assumptions in a collaborative manner with other participants helps one "to appreciate more the inherent complexity of communication and mutual understanding." By mutually agreeing to critically and respectfully examine different viewpoints, participants become more aware of the nature and limitations of their mental models as linguistic, context-specific constructs (Schein, 1993: 43). Utterances of surprise are indicators of such an introspective, reflective moment, as participants come to realize the implicit assumptions in their statements (Isaacs, 1999) and gain conscious access to their own mental models (Schein, 1999: 211). By encouraging dialogue as a specific, reflective conversational mode distinct from debate or discussion, the quality of conversation may be transformed, along with the thinking that lies beneath it (Isaacs, 1993: 24–5).

Acknowledging different mental models makes them intelligible and allows for the development of a shared understanding of a particular state of affairs. Isaacs (1999) suggests that this generative potential stems from developing a shared language by crossing boundaries of individual mental models. He proposes that dialogue as a "discipline of collective thinking and inquiry" would allow us to develop new

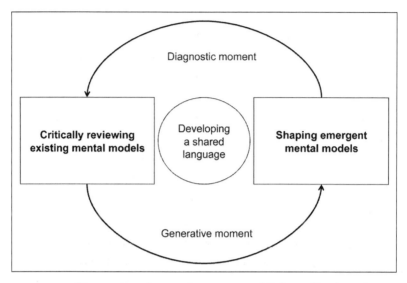

FIGURE 5.4 *Diagnostic and generative moments of dialogue (Jacobs and Heracleous, 2006; used with permission).*

possibilities for thinking and action (Isaacs, 1993: 24). Because assumptions and mental models are more visible and, therefore, intelligible, more collaborative inquiry into their determinants can occur. Rather than focusing instrumentally on outcomes, dialogue can allow people to participate in the creation of shared meaning through processes of collectively exploring and reflectively inquiring into patterns of collective thinking (Isaacs, 1999). Such shared learning experiences can provide a basis for developing "an overarching common language and mental model" (Schein, 1993: 41). The recursive process of inquiring into existing mental models and thereby developing a shared language of diagnosis contributes subsequently to developing a shared understanding. Figure 5.4 shows the dual nature of this dialogue.

Creating the conditions for dialogue. How can the conditions for dialogue be designed? A distinction can be made between an organization's culture, on one hand, and designing a specific workshop or experiential exercise, on the other. With regard to the former, Schein's (1988, 1993) work refers to the evolution of management teams in general and of conversation within such groups in particular. The maturity of a group relates to its problem-solving process and its handling of critical incidents. Lack of openness in communication by people in positions of authority makes reflective dialogue highly unlikely. Mature groups, according to Schein, score highly in the following dimensions: capacity to deal with their environment; basic agreement on mission, goals and values; capacity for self-knowledge; optimal use of resources; optimal integration of communication, decision-making, authority, influence and norms; as well as the capacity to learn from experience at a collective level (Schein, 1988: 80–1). Openness, transparency in terms of problem-solving and acknowledging differences are key elements for managers to role model conversations for understanding rather than closure.

With regard to designing specific experiential exercises, Isaacs and Smith (1994) outline how dialogue can be nurtured within an overall organizational context. To start with, participants should be invited but not forced to participate. They should have the choice whether to take part in the conversation in the first place. Secondly, listening by paying close attention not only to what is being said, but also more importantly to what is said beneath the words (the connotations or implicit associations of verbal exchanges). Thirdly, reflective dialogue requires the observation of the observer, which is a kind of second-order observation. Listening has been identified as a central aspect of the discourses of communities of practice. Rather than being a functional silence in the turn-taking of a conversation, listening provides the relational basis for joint meaning-generation (Jacobs and Coghlan, 2005; Jacobs, 2003). Finally, reflective dialogue entails the suspension of assumptions. Rather than imposing or advocating one's own views, suspension of assumptions is at the core of the diagnostic element of dialogue.

Within reflective dialogue, disagreement is seen as an opportunity, not a threat to consensus, providing the opportunity to inquire deeper into the privately held assumptions that tend to underlie superficial disagreements. Dialogue as a reflective form of conversation, therefore, holds promise in potentially altering the mental models of those participating in such a conversation. Or, as Schein (1996: 31) puts it, the "most basic mechanism of acquiring new information that leads to cognitive restructuring is to discover in a conversational process that the interpretation that someone else puts on a concept is different from one's own." Below, we demonstrate through an empirical example how the practice of crafting strategy as embodied recursive enactment can facilitate reflective dialogue, and in this enable strategic thinking and innovation.

An illustration from practice. In early 2003, the CEO of a Swiss-based private banking group had planned to launch a major strategy initiative in terms of the group's overall go-to-market strategy. The "I know my banker" initiative was designed to operationalize the bank's aspiration to move towards a more customer-focused service provisioning. The goal was to provide a distinctive, differentiated private banking service offering to customers that, in the context of broader trends in the banking industry, would be serviced with standardized banking products. To kick off the initiative, the CEO invited his heads of departments, as well as their direct reports, to a one-day management retreat aimed at familiarizing them with the concept and aligning management accordingly.

The workshop was designed so as to enable participants to explore dialogically the concept "I know my banker" and its consequences in more detail, so that by the end of the workshop they would develop shared mental maps on this theme, and strategic action consequences would take shape. In a first round of conversations the participants engaged in an intense debate. While some had assumed that the private banking service should benefit all its customers, others kept emphasizing that this initiative should only be applied to a carefully selected segment of the group's customer base. A second round of conversations revealed further ambiguity about the actual intent of the change initiative. While some participants took the concept at face value and speculated on ways that would encourage customers to actually get to know their bankers better – and what that might mean for them as bankers – others followed a more traditional, instrumental path along a "know your customer" logic. A subsequent third conversation finally made the major differences in mental maps related to this theme even more tangible. While on one hand, some participants argued that "I know my banker" was all about technical systems, customer relationship marketing or data mining, others argued from a relationship and trust-building angle. Proponents of the latter view employed metaphors to emphasize the need to establish the "same wavelength" or "getting into the jacuzzi" with customers. The CEO appreciated the workshop conversation that had revealed initial divergences of thinking, building new, shared perspectives, and had a significant impact in terms of subsequent bank strategic actions.

Acknowledging the lack of shared understanding revealed by the workshop conversations, the CEO decided to postpone the launch of the change initiative for a few months. The two emergent views (technocentric vs. anthropocentric) on the subject matter allowed him to adjust the change initiative so as to emphasize the relational aspects while acknowledging the technical implications for the back office functions. After careful reconsideration and redesign along these aspects, the "I know my banker" program was launched successfully in close collaboration with the heads of departments later that year. The workshop dynamics illustrate some of the interrelations of dialogue, mental maps and strategic innovation (Figure 5.5). Designed as an implementation kick-off event, the workshop provided a conversational setting in which an arguably "clear" concept ("I know my banker") was shown to in fact be ambiguous, and further explored through dialogical interactions. It was through the diagnostic moment of the dialogical process of meaning-creation and negotiation that differences in viewpoints on the issue at hand were made explicit. While on one hand proponents of a technocentric, selective view argued for a rather incremental change, proponents of an

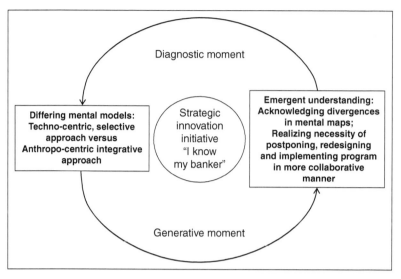

FIGURE 5.5 *Diagnostic and generative moments at SwissBank (Jacobs and Heracleous, 2006; used with permission).*

anthropocentric, integrative view advocated a more radical shift in the service offering. Both views – emerging from the workshop conversations – can be considered as manifestations of underlying mental maps relating to participants' understanding of the nature of human relations, the nature of their business, their customers, of the level and type of service they aimed to offer. Revealing and acknowledging these differences through reflective conversations made it possible for participants to engage in more generative conversations that contributed to a more shared view on the theme – and in turn, allowed the management to make necessary adjustments prior to the actual launch of the initiative.

Reflective dialogue and crafting strategy. While complexity reduction on the one hand is necessary for taking action in the first place, it also encourages a certain myopia by downplaying disconfirming information. In a strategic context, this means that current strategy paradigms tend to be perpetuated while alternative routes and ideas for strategy development might not be explored. In order to alter mental models of managers, a specific form of conversation for understanding is suggested. Dialogue as a reflective form of conversation allows us to critically review and inquire into the underlying assumptions of individual and collective mental models. During such an inquiry, a collective language is likely to emerge. It is through this common language that emergent, new mental models can take shape. Thus, fundamental strategic innovation per se cannot be designed, but only be designed for. We argue that crafting as embodied recursive enactment offers a practice that can create the conditions of possibility for reflective dialogue.

Conclusion

Crafting strategy typically changes the mode of interaction and communication as well as the mode of reasoning. It does so by relying on a playful interaction that is nevertheless serious in intent; a dialogic form of communication that offers space to critically reflect on and alter taken-for-granted mental models as well as by engaging participants in a material form of analogical reasoning.

As exemplified in the case of PackCo, the metaphorical models generated and shaped within the reasoning process were not only discursively expressed, but involved participants' bodies in order to construct them and had a physical existence beyond the actual utterance. We refer to these kinds of metaphors as embodied metaphors precisely because they are built through the body and since they have a body themselves. We will elaborate on and explore in more detail how embodied metaphors can be utilized in understanding organizations in the following chapter.

REFERENCES

Baden Fuller, C. and Stopford, J.M. 1994. *Rejuvenating the mature business: The competitive challenge.* Boston, MA: Harvard Business School Press.

Barrett, F. J. and Cooperrider, D. L. 1990. Generative metaphor intervention: A new behavioral approach for working with systems divided by conflict and caught in defensive perception. *Journal of Applied Behavioral Science*, 26: 219–39.

Brown, J. S. and Duguid, P. 1991. Organizational learning and communities-of-practice: Toward a unified view of working, learning, and innovation. *Organization Science*, 2(1): 40–57.

Chandler, A. 1962. *Strategy and structure: Chapters in the history of American industrial enterprise*. Cambridge, MA: MIT Press.

Choi, D. and Valikangas, L. 2001. Patterns of strategy innovation. *European Management Journal*, 19(4): 424–29.

Fish, S.E. 1980. *Is there a text in this class? The authority of interpretive communities*. Cambridge, MA: Harvard University Press.

Forbus, K. D., Gentner, D., and Law, K. 1995. MAC/FAC: A model of similarity-based retrieval. *Cognitive Science*, 19(2): 141–205.

Ford, J. and Ford, L. 1995. The role of conversations in producing intentional change in organizations. *Academy of Management Review*, 20(3): 541–70.

Gadamer, H. G. 2002. *Truth and method*. New York: Continuum.

Geertz, C. 1973. *The interpretation of cultures: selected essays*. New York: Basic Books.

Gentner, D. and Markman, A. B. 1997. Structure mapping in analogy and similarity. *American Psychologist*, 52(1): 45–56.

Gentner, D., Holyoak, K. J., and Kokinov, B. N. 2001. *The analogical mind: Perspectives from cognitive science*. Cambridge, MA: MIT Press.

Gergen, K.J., Gergen, M.M., and Barret, F.J. 2004: Dialogue: Life and death of the organization. In Grant, D., Phillips, N., Hardy, C., Putnam, L., and Oswick, C. (eds), *Handbook of Organizational Discourse*. Thousand Oaks, CA: Sage.

Gergen, K.J., McNamee, S., and Barrett, F.J. 2001. Toward transformative dialogue. *International Journal of Public Administration*. 24 (7/8): 679–707.

Heracleous, L. 2006. *Discourse, interpretation, organization*. Cambridge University Press.

Holyoak, K.J. and Thagard, P. 1997. The analogical mind. *American Psychologist*, 52(1), 35–44.

Hoskisson, R. E., Hitt, M. A., Wan, W. P., and Yiu, D. 1999. Theory and research in strategic management: Swings of a pendulum. *Journal of Management*, 25: 417–56.

Huizinga, J. 1950. *Homo ludens: A study of the play-element in culture*. London: Routledge & Kegan Paul.

Isaacs, W. 1993. Taking flight: Dialogue, collective thinking and organizational learning, *Organizational Dynamics*, 22(2): 24–40.

1999. *Dialogue and the art of thinking together*. New York: Doubleday.

Jacobs, C. D. 2003. *Managing organizational responsiveness – toward a theory of responsive practice*. Wiesbaden: DUV.

Jacobs, C.D. and Coghlan, D. 2005. Sound from silence – on listening in organizational learning. *Human Relations*, 58(1):115–38.

Jacobs, C.D. and Heracleous, L. 2005. Answers for questions to come: Reflective dialogue as an enabler of strategic innovation. *Journal of Organizational Change Management*, 18(4): 338–52.

2006. Constructing shared understanding – The role of embodied metaphors in organization development. *Journal of Applied Behavioral Science*, 42(2): 207–26.

Jacobs, C. and Statler, M. 2005. Strategy creation as serious play. In Floyd, S.W., Roos, J., Jacobs, C., and Kellermanns, F. (eds.), *Innovating Strategy Process*. Oxford: Blackwell.

2006. Towards a technology of foolishness: Developing scenarios through serious play. *International Studies of Management and Organization*, 36(3): 7–92.

Janis, I.L. 1972. *Victims of groupthink: A psychological study of foreign-policy decisions and fiascos*. Boston, MA: Houghton.

Johnson-Laird, P.N. 1983. *Mental models: Towards a cognitive science of language, inference, and consciousness*. Cambridge, MA: Harvard University Press.

Kim, D.H. 1993. The link between individual and organizational learning. *Sloan Management Review*, 35(1): 37–50.

Kuhn, T. 1962. *The structure of scientific revolutions*. University of Chicago Press.

MacIntosh, R. and MacLean, D. 1999. Conditioned emergence: a dissipative structures approach to transformation. *Strategic Management Journal*, 20 (4): 297–316.

March, J.G. 1979. The technology of foolishness. In March, J.G. and Olsen, J.P. (eds.), *Ambiguity and choice in organizations*. Bergen: Universitetsforlaget, 69–81.

Markides, C.C. 1998. Strategic innovation in established companies. *Sloan Management Review*, 39(3): 31–42.

Minsky, M.L. 1986. *The society of mind*, New York: Simon & Schuster.

Mintzberg, H. and Waters, J. A. 1985. Of strategies, deliberate and emergent. *Strategic Management Journal*, 6: 257–72.

Papert, S. 1980. *Mindstorms: Children, computers, and powerful ideas*. New York: Basic Books.

Piaget, J. and Inhelder, B., 1958. *The growth of logical thinking from childhood to adolescence: An essay on the construction of formal operational structures*. New York: Basic Books.

Rumelt, R. P., Schendel, D. E., and Teece, D. J. (1944). *Fundamental issues in strategy: A research agenda*. Boston, MA: Harvard Business School Press.

Schein, E.H. 1988. *Process consultation Vol. I: Its role in organization development*. Reading, MA: Addison-Wesley.

1993. On dialogue, culture, and organizational learning. *Organizational Dynamics*, 22(2): 40–51.

1996. Kurt Lewin's change theory in the field and in the classroom. *Systems Practice*, 9(2): 27–47.

1999. *Process consultation revisited: Building the helping relationship*. Reading, MA: Addison-Wesley.

Statler, M., Jacobs, C., and Roos, J. 2008. Performing Strategy: Analogical reasoning as strategic practice. *Scandinavian Journal of Management*, 24: 133–44.

Sutton-Smith, B. 1997. *The ambiguity of play*. Cambridge, MA: Harvard University Press.

Tsoukas, H. 1991. The missing link: A transformational view of metaphors in organizational science. *Academy of Management Review*, 16(3): 566–85.

1993. Analogical reasoning and knowledge generation in organization theory. *Organization Studies*, 14(3): 323–436.

Vosniadou, S., and Ortony, A. 1989. *Similarity and analogical reasoning*. Cambridge University Press.

Vygotsky, L.S. and M. Cole. 1978. *Mind in society: The development of higher psychological processes*. Cambridge, MA: Harvard University Press.

Weick, K.E. 1995. *Sensemaking in organizations*. Thousand Oaks, CA: Sage.

Wenger, E. 1998. *Communities of practice: Learning, meaning, and identity*. Cambridge University Press.

2000. Communities of practice and social learning systems. *Organization*, 7(2): 225–46.

Winnicott, D.W. 1971. *Playing and reality*. London: Tavistock.

Hephata Foundation

Understanding the strategic context of a non-profit health and educational service provider

Context

Hephata is a non-profit foundation that offers health and education services in the largest German state of North Rhine-Westphalia. As part of Hephata's biannual strategy retreat, the foundation's leadership team – comprising of two executive officers and their direct reports – gathered for three days in order to jointly identify Hephata's strategic challenges and to agree on how to design a structured strategy process. In particular, the goal of the workshop was to define the foundation's strategic initiatives and projects for 2010; to develop and define the performance measures to evaluate these, as well as to approve the formal process on defining strategic initiatives and projects.

Strategic goal of intervention

Within this two-day strategy retreat, a three-hour embodied metaphor intervention was solicited on the first day to develop a shared understanding of Hephata's overall and division-specific strategic environment. In turn, the intervention aimed to identify the main environmental trends the organization needed to respond to and to trigger a discussion on the relative relevance of these trends for Hephata's strategy.

Embodied metaphors

A first model portrayed the general demographic trend towards *a decreasing birth rate and the specific consequence in terms of recruiting suitable and sufficient talent to the organization.* The foundation not only had difficulties in recruiting sufficient new hires in general, but moreover it lacked a sufficiently large layer of "high performers." Hephata's staff consisted of many old and a few young staff – a development that was even more pronounced in more rural regions. The model prepared by a team of five participants, and debriefed to the plenary, consisted in two main elements, each being structured in three stages. In the back of the model, three towers increasing in height from left to right portrayed the increasing demands, challenges and workload of the organization. In the front of the model, three staff populations

FIGURE D.1 *Embodied metaphor 1 from Hephata.*

were portrayed, decreasing in numbers and abilities from left to right. Opposite to the highest tower of workload sat only two person figures, with strange heads and hats to portray their limited ability to cope with this workload. Thus, the model summarized two concurrent developments: an increase in workload and a decrease in numbers and qualification of staff.

A second model portrayed the *increasing need for negotiation and lobbying vis-à-vis funding and supervisory authorities* that were thought of as inflexible and skeptical to innovation. Acknowledging both an increase in regulation and a decrease in resources allocated by the authorities, Hephata had to fight for implementing novel ideas in service offerings. This ambiguity between regulation and resources revealed an ambivalence with regard to elected politicians. While politicians spoke of strengthening the rights for people with disabilities, the financial support for organizations providing specialized services to this population had been cut back. The model featured a person figure with a megaphone – portraying a politician – who

FIGURE D.2 *Embodied metaphor 2 from Hephata.*

shouted ambiguous information to supervisory and funding authorities – sitting with their back to him on a bench – who themselves
were watching the service providers from a distance and through a
window. In turn, Hephata's challenge consisted of effectively balancing all these ambivalent claims from service users, funding and
supervisory authorities and politicians alike.

A third artifact portrayed the *increasing differentiation and spe-
cialization in service user requirements and needs*. So far, Hephata had
responded very early to the increase in emancipation and individual-
ization of people with special needs by de-institutionalizing its services
and by working towards an increase in autonomy and involvement of
service users. This development has continued at an increased pace
since service demands have become ever more customized and thus
fragmented – symbolized by a clustered set of bricks of different shapes
and colors. The organizational challenge consisted in handling the
increase in complexity of service provision and in integrating the

FIGURE D.3 *Embodied metaphor 3 from Hephata.*

different service offerings. The corresponding leadership challenge was portrayed through a joker head on a wooden stick, trying to monitor and guide these developments.

A fourth group tackled the *challenge of increasing demands in service requests while simultaneously, resources decreased.* Given the total increase in complexity and number of service offerings, the funding bodies had not fully covered the corresponding increase in costs. Thus, the challenge of an ever more cost efficient organization became very evident. An increase in demand was mirrored by a decrease in financial and human resources. Or, as the model portrayed, more had to be done with less.

FIGURE D.4 *Embodied metaphor 4 from Hephata.*

Insights gained: How was this session strategically consequential for the organization/the team?

Within the overall strategy retreat, this collaborative, multimodal analysis of the organization's environment allowed participants to appreciate aspects of their competitive landscape and interrelation-ships among actors, in a nuanced and vivid way. Despite the apparent simplicity of the models, they triggered a quite intense discussion of each of the environmental trends that in turn provided a solid ground for a systematic development of Hephata's strategy for 2010 and beyond.

CHAPTER SIX

Understanding organizations through embodied metaphors

In Chapter 2 we outlined the key theoretical antecedents to crafting strategy through embodied metaphors, drawing from literature on metaphor and embodied realism. We portrayed metaphor as a creative force, addressing the cognitive, spatial and embodied dimensions. We also addressed the theoretical development of metaphor in the context of organization development interventions, a context we exemplify in this chapter. We operationalize the embodied metaphor approach in a study of three organization development workshops where groups of actors were engaged in constructing metaphors in the flesh: physical entities whose target domains were their task, their organization in its business landscape, and the identity of their division. In doing so, participants drew on a variety of source domains, and the resulting metaphors produced insights for them in terms of developing shared views of their target domains, as well as for us as researchers through a three-stage analytical process involving contextual understanding, within-case analysis and cross-case analysis.

We analyzed grand metaphors and constituent metaphors constructed by these teams, and found that actors' first-order perceptions

This chapter is based on Heracleous and Jacobs (2008).

of organizational dimensions such as power, importance, relatedness, coherence, belongingness, robustness/duality of relationships,
and uniformity, are manifested in particular ways in these embodied
metaphors, through the spatial arrangement of physical objects. We
found that analysis of embodied metaphors can enable access to actors'
first-order conceptions of organizational dimensions, revealing alternative qualities and interrelations among them, and posing substantial challenges to established conceptions of ontology and method in
organization theory. In doing so, the embodied metaphor approach
offers a viable, novel alternative to the dominant positivist paradigm
of conceptualizing and researching organizational dimensions as well
as understanding organizations.

Case study approach and data set

Given that access to rich data and to actors' own perspectives (Miles
and Huberman, 1994) is essential to our research topic, we have pursued an interpretive case study design (Stake, 1995; Yin, 1994). The
empirical data set consists of embodied metaphors constructed at
three management workshops carried out between July 2001 and June
2002 with groups of managers from the same organization. The teams
involved were the strategy development team, the business operations
team and the technical division of CellCo, a European mobile telephony provider. All three workshops aimed at exploring and addressing
the strategic and operational implications of the major changes in
CellCo's business landscape, and were facilitated by members of the
Imagination Lab Foundation, of which the second author of the book
was an associate.

CellCo had become by 2000 the fastest growing top-three player in
its domestic market, with a market share of nearly 25 per cent, project-
ing the image of a dynamic, innovative and unconventional company.
Then two major changes significantly shifted its business landscape.
Taking on a large debt, CellCo purchased one of the domestic 3G

licenses through competitive bidding. Shortly after this purchase, CellCo was acquired by FixCo, a large, foreign European competitor that was the market leader in its domestic market. Capitalizing on the strong brand recognition of CellCo, FixCo decided to group its entire international mobile telephony operations under the auspices of a newly formed organizational entity called CellCo Global. Although CellCo had been assured of retaining a relatively high degree of autonomy within CellCo Global, management had been concerned by the implications of the change in ownership for strategic direction as well as operational priorities. The specific focus of each retreat was based on the nature of the team involved and their perceived organizational challenges. While six managers of the strategy team met for two days to develop a shared view on a renewed, ideal strategy development process at CellCo, nine managers of business operations and ten managers of the technical division each explored for two-and-a half days a shared view on the adjusted, post-merger business landscape of their respective domains.

Physical entities were constructed by these groups of organizational actors, employing analogically mediated inquiry. This is a group of approaches in which participants are actively involved in constructing or sculpting physical, and simultaneously metaphorical, symbols that are then decoded or interpreted with the assistance of organization development practitioners who act as workshop leaders and facilitators (Barry, 1994; Broussine and Vince, 1996; Buergi, Jacobs, and Roos, 2005; Doyle and Sims, 2002). In terms of approaches to tropological analysis, we studied what Oswick, Putnam, and Keenoy (2004) refer to as "exposed tropes in use," where tropes are not imposed on organizational phenomena, but are rather studied inductively; and where "resonant" tropes such as metaphor rather than "dissonant" tropes such as irony are focused on.

In this research we have operationalized the concept of embodied metaphors in terms of these constructions. Even though metaphors are inherently embodied, as Lakoff and Johnson (1980, 1999) have shown, the constructions we have studied offer opportunities for gaining further insights because they are also *literally* embodied. The notion of embodied metaphors echoes what others refer to as multimodal metaphors. Forceville (2009), for instance, distinguishes monomodal (typically verbal) metaphors whose target and source domains are represented in a single mode, from multimodal metaphors involving more than one mode.

We have labelled the constructions we studied as "embodied metaphors" for the following reasons: first, they are actual structures constructed through engagement of the body, involving a direct phenomenological, experiential relationship between the participants and the resulting constructions. Embodied engagement as our mode of being in the world (Johnson, 1987; Lakoff and Johnson, 1999) is actualized in the making of these constructions. Secondly, these constructions are not simply semantic or spatial metaphors such as cognitive maps (Huff, 1990), but are tangible entities extending into three-dimensional space. They are metaphors in the flesh that are recursively and simultaneously constructed and interpreted. They embody the blending of source and target domains, and engender meanings both in the construction process and subsequent interpretations. They are material exemplars of metaphorical image-schemas, since they draw from particular source domains to represent target domains such as organizational identity or divisional identity or group task, as perceived by organizational actors. Embodied metaphors thus exhibit the meta-theoretical perspective of embodiment that holds embodied experience to be central to thought and interpretation. Further, the process of constructing these metaphorical structures through the engagement of the corporeal body actualizes the experiential perspective on embodiment (Rohre, 2007) and results in these constructions as unique artifacts, metaphors-in-the-flesh providing access to agents' thoughts and interpretations.

Participants in each workshop had available 3,000 pre-selected construction toy materials of a variety of colors, sizes and shapes (including materials with preconfigured meaning, such as person figures or animals). After some exercises aimed to help participants familiarize themselves with the materials, the practice of crafting embodied metaphors involves four iterative stages that operate at both the individual and collective levels and build up to detailed conversations on the core strategic issues and challenges as perceived by participants. First, participants are invited to construct and then debrief or intepret their individual constructions relating to the goal of the workshop. Secondly, the groups are invited to integrate their individual constructions into a collective construction whereby redundancies should be eliminated but differences and diversity maintained. This latter step represents the central part of the process since consonances and dissonances in terms of the strategic issue are exchanged and negotiated. Thirdly, in a recurring cycle of steps one and two, individual and then collective models of key stakeholders and relationships to the core construction supplement the emergent strategic landscape. Finally, the overall construction is debriefed and probed by means of "what-if" scenarios suggested by participants themselves (for further details on the approach, see Buergi, Jacobs, and Roos, 2005; Jacobs and Heracleous, 2006; Buergi and Roos, 2003; Roos, Victor, and Statler, 2004).

Analytical strategy

Studying embodied artifacts in social interaction

Gibbs (1999) emphasizes the relevance of our physical experience for our interpretation and understanding and holds that meaning is motivated by "people's recurring bodily experience in the real world" (1999: 39). Thus, he rejects a concept of cognition as purely internal and disembodied, and rather advocates the examination of the interrelationship between language, thought and embodied action (Gibbs, 2003: 2). Processing linguistic meaning involves not only the understanding of what a word means, but also an acknowledgment of the role of physical experience and the body in intersubjective meaning-generation (2003: 13).

Equally emphasizing the relevance of bodily and material resources in the generation and negotiation of meaning, Heath and Hindmarsh (2002) view the recursive interrelationship between language, body and artifacts as crucial to understanding social interaction emphasizing the necessity of studying how objects and artifacts shape meaning (2002: 102). Such emergent "architecture of intersubjectivity" (Heritage, 1984: 254) gives objects and artifacts their local, specific meaning, relevance and significance. Thus, objects and artifacts are considered co-constitutive of meaning-generation in discursive interaction, that in turn shapes the meaning, relevance and significance of these material features in a "local ecology of objects and artefacts" (Heath and Hindmarsh, 2002: 117).

Analyzing objects and artifacts comes with both certain advantages as well as trade-offs, and deserves some further specifications. While some materials such as plasticine are more "neutral" in terms of preconfigured meanings, others such as construction toy materials may be more effective in terms of connectivity and likelihood of swiftly inducing rich imagery. While the participants may be partly constrained by the nature of materials available, they are also enabled by these same materials in externalizing and debating their views. Methodologically speaking, the constraints relating to preconfigured meanings inherent in the materials can be considered limitations, but on the other hand participants are able to ascribe local meaning to their constructions through drawing from and combining these preconfigured meanings into broader metaphors and storylines, and therefore emergent, creative sensemaking is facilitated by these same materials.

Due to the nature of the method, the materials available become part of, and influence participants' constructions. For example, stereotypical views of accountants, dungeons, dragons, or lions, that are represented by materials seen as embodying such "prefabricated" meanings, will influence how these materials are used. We view the materials however as not simply constraining, but also enabling, in that they offer effective ways to externalize such views and make them part of the constructions as integral elements of the storylines presented, and to make them amenable to conscious debate. So, while stereotypical meanings are no doubt part of agents' cognitive repertoire, they are also situationally activated and employed to present participants' own views, on their own terms, about the target domains of the embodied metaphors.

The process itself involves successive levels of complexity in what participants are invited to construct, aims to gradually increase confidence and dexterity with the materials, ensures that each single participants at any time has available a variety of construction materials, and finally invites participants to remove redundancies in their individual constructions so that diversity can be maintained in the group constructions. These features of the process help to reduce the likelihood that participants will simply behave as automata and put together elements of the construction mindlessly, or even in a manner determined by the dominant paradigms in their organizations.

Thus, established patterns of sensemaking and "on-line" construction of embodied metaphors are not mutually contradictory, as the latter draws from the former in a manner that fosters creative constructions using available materials, but on participants' own terms as they are invited and enabled to tell their own story. Even though a method inspired by embodied realism might be seen as "imposed" on the setting, as nomothetic research is (in the sense that the procedures involved are pre-designed and the instruments and materials pre-existing), the responses in the former case are much more emergent and unexpected than those of nomothetic research, offering the ability to collect rich data and the potential for novel insights.

Analyzing embodied metaphorical mappings

When analyzing embodied metaphors that resulted from the generic process outlined above, we distinguish between process and product of metaphorical processing (Gibbs, 1999). Furthermore, we follow Gibbs' (1999) methodological recommendation in acknowledging the specific time course in the experience of metaphor processing by focusing specifically on the stage most relevant to our analysis, namely that of *interpretation* which involves the conscious, intersubjective development and active attribution of a particular meaning to a metaphorical utterance or text (Gibbs, 1999: 39).

Both process and product involve participants mapping a source to a target domain by crafting physical artifacts that are concurrently being interpreted by them. Our analysis focuses on the artifactual level of metaphorical mapping, that is, embodied metaphors as our primary form of text. In a gesture of second-order interpretation, we interpret these by sticking as closely as possible to the first-order interpretations of participants by considering the linguistic process of meaning negotiation as necessary interpretive context.

As an illustration of our analytical protocol, we outline below an extract from a transcribed vignette of the embodied metaphor of the "safari park," a constituent element within the "Strategy process is a journey of disoriented animals" construction, the grand metaphor of the strategy development team in CellCo. Total time frame of the vignette was fourteen minutes; we focus in this extract on selected sequences that are indicative of our analytical approach. We adapted Heath and Hindmarsh's (2002) transcription protocol for our analytical purposes which recommends capturing the content of what participant said as well as what they physically built or manipulated in their meaning negotiation.

The process of embodied metaphorical mapping involved three related, yet distinct stages. The first stage of initial mapping refers to the construction of individual, unrelated artifacts, while the second

TABLE 6.1: *Process steps of embodied metaphorical mappings*

Stage of embodied metaphorical mapping	Stage of constructing embodied metaphors	Agents' actions and artifactual manifestations (example from safari park episode)
Initial mapping	Constructing individual, unrelated artifacts and attributing meaning to them.	• I(1): Four animals (SD); 70 national operators (TD). • I(2): Astronaut (SD); aligned managers (SD). • I(3): Green platform (SD); end-point of strategy process (TD). • I(4): Blue book (SD); corporate strategic framework document (TD).
Relational mapping	Interrelating artifacts by physical positioning, performative gestures and/or narrative connections.	• R(1):Green platform of safari park as final destination for traveling animals (SD); end-point of strategy process for 70 managers (TD). • R(2): Blue book within safari park but invisible (SD); corporate strategic framework as guiding strategic behavior (TD).
Integrative mapping	Integrating relational mappings into constituent/ grand metaphor by physical positioning, performative gestures and/or narrative connections.	• IM(1): Safari park as constrained habitat for animals (SD); strategic alignment with degrees of freedom as goal of ideal strategy process (TD).

(Heracleous and Jacobs [2008]; used with permission.)

stage of relational mapping interrelates these artifacts physically and narratively. Finally, integrative mapping refers to the physical and narrative integration of these relational mappings into constituent and grand metaphors. Table 6.1 provides a synopsis of these different steps in the process of embodied metaphorical mapping and high-lights examples from the safari park episode (SD stands for source domain, TD for target domain, I for initial mapping, R for relational mapping, and IM for integrative mapping).

Tables 6.2 to 6.4 expand each of the three stages by drawing on transcribed conversations and videotape analysis from the safari park episode. We illustrate the stages with extracts from this vignette, whereby the four examples are organized in their actual time sequence.

A first, initial mapping refers to participants actively constructing individual artifacts and concurrently assigning meaning to them. For instance, in the sequence reported below, four animal figures (SD) were constructed and positioned at the starting point of an ideal strat-egy process, to represent the target audience of such process, that is seventy country managers of the organization (TD).

Secondly, these initial mappings were then mapped relationally whereby initial metaphors were interrelated by producing (or delib-erately rejecting) inter-metaphor relationships. Here, the initial map-ping of the four animals led participants to deliberately identify a green landscape platform for the metaphor of a safari park (SD), represent-ing the end-point of a (yet to be specified) strategy process (TD).

Thirdly, the interrelated metaphors of animals and safari park were then integrated to form a constituent element of the grand metaphor, i.e. the strategy process as a journey. Such integrative mapping con-verges subsidiary mappings into constituent metaphors that in turn from a grand metaphor.

This analytical protocol allowed us to understand the detailed meaning negotiation at an artifactual informed by what was said. Further, it allowed us to identify the safari park as a constituent meta-phor within the grand metaphor. Importantly, it allowed us to track not only the mapping from source to target domain, but to understand the emergent meaning (EM) resulting from such mapping, that is, an ideal strategy process in terms of a journey of disoriented animals.

TABLE 6.2: *Examples of initial mappings*

Participant	Verbatim transcript	Agents' actions and artifactual manifestations
1	"These are all individual national operators – 70 individual representatives in our company ... still respecting their individuality."	Puts four animal figures, a sheep a cow, a tiger and a giraffe at the front end, i.e. the starting point of the model [I(1)].
3	"But when they come out of the [strategy] process are they all one mind? Futuristic people?"	Holds up an astronaut person figure [I(2)].
1	"Not necessarily. They don't have to be all the same, but they all have something in common..."	Debate.
3	"Well, how do we represent that ...?"	Debate.
4	"They understand, ... they understand that ... they are in the same ... safari park!"	Puts a green landscape platform at the end of the model [I(3)].
1,2,3,5	"Yes, yes..."	Debate.
1	"... and in fact, in a safari park, with limited resources, you have to be observant to each other in order to survive ..."	Debate.

(Heracleous and Jacobs [2008]; used with permission.)

Based on the above analytical protocol, we developed a case database that contained contextual information on the company, video recordings and video stills for each retreat gathered by Imagination Lab Foundation associates, as well as a systematic inventory of grand embodied metaphors and their constituent metaphors, as constructed by participants. We drew on these materials to develop detailed case

TABLE 6.3: *Examples of relational mappings*

Participant	Verbatim transcript	Agents' actions and artifactual manifestation
2	"… Ok, we start at the very beginning of the process with all these different companies."	Puts the four animals to the front end of the model.
3	"Do you mean companies or people?"	Debate.
1	"Representatives of their companies and cultures I guess…"	Debate.
2	"Yes, all the differences are represented here!"	Points to the four animals.
2	"Different types of people, personalities, different people. They all point and move in different directions."	Shuffles the animals so that they face different directions.
2	"Now, what happens crucially is that these people were facing different directions …"	Takes animal figures from the front end …
2	"… now we have an understanding for the concepts within which they are operating, and know of each other's work and that where they are all coming from. That we are all now moving in the same direction."	… and puts them onto the green platform at the end of the model; the animals all facing forward [R(1)].
4	"Actually, it is the corporate strategic framework that we produce which will enable them to construct the park. This is not necessarily aligning them in all directions. But we keep them in the park through this."	Lifts a blue book brick and puts it underneath the green platform [I(4)].

4	"Then, they can go wherever they like but this tells them how to behave in there."	Puts the blue book in the middle of the green platform.
1	"Alignment is a huge issue! They are not gonna come out thinking and doing exactly the same thing. But they are gonna come out with a common understanding that there is one company and some guiding principles that they can all adopt which allows them to run and be creative and innovative within the park."	Debate.
3	"So just taking a step back, I see something very different from what you [participant 4] describe!"	Debate.
3	"I think this becomes incidental to these 70 people – because of the process we are guiding them through."	Points to the blue book and lifts it.
4	"Yes."	Debate.
3	"It is incidental inside the park and should actually be covered up."	Takes the blue book and puts its into a little holder on the green platform and covers it with a smaller board [R(2)].
1	"Yes, it should be common guiding principles that tell you how to behave in the park, not the corporate strategic framework."	Debate.

(Heracleous and Jacobs [2008]; used with permission.)

TABLE 6.4: *Examples of integrative mappings*

Participant	Verbatim transcript	Agents' actions and artifactual manifestation
1	"In nature, the lion would attack the gazelle. So in CellCo, France doesn't care whether we are in the same company. If you step on their turf, out you are! They will eat you alive, although you are part of the same company. In the park, the gatekeepers have to make sure that the lions don't eat all the gazelles. If you want to survive in the park, we have to have some ground rules, guiding principles of behavior."	Debate.
3	"I think what we have now described here is the transformation of these 70 disparate people. Guided them through a passionate and different process."	Takes animal figures from the back end of the model to the front.
3	"And what we have done is to transform them so that the bet is, they will help transform others, and – actually that's it. That is the whole bet! … Incidental to this process is that we will try and capture what happens to these 70 people by building some simple rules and so forth. All we really want to do is transforming 70 people."	Moves animal figures back to the green platform [IM (1)].

(Heracleous and Jacobs [2008]; used with permission.)

write-ups for each retreat. These formed the basis for a subsequent systematic and iterative process of interpretation (Miles and Huberman, 1994) involving three stages.

First, as an initial analytical moment and in order to sharpen our hermeneutic apparatus, we reviewed the individual constructions of participants with regard to their respective target domains, in order to get a sense of the context-specific metaphorical terminology employed when attributing meaning to the embodied metaphors produced, as illustrated above. Secondly and for each case, we systematically analyzed both the collective constructions (which we label the "grand metaphors"), as well as their primary constituent metaphors. We selected five such constituent metaphors in each case for deeper analysis, whereby the selection of these constituent metaphors was informed by the emphasis given to a particular element by participants; the physical prominence with respect to the entire model as well as the centrality of that element for the overall narrative, as exemplified in the vignette above. We analyzed metaphorical mappings in terms of the interactions between source domains and target domains, and the emergent meanings resulting from these interactions.

Finally and as a form of cross-case analysis, we juxtaposed within-case findings in terms of how organizational dimensions were embedded in, and represented by, the group embodied metaphors. Table 6.5 outlines this analytical process.

Analysis and findings

Within-case analysis of metaphorical mappings

Strategy development team: "Strategy development
is a troop of confused animals"

The target domain of the grand metaphor was a renewed, ideal strategy development process (target domain of grand metaphor,

TABLE 6.5: *Outline of three analytical moments*

Analytical moment	Unit of analysis	Purpose	Outcome
Focus on process of individual constructions	Process of individual constructions treated as context for group constructions.	Understanding the emergent, situationally specific vocabulary.	Sharper hermeneutic apparatus for subsequent analysis.
Within-case analysis	Collective constructions (grand metaphors and their constituent metaphors).	Analyzing within-case metaphorical mappings in terms of source domains, target domains, and emergent meanings.	Case-specific understanding of embodied metaphors and their portrayal of conventional organizational dimensions.
Cross-case analysis	All three collective constructions, juxtaposition of spatial features of these constructions across cases.	Cross-case pattern recognition and exploring validity of these features across cases.	Insights on organizational dimensions as embodied in constructions.

(Heracleous and Jacobs [2008]; used with permission.)

hereafter TG). This was portrayed as a troop of confused animals (source domain of grand metaphor, hereafter SG) that undertook an energetic journey to reach safe and common ground in a safari park environment. The emergent meaning of the grand metaphor (EMG) arising from the combination of source and target domain was the aspiration of the team to design a dynamic strategy development process that – in contrast to conventional strategy-making – drew otherwise disinterested and confused organizational members into passionate strategic conversation that allowed individual differences in outlook and identity while operating within the parameters of a collective framework.

Each of these dimensions of strategy development as the target domain was further cognitively structured or given meaning by five constituent metaphors, in this case structured as stages of the strategic journey. The first constituent metaphor, the point of departure, consisted in a "group of disoriented animals" (source domain of constituent metaphor S1, hereafter numbered accordingly), representing the confusion of organizational members at the beginning of the strategy development process (dimension of target domain of constituent metaphor T1). By combining source and target domain, participants conveyed that organizational members were a somewhat depersonalized, confused group of individuals who were unclear about the needed processes and outcomes of strategy-making in CellCo and thus in need of some guidance (EM1).

This stage of the journey led the traveler to a "chocolate bar and a shaken bottle of Cola," symbolizing a dynamic, passionately desired strategy-making process. Secondly, the "transformative engine" (S2) contained at its entrance a large, monochrome block of bricks (S2) representing myopic, conventional strategic development (T2). Blending source and target domains, participants made reference to their belief that conventional strategy development had been perceived as myopic and lacking passion. Physically juxtaposing monochrome with multicolor elements illustrated this duality (EM2).

A set of person figures with extra sets of "eyes" at the center of the engine (S3) represented those strategists "with vision" (T3) to lead strategy discussion groups, arriving at a multicolored set of bricks portraying new, creative perspectives of strategic thinking. Thirdly, having gone through this engine, the strategic traveler reached an interconnected set of wheels (S3) that represented the "massive gearing effect" (EM3) such a renewed strategizing process (T3) could have for the organization. A set of interconnected, interoperable wheels suggested a combination of source and target domains that revitalized and illustrated the effects of an otherwise dead metaphor: the notion of a gearing effect (EM3).

The end-point of the journey was represented as a "safari park" (S4) symbolizing the outcome of the strategizing process, namely strategic alignment (T4) of organizational constituent functions, combined with specific degrees of freedom. The emergent meaning from the metaphorical mapping of this final constituent metaphor showed that the animals still differed in their shape and identity, but had now arrived in a fenced-in territory that provided them with different degrees of freedom, within certain parameters (EM4). Thus, initially disoriented animals having travelled through a revitalized strategic development process would in the end have a shared strategic framework.

Surrounding this "strategy as journey" embodied metaphor were further related representations. A group of conventional strategic business planners was portrayed as skeletons with black hats positioned in a repetitive cycle (S5) of producing pointless and ineffectual (EM5) corporate strategic documents (T5). Skeletons and black hats suggested bloodless uniformity that produced somewhat meaningless outcomes (EM5).

Business Operations team: "CellCo is a conquest of FixCo"

Participants viewed CellCo (TG) as a castle, the most recent conquest (SG) of the "FixCo Empire". A previously strong, defendable fortress had become vulnerable and had now been conquered – with its members now taking orders from the conqueror, the new owner of the castle (EMG).

This grand metaphor consisted of five constituent metaphors. Having entered the CellCo castle through a castle gate entrance with CellCo's brand icon on top symbolizing the organization's image to the world, business functions such as call centers or customer service were portrayed as disconnected platforms to represent their lack of organizational alignment or co-ordination. For instance, a call center

(T1a) was portrayed as six PC agents, while a person figure wearing a crown and holding a whip (S1a) to represent strict, authoritarian management (EM1a) represented the call center manager. The central castle square hosted the "heart" of CellCo's service, the mobile network. A white tower hosted several person figures with black hats, all in the same posture and facing in the same direction (S1b), to represent the accounting department (T1b) – and the new, dominant view of business logic and shareholder value. The accounting function was portrayed as a remote, yet powerful, politically ambiguous, uniform and faceless activity in CellCo (EM1b).

The brand (T2) that had driven CellCo in the past was symbolized by a tall, mobile lighthouse on wheels, deliberately positioned outside the castle walls (S2). While the brand was still relevant and influential, it was somewhat remote and disconnected (EM2).

Also outside the castle was a set of scattered grey bricks (S) representing a "grey invasion" of bureaucracy and business logic (EM) in CellCo (T). On the castle square was a set of disconnected wheels (S) also representing dysfunctional bureaucracy (EM). Close to them, yet outside the castle, were two animal figures, an elephant and a tiger, facing in opposite directions (S3), representing the perceived ambiguity and risk (EM3) with respect to the 3G license purchase (T3) that could turn out either as "an elephant around our neck" or as a "tiger of growth."

Next to the castle's main compound was an annex building located on a smaller platform. It hosted a set of upward facing purple tubes (S) representing "projects in the pipeline" that were as yet unused since they were not physically connected to any of the functional domains (T). An unpopulated carousel with yellow seats (merry-go-round) (S) represented the potential (and past) fun (EM) of working in the organization (T). Next to the carousel, and by far the largest population in this annex building, was a "herd" of person figures (S4) symbolizing members of operations staff (T4). They were all positioned within a fenced area, facing different directions (S), thus indicating a lack of direction and coherence (EM4). While some of them wore brand icon hats (S), others were "brandless," thus considered outsiders who were nevertheless inside (EM).

On top of a pyramid-type construction (S) representing formal hierarchy (T), was a person figure wearing a crown and holding a whip with his back to the team (S5), representing the head of business operations (T5). This authoritarian figure (EM5) did not wear any brand icons at all, also symbolizing a certain foreignness to "branded" members of the organization (EM5). On the bottom of this winners' podium, and interestingly on the same platform as operations staff, was a ghost figure (S), "the ghost of the founder," symbolizing the founder's image (T) at an earlier time of being "one of the lads" (EM).

Technical Division Team: "Technical division is a conglomerate of dispersed machines"

The grand metaphor employed by the technical division management team of CellCo to represent its identity (TG) was that of a conglomerate of distinct, poorly connected machines (SG), indicating the division's disconnectedness and lack of coherence (EMG).

A first platform hosted the service solutions building, which had two main parts. Through a large entrance gate, customer enquiries were channeled into the design function (T1), represented as a cluster of person figures seated at work benches (S1). Two policemen (S1) guarded a massive gate separating the design function from the production unit (T1), shown as a large, opaque "sausage machine" (S1). They acted as gatekeepers to enforce the final decision of the "central design authority" (EM1) represented by a blue, transparent globe (S) symbolizing a brain (EM). The approved output of the design process was the necessary input to the production "sausage machine," whose output in turn was sent via a turntable to the next island of technical operations. Solutions delivery was portrayed as a mechanistic, opaque process consisting of two phases of design and production, that were kept distinct (EM1). While the connection (T) through a turntable pivot (S) was portrayed as close and stable (EM), the connection to the third island was rather thin and fragile (EM).

The platform of operations hosted another machine at its center; this time in the form of a surgery operating theatre with a patient being treated (S2). The patient – closely monitored by three body-guard doctors wearing crowns (S), to indicate the utmost importance of the patient and their medical treatment (EM2), represented the "heart of CellCo technical operations," the mobile network (T2). The surgical theatre (S2) was surrounded by service and support functions, such as service management and a help desk. The entire island was surrounded by a large fence and its only entrance was guarded by a warrior figure (S), the whole set-up representing the fragility, security and safety needs (EM2) of the network (T). The highest element of this area was the CellCo branded platform with three person figures overlooking it (S), representing the network management center (T). On separate stand-alone platforms were two radio masts surrounded by maintenance and upgrade personnel (S).

The main element of the third platform – representing the infra-structure development unit (T3) as complementing the current mobile network with the newly purchased 3G technology, was a 4WD vehicle exploring a wild landscape that needed to be developed for use as a site for a radio mast (S3). Mapping the physicality of infrastructure development onto the metaphor of an exploration revived the dead metaphor of development and exploration (EM3).

Two smaller sites next to this central element hosted the central planning and strategy function (T), represented by person figures with computers and mobile phones (S), all wearing identical gear; and the regional infrastructure offices (T), represented by a vehicle carrying construction workers (S). While the planning departments between the two entities (T) were connected through a stable con-nection (S), the link to the finance function in the central planning entity (T) was portrayed by a broken chain (S). Next to the regional office platform were the "broken bridges over the River Styx" (S4), symbolizing the problematic relationship (EM4) between infrastructure expansion and technical operations (T4). While technical operations needed to ensure 24/7 service, infrastructure expansion needed migration time to set up the new 3G services.

Outside this central grand metaphor representing the identity of the technical division were several significant agents. CellCo Global (T5) under the auspices of the new owners was portrayed as an unstable vehicle, crowded with person figures waving various flags while facing in all different directions (S5), indicating the lack of stability, direction and clarity of profile of the new entity (EM5). Table 6.6 outlines our analysis.

Cross-case analysis

As Lakoff and Johnson (1980) note, spatial dimensions are inherent in the orientational metaphors we employ, deriving from our experience of our physical existence. The dimensions we identify below are consistent with this discussion (for example spatial elevation symbolizes importance; spatial proximity symbolizes organizational relatedness), but also go beyond it in the sense that we address dimensions and their meaning to organizational participants that are not directly discussed by Lakoff and Johnson (for example, directional uniformity symbolizes coherence; similarity in spatial level symbolizes a sense of belongingness). Even though it would be interesting to examine in detail how these additional spatial aspects may relate to orientational metaphors and their qualities of systematicity, discussed by Lakoff and Jounson (1980), such an analysis would go beyond the particular scope of this chapter.

Thus, we propose that the study of the emergent meanings arising from the blending of source and target domains provides access to actors' first-order views regarding organizational dimensions. Below, a variety of organizational dimensions are represented in embodied metaphors through specific physical and spatial manifestations.

TABLE 6.6: *Outline of source domains, target domains and emergent meaning in grand and constituent metaphors*

	Strategy Development Team			Business Operations Team			Technical Division Team		
	Emergent meaning	*Target domain*	*Source domain*	*Emergent meaning*	*Target domain*	*Source domain*	*Emergent meaning*	*Target domain*	*Source domain*
Grand metaphor	Strategy-making is a journey of confused individuals eventually reaching common ground (EMG).	Strategy development process (TG).	Journey of confused animals searching for guidance and direction, eventually reaching common ground (SG).	The strong fortress of CellCo has become the conquest of FixCo (EMG).	Identity of CellCo (TG).	Castle in the center, buildings and towers of different shapes, sizes and height; conqueror observing conquest (SG).	Technical division consists of three scarcely connected operating entities (EMG).	Identity of technical division (TG).	Conglomerate of dispersed machines (SG).
Constituent metaphors	Organizational members are an anonymous group of individuals seeking strategic guidance (EM1).	Organization members at beginning of strategy development (T1).	Troop of disoriented animals (S1).	Call centers are pressurizing, strictly managed environments. Accounting dept is a remote, monitoring, powerful dept (EM1a,b).	Call centers (T1a), accounting department and logic (T1b).	Uniform figures kept in order by the whip (S1a). White monochrome tower detached from main building, populated by black hats monitoring events in castle (S1b).	Solutions delivery operates as a mechanistic, intransparent process in two phases that are kept distinct (EM1).	Design and production function of solutions delivery (T1).	Person figures seated at work benches, policemen, sausage machine as black box (S1).

TABLE 6.6 (cont.)

	Strategy Development Team			Business Operations Team			Technical Division Team		
	Emergent meaning	*Target domain*	*Source domain*	*Emergent meaning*	*Target domain*	*Source domain*	*Emergent meaning*	*Target domain*	*Source domain*
Constituent metaphors	Strategy-making is a passionate, energetic transformation process (EM2).	Strategy-making as transforming force (T2).	Combustion engine, transforming fuel into kinesthetic energy (S2).	Even though still relevant, the brand has become distant and detached from the organization (EM2).	CellCo brand (T2).	A lighthouse detached from main building (S2).	The mobile network is our most valuable asset, and needs protection and constant monitoring (EM2).	Mobile network (T2).	Patient; heart (S2).
	Renewed, revitalized strategizing is essential to the journey (EM3).	Renewed strategy development process (T3).	Set of gearing wheels, transmitting energy between entities (S3).	Success or failure of the 3G investment is highly risky and ambivalent (EM3).	3G investment (T3).	An elephant as a heavy, inflexible burden and a tiger as an agile predator (S3).	Infrastructure expansion is a dangerous but exciting expedition (EM3).	Infrastructure expansion to provide 3G services (T3).	Expedition, exploration of landscape in 4WD vehicle (S3).

Strategic alignment provides a common framework while simultaneously allowing for degrees of freedom (EM4).	Relation of strategists and organization in renewed strategy process (T4).	Safari park as a fenced territory with degrees of freedom for different animals (S4).	Operations staff are a uniform, anonymous group of people seeking guidance (EM4).	Members of operations department (T4).	Group of farmed cattle, person figures behind a fence (S4).	Relationships and connections are dysfunctional, fragile, and with potentially dangerous consequences (EM4).	Relationships and connections among subunits (T4).	Unfinished bridges over mystic River Styx (S4).
Existing, conventional strategy-making is a bloodless, repetitive exercise (EM5).	Conventional strategy planning process and outcome (T5).	Group of skeletons with black hats in an endless cycle (S5).	Head of operations is powerful, authoritarian and remote from team (EM5).	Head of business operations department (T5).	Elevated warrior king wielding whip, overlooking and with back turned to operations team (S5).	CellCo Global lacks stability, direction and shared profile (EM5).	CellCo Global (T5).	Unstable vehicle with passengers all waving in different directions (S5).

(Heracleous and Jacobs [2008]; used with permission.)

Spatial elevation and centrality symbolizes importance

In all three models, we find that the spatially highest elements indicate high importance as perceived by actors. Interestingly, all three teams positioned FixCo as the highest element of each collective construction. Further, all three embodied metaphors show individuals, functions or organizations with power as being located higher up. For example, each tower of FixCo in all three models hosts the CEO of FixCo on top of the tower, overlooking the constructions representing CellCo. In addition, we find that the more central an element is positioned, the more importance is attributed to it. For instance, the strategy team placed the "transformative engine" at the core of its model, while the business operations team emphasized the mobile network. Interestingly, the technical division left the central space in its construction unpopulated, perhaps related to their view of the division's identity as an incoherent collection of three scarcely connected entities.

Spatial proximity symbolizes organizational relatedness, and vice versa

We found that significant elements positioned closely together have a perceived close relationship, functional or otherwise. For example, the strategy development team placed the "dungeon of formal hierarchy" right under the "transformative engine," which suggests that management, specifically the actors represented in the dungeon, were perceived as pivotal to the success of the transformation effort. The business operations team positioned the brand tower deliberately outside and remotely from the castle, to indicate the increasing ambiguity and felt distance to the brand. The technical division positioned the three conglomerations of machines representing the division in a way that indicated that a meaningful physical connection between the three was difficult, manifesting their views on organizational disconnectedness and incoherence.

Directional uniformity symbolizes coherence, and vice versa

The expressive repertoire of all three groups' embodied metaphors shows that uniformity in directional orientation indicates coherence, common views, and organizational connectedness, and the opposite indicates lack thereof. Examples include the representations of operations staff close to the CellCo castle of the business operations team; and the technical division team portraying CellCo Global as an overpopulated vehicle with individuals facing in all directions. Further, the strategy journey of confused animals, initially facing in all directions, ended with animals on the same ground facing in the same direction, within well specified parameters.

Similarity in spatial level symbolizes a sense of belongingness

All three models exemplified the assumption that a similar spatial level represents belongingness and group membership, while difference in spatial level indicates remoteness or distance. For instance, the strategy development team portrayed members of the formal hierarchy all sitting in different chambers of a dungeon, irrespective of their differences in the formal hierarchy. The business operations team placed the ghost of the founder at the same height as the "cattle of operations staff" to indicate a (lost) sense of equality.

Solid physical connections symbolize coherent, smooth
organizational relations, and vice versa

The three embodied metaphors portrayed connected, coherent relations with physically intact connections, and dysfunctional or indeterminate relations with disconnected or fragile connections. For instance, the strategy development team portrayed the relationship between the strategy development and the organization by a set of interconnected wheels having a "massive gearing effect on the organization." By contrast, the business operations symbolized the different projects in the pipeline with a set of purple tubes that were as yet unconnected to any business functions, thereby compromising their potential benefit. Similarly the technical division portrayed a most difficult relationship between the infrastructure development and the operations subunit by "unfinished bridges over the River Styx." We also found that while embodied metaphors employ physical entities such as fences to indicate boundaries (for example fences around the business operations staff, around the mobile network, and around the safari park), most metaphors also employ some empty space to leave the nature and quality of the interconnection or boundaries open and ambiguous.

Dual structures symbolize dual aspects of relationships

In several models, participants constructed models exhibiting duality to represent dual aspects of relationships and ambiguity. For instance, the business operations team portrayed the 3G license as both tiger and elephant, indicating the ambiguity and strategic risk of whether the investment would turn out to be a lethal mistake or an avenue to success. Further, the panda and dragon at the entrance gate of the suppliers' plant symbolizes dual qualities in this relationship, that can turn from friendly to hostile and vice-versa.

Monochromatic constructions symbolize uniformity and convention, polychromatic constructions indicate diversity and creativity

All models employ monochrome as well as multi-colored elements, to express both uniformity and convention (such as the sinister army of FixCo, or the monochrome accounting tower populated by accountants all wearing black hats, monitoring CellCo) or creativity and diversity (the multicolored block of bricks in the transformative engine to indicate creative strategic thinking, or the jungle expedition of infrastructure expansion). The business operations team employed the color grey to indicate the conventional, rational, unemotional aspects of bureaucracy that contrast strongly with the previous experience of fun (on the colorful carousel). Table 6.7 summarizes and exemplifies these findings.

TABLE 6.7: *Organizational dimensions manifested in embodied metaphors*

Physical manifestation	Example	Orientational metaphor	Rhetorical function in identity narrative	Example
Elevation	FixCo tower	Up-down: "up is powerful, down is powerless."	Power, observation	"FixCo, the new owners are observing us."
Centrality	Transformative engine	Central-peripheral: "central is important, peripheral is less important."	Importance	"The transformative engine is the core of the strategy development process."
Proximity	Dungeon of management	Close-remote: "close is related; remote is unrelated."	Relatedness	"Management is pivotal to the transformation process."
Directional uniformity	Disoriented animals	Same-different direction: "same direction is coherent; different direction is incoherent."	Coherence	"Country managers are very different."
Similarity of spatial level	Ghost of the founder	Up-down-level: "difference in level is different; same level is equal."	Belongingness	"He used to be one of us."
Solidity of physical connection	"Gearing wheels"	Robust-shaky: "robust is solid; shaky is less solid."	Robustness of relations	"Strategy process has a massive gearing effect."
Dual structures	"3G licence"	Same-different direction: "same direction is coherent; different direction is incoherent."	Duality of relationships	"We don't know whether it is the tiger of growth or an elephant around our neck."
Use of colors	"Grey invasion of accountants"	Same-different color: "same color is same; different color is different."	Uniformity/creativity	"Grey invasion of accountants."

(Heracleous and Jacobs [2008]; used with permission.)

Discussion and implications

In this chapter we proposed and developed a novel approach to understanding organizational dimensions, the "embodied metaphors" approach based on embodied realism. This offers an alternative to the conventional positivist model through which organizational dimensions have traditionally been conceptualized and researched. As we have shown, when constructing embodied metaphors, actors' assumptions and interpretations about their organizations and environments, groups and selected individuals, and the interrelations among them are spatially manifested in a recursive process of construction and interpretation. Through researching the interactions of the source and target domains and the emergent meanings afforded by these embodied metaphors, we found that these constructions offer insights to our understanding of a variety of organizational dimensions that conventional positivist approaches cannot access. In particular, we found that analysis of embodied metaphors can enable access to actors' first-order conceptions of organizational dimensions and reveals alternative qualities and interrelations among them; and in so doing poses substantial challenges to established conceptions of ontology and method in organization theory.

Enabling access to actors' first-order conceptions of organizational dimensions

An embodied metaphors approach allows researchers to gain a meaningful understanding of the actors' frames of reference, what Dilthey and Weber referred to as *verstehen*. Dilthey (1989) suggested that whereas the natural sciences explain nature, human studies can understand "lived experience" through its observable expressions. Further, in Weber's (1991) view, the aim of achieving an in-depth, first-order understanding was what could distinguish the social from the natural sciences, by producing knowledge that would be "adequate at the level of meaning." Metaphorical mappings, such as portraying the rest of the organization as a dragon to be kept at bay; the competitive environment as containing a threatening and unpredictable UFO spider; competitors variously represented as mirror, sheep or predator animals; or suppliers as both evil dinosaur or friendly panda, attribute imputed qualities to these domains that are hard to convey or capture otherwise.

Further, embodied metaphors not only enable access to actors' first-order conceptions, they also illuminate and highlight the relevance of different qualities and interrelations among actors that are not conventionally researched (or arguably researchable) within a positivist view. For example, portraying the CEO as a headless chicken, a warrior with laser gun or a king of the castle comes with narrative connotations relevant to understanding extant organizational relationships and dynamics in the various divisions. Portraying a division head as an elevated warrior king wielding a whip gives insights as to how the actors constructing the embodied metaphor perceive this individual.

Reflections on ontology and method

We operationalized the approach of embodied realism in terms of analysis of embodied metaphors and suggested that this kind of analysis can offer a novel perspective to understanding organizational dimensions. We offered this approach as an alternative to the one offered by the traditional positivist paradigm, a suggestion consistent with *methodological* pluralism. If we take the trajectory of the argument to its logical conclusion, however, we can see that taking embodied realism seriously would render *paradigmatic* pluralism less tenable and inherently problematic, because it radically questions established conceptions of ontology and epistemology, as we hinted earlier in our discussion summarized in Table 2.1.

This can become clearer if we explore the ontology and attendant epistemology of positivism through the following metonymic metaphor that can be found in the *Publication Manual* of the American Psychological Association (1994: 291): "Like a wall that is built one brick at a time, the peer-reviewed literature in a field is built by single contributions that together represent the accumulated knowledge of a field. Each contribution must fill a place that before was empty, and each contribution must be sturdy enough to bear the weight of contributions to come." Similarly to the positivist conception of organizational dimensions, this is not only an essentially metaphorical view ("scientific knowledge is a brick wall"), it is also an embodied one *par excellence*, being based on our lived, physical experience. It is also a metonymy, where the part focused on (in this case, the process of building scientific knowledge as the process of building a wall) stands for the whole. The implication complex of conceptual correspondences transferred from the source to the target domain relates to aspects such as the nature of peer-reviewed literature and scientific knowledge (solid and unitary), the process of its development (methodical, ever advancing upwards and aiming towards completion), the actors involved (the knowledgeable craftsmen being the reviewers who decide which articles or "bricks" are fit and worthy enough to form part of the wall of knowledge), and lastly the articles themselves (which ideally should be like sturdy bricks: enduring contributions that uniformly follow the conventions of normal science, so that they can be deemed worthy of inclusion in the wall of knowledge).

Further, from an experiential or embodied perspective, a more implicit aspect of this metaphor is the orientational nature of building a brick wall, from low, advancing upwards. As Lakoff and Johnson (1980: 14–21) have shown (and manifested in different ways in the embodied metaphors we analyzed), most positive or desirable states or situations are "up," whereas most negative or undesirable ones are "down," implying that more scientific knowledge is always more desirable than less. The metaphor "scientific knowledge is a brick wall" therefore draws from the orientational nature of human thought and expression; and its attraction arises from the human desire for control and predictability that would result from complete knowledge. This implication can shed light on the idealism often surrounding the desire for a cumulative, unitary body of scientific knowledge, each contribution building on the ones that preceded it, advancing inexorably towards an end state of full understanding (e.g. Donaldson, 1996; Pfeffer, 1993).

Can there be fruitful dialogue across paradigms that do not share this teleological, instrumental, unitary view of science? Even though metaphorical analyses such as the one that we have carried out challenge the fundamental nature of positivist science and further buttress the view of its essentially metaphorical nature (Morgan, 1980, 1983, 1986), accepting that this is the case would be anathema to scientists schooled in positivism and all its arsenal of ideas on ontology, epistemology and method, because it would question the very basis of their identity as scientists, and their conception of what science is all about.

This situation has led scientists in different paradigms to talk past each other rather than to each other, forming a rather shaky basis for fruitful cross-paradigm debate, as evidenced by Rakova's (2002) critique of embodied realism from the perspective of traditional, objectivist analytical philosophy. Johnson and Lakoff's (2002) response showed how the most essential propositions of embodied realism that call into question established beliefs can be wholly misunderstood, if read from the perspective of analytical philosophy and essentialist realism.

Taking embodied realism seriously might thus render cross-paradigmatic debate that goes beyond method to considerations of epistemology and ontology problematic, especially if perceptions of the nature of paradigms remain implicit and undiscussed. A turn to reflexivity, striving to be explicit about such issues as how these inherent features shape approaches to inquiry and the knowledge(s) produced, would be a good start, but would be insufficient if not accompanied by a willingness to examine how these modes of knowledge can best interact and inform each other. This would lead to the acceptance not only of methodological pluralism but also of ontological and epistemological pluralism, a rather radical notion for many social scientists committed to their craft and its view of the world.

REFERENCES

American Psychological Association. 1994. *Publication manual of the American Psychological Association*, 4th edn. Washington, DC: APA.

Barrett, F. J. and Cooperrider, D. L. 1990. Generative metaphor intervention: A new behavioral approach for working with systems divided by conflict and caught in defensive perception. *Journal of Applied Behavioral Science*, 26: 219–39.

Barry, D. 1994. Making the invisible visible: Using analogically-based methods to surface unconscious organizational processes. *Organization Development Journal*, 12(4): 37–47.

Broussine, M. and Vince, R. 1996. Working with metaphor towards organizational change. In Oswick, C. and Grant, D. (eds.), *Organisation development: Metaphorical explorations*. London: Pitman, 57–70.

Buergi, P. and Roos, J. 2003. Images of strategy. *European Management Journal*, 21(1): 69–78.

Buergi, P., Jacobs, C., and Roos, J. 2005. From metaphor to practice in the crafting of strategy. *Journal of Management Inquiry*, 14: 78–94.

Burke, W. W. 1992. Metaphors to consult by. *Group and Organization Management*, 17: 255–9.

Dilthey, W. 1989. *Introduction to the human sciences*. Makkreel, R. A. and Rodi, F. (eds.), Princeton University Press.

Doyle, J. R., and Sims, D. 2002. Enabling strategic metaphor in conversation: A technique of cognitive sculpting for explicating knowledge. In Huff, A. S. and Jenkins, M. (eds.), *Mapping strategic knowledge*. London: Sage, 63–85.

Donaldson, L. 1996. *For positivist organization theory*. London: Sage.

Forceville, C. 2009. Non-verbal and multimodal metaphor in a cognitivist framework: Agendas for research. In Forceville, C. and Urios-Aparisi, E. (eds.), *Multimodal metaphor*. Berlin/New York: Mouton de Gruyter, 19–44.

Gibbs, R. W. 1999. Researching metaphor. In Cameron, L. and Low, G. (eds.), *Researching and applying metaphor*. Cambridge University Press, 28–47.

    2003. Embodied experience and linguistic meaning. *Brain and Language*, 84, 1–15.

Heath, C. and Hindmarsh, J. 2002. Analysing interaction: Video, ethnography and situated conduct. In May, T. (ed.), *Qualitative Research in Action*. London: Sage, 99–121.

Heracleous, L. and Jacobs, C. 2008. Understanding organizations through embodied metaphors. *Organization Studies*, 29: 45–78.

Heritage, J. 1984. *Garfinkel and ethnomethodology*. Cambridge: Polity.

Huff, A. S. 1990. *Mapping strategic thought*. Chichester: Wiley.

Jacobs, C. and Heracleous, L. 2006. Constructing shared understanding – the role of embodied metaphors in organization development. *Journal of Applied Behavioral Science*, 24(2): 207–26.

Johnson, M. 1987. *The body in the mind: the bodily basis of meaning, imagination, and reason*. University of Chicago Press.

Johnson, M. and Lakoff, G. 2002. Why cognitive linguistics requires embodied realism. *Cognitive Linguistics*, 13: 245–63.

Lakoff, G. and Johnson, M. 1980. *Metaphors we live by*. University of Chicago Press.

1999. *Philosophy in the flesh*. New York: Basic Books.

Marshak, R. 1993. Managing the metaphors of change. *Organizational Dynamics*, 22(1): 44–56.

Miles, M. B. and Huberman, A. M. 1994. *Qualitative data analysis: An expanded sourcebook*. Beverley Hills, CA: Sage.

Morgan, G. 1980. Paradigms, metaphor and puzzle solving in organization theory. *Administrative Science Quarterly*, 25: 660–71.

1983. More on metaphor: Why we cannot control tropes in administrative science. *Administrative Science Quarterly*, 28: 601–7.

1986. *Images of organization*. Beverly Hills, CA: Sage.

Oswick, C., Putnam, L., and Keenoy, T. 2004. Tropes, discourse and organizing. In Grant, D., Hardy, C., Oswick, C., and Putnam, L. (eds.), *Sage handbook of organizational discourse*. London: Sage, 105–27.

Palmer, I. and Dunford, R. 1996. Conflicting uses of metaphors: Reconceptualizing their use in the field of organizational change. *Academy of Management Review*, 21: 691–717.

Pfeffer, J. 1993. Barriers to the advance of organization science: Paradigm development as a dependent variable. *Academy of Management Review*, 18: 599–620.

Rakova, M. 2002. The philosophy of embodied realism: A high price to pay? *Cognitive Linguistics*, 13: 215–44.

Roos, J., Victor, B., and Statler, M. 2004. Playing seriously with strategy. *Long Range Planning*, 37: 549–68.

Rohrer, T. 2007. The body in space: Embodiment, experientialism and linguistic conceptualization. In Ziemke, T., Zlatev, J., and Frank, R. (eds.), *Body, Language and Mind*, Vol. 1. Berlin: Mouton de Gruyter.

Stake, R. E. 1995. *The art of case research*. London: Sage.

Weber, M. 1991. The nature of social action. In Runciman, W. G. (ed.), *Weber: Selections in translation*. Cambridge University Press, 7–32.

Yin, R. 1994. *Case study research: Design and methods*, 2nd edn. Beverly Hills, CA: Sage.

CHAPTER SEVEN

Sensemaking through embodied metaphors in organization development

In this chapter we illustrate how embodied metaphorical mapping can be effectively employed in organization development (OD) interventions. Conceptually, we suggest that an embodied metaphor approach complements and extends the traditionally deductively oriented approaches to employment of metaphor in organization development. This is accomplished by emphasizing induced rather than naturally occurring metaphors, building on a developed base of diagnostic technologies, enabling a collaborative effort of metaphorical selection and diagnosis, and enabling the employment of embodied metaphors to address specific, targeted issues of consequence to participants. We illustrate these considerations by discussing the case of a management retreat of a Swiss bank.

Sensemaking through embodied metaphors

As outlined in Chapter 2, we view metaphors as conceptual constructions that play a central role in the development of thought and inter-subjective meaning-making. Furthermore, and in line with

This chapter draws on Jacobs and Heracleous (2006).

social constructionism, we concur with the view that correspondence between source and target domain may be created, rather than just revealed (Black, 1979), making metaphor a prime means of gaining new perspectives on existing challenges. This generative potential of metaphors in terms of allowing for novel perceptions, explanations and inventions has been acknowledged in organization development (Burke, 1992; Marshak, 1993) but not extensively utilized. In addition to their generative potential, metaphors provide lenses for interpreting the world, embodying implicit evaluations and helping to concretize vague or abstract ideas (Armenakis and Bedeian, 1992; Hirsch, 1986).

Whereas a deductive approach to metaphors attempts to apply a generic set of (pre-existing, universal) metaphors to organizational situations (for example, viewing organizations as machines, as organisms, as political systems, or as brains, and exploring the implications of these views for a change process), an inductive approach operates on the assumption that organizational members already generate and use metaphors in view of their context and experience that can be employed for the purposes of system diagnosis and change. The embodied metaphor approach operates from an inductive approach to metaphorical reasoning in organizations, since organizational metaphors are intimately related to context and experience (Heracleous and Jacobs, 2008; Lakoff and Johnson, 1980). Embodied metaphors therefore inductively build on at the ultimately local, contextual, and situated nature of metaphor, rather than being based on assumptions of metaphorical generality and universality.

In facilitating processes of sensemaking, embodied metaphors combine cognitive-semantic, spatial and embodied aspects of metaphorical reasoning. The process of constructing embodied metaphors echoes Weick's (1995) properties of sensemaking. When groups of managers are invited to construct representations of their organization and its environment, for example, the process literally invites a physical construction of organizational identity, draws on past experience and learning, encourages various perspectives to be brought to bear on collective reasoning, is ultimately a social construction process that taps into an ongoing conversation, facilitates the exploration of an enacted organization/environment boundary, and finally, allows for a collective, social plausibility check on the various interpretations and constructions. Their capacity to facilitate sensemaking renders embodied metaphors most suitable for organization development processes.

Organization development processes and embodied metaphors

From a traditional perspective of organization development as involving an analytical distinction of people and organizational processes on one hand (the human-processual approach), versus technology and organizational structures on the other (the techno-structural approach) (Friedlander and Brown, 1974), an embodied metaphors approach lies within the human-processual domain. Organization development has from early on recognized the importance of people and cognitively related interventions (Alderfer, 1977). In addition, the organization development field has continuously encouraged new approaches. According to Friedlander and Brown (1974), "broader applications of a theory of planned change will require expanded intervention technologies" (1974: 335), and more recently Porras and Silvers (1991) note that "we encourage the use of new tools in OD, especially when those tools are derived from a sound theoretical base" (1991: 65). Interventions based on embodied metaphors aim to expand organizational members' ways of seeing through active, collaborative construction of metaphorical structures, thus potentially leading to reframing, or change in perceptions of reality (Porras and Silvers, 1991).

There is a wide range of OD approaches that advocate the use of metaphors in organizational diagnosis and intervention (e.g., Broussine and Vince, 1996; Clark and Salaman, 1996; Keizer and Post, 1996; Marshak, 1993; Morgan, 1996; Oswick, 1996; Palmer and Dunford, 1996. The dominant approach with regard to the use of metaphors in organization development suggests that change agents should take a leading part in diagnosing the organization through an understanding of the language-based metaphors used by organizational actors and can foster change through diffusing appropriate metaphors given the context and type of change aimed for (Cleary and Packard, 1992; Marshak, 1993; Sackmann, 1989). Furthermore, usually attention is paid to naturally occurring metaphor use, rather than engaging in a process that induces metaphorical creations, and the emphasis is on a metaphorical intervention designed by the OD practitioner rather than a collaborative effort of jointly developing and interpreting metaphors with organizational members. Finally, metaphorical diagnosis is usually employed with regard to the whole organization rather than a targeted issue that the organization is facing.

As Howe (1989) notes, "At present, practice seems to be guided largely by intuition and accumulated experience" (1989: 81). More than twenty years after this statement was made, there is still a lot to be learned about relevant intervention technologies. The concept of embodied metaphors complements existing approaches by emphasizing the relevance of actively induced metaphors, emphasizing the social dimension of such literal social construction processes through engaging participants in a collaborative effort, and aiming to elicit metaphors to assist with a targeted issue rather than a diagnosis and change of the whole system.

Table 7.1 and Figure 7.1 summarize these considerations.

In the case section, we will draw on a management retreat of a bank in Switzerland to illustrate the use and operations of embodied metaphors.

Constructing shared understanding through embodied metaphors at SwissBank

While in Chapter 5, we drew on the SwissBank management retreat to demonstrate the concept of reflective dialogue, we focus below on

TABLE 7.1: *Two perspectives on metaphors in OD*

Traditional use of metaphor in OD	Embodied metaphors in OD
Emphasis on naturally occurring, language-based metaphors.	Emphasis on induced embodied metaphors.
Relatively little available knowledge on diagnostic and intervention technologies.	Builds on a developed base of diagnostic and intervention technologies.
OD practitioners select appropriate metaphors for change task and setting.	Metaphors selected arise from collaborative effort.
OD practitioners lead metaphorical diagnosis.	Metaphorical diagnosis through shared sensemaking.
Emphasis on whole system.	Can be employed for targeted issue diagnosis and intervention.

(*Source: Jacobs and Heracleous, 2006*; used with permission.)

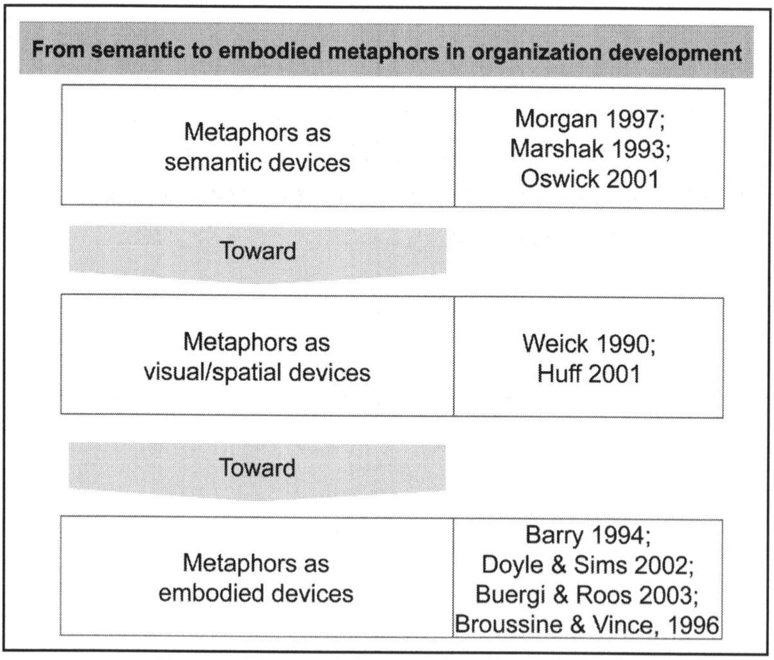

FIGURE 7.1 *Metaphors in OD (Jacobs and Heracleous, 2006; used with permission).*

the process and outcomes of embodied metaphorical mapping of the same setting. As discussed in detail above, the workshop aimed at exploring and specifying the concept of "I Know My Banker." As an integral part of the workshop, participants were asked to construct a model of their individual view of the concept and subsequently to construct, negotiate and agree on a joint representation of the concept at each table. After having debriefed to their peers at each table, participants were encouraged to critically reflect on commonalities, differences, and blind spots. Ideally, the facilitator role models these steps at each table. Then, participants were asked to construct a joint model of the concept by integrating their existing individual models to a collective one. In particular, redundancies were to be eliminated, for instance if each participant has built a model of a customer, they were asked to agree on a single representation of customers in the final collective construction. These constraints catalyze meaning negotiation as they progressively move towards univocality (which may still not be fully achieved in the final construction, since metaphors are intrinsically multi-faceted). The result of the collective construction process then results in a number of different collective constructions (depending on how many groups of participants there are) that are then again being debriefed in plenary. Similarly, commonalities, differences, and blind spots are to be investigated by fellow participants.

In constructing and discussing their models, SwissBank participants created a variety of embodied metaphors and engaged in processes of sensemaking. These physical constructions portrayed the need "to raise customers up to the same level" as bankers, to improve mutual understanding by "getting on the same wavelength," or to develop a much closer relationship by even "getting into the jacuzzi" with customers. Figures 7.2 and 7.3 give two examples of these metaphors illustrating how participants portrayed the concept of "I Know My Banker."

When faced with such incompatible metaphors and overall orientation, significant effort is required of the facilitator to explore these

1. **Circle 1:** By putting oneself in the client's shoes, their needs and aspirations can be identified or anticipated. The different areas for example could be leisure or investing in real estate. This variety of needs is represented by the *orange circle* encompassing the different needs of the client.

2. **Circle 2:** The second circle represents the bank as a very complicated machine with its different functional areas of marketing, financials, logistics, IT, etc. The nature and functioning of the machine itself is of no interest to the client. The front line should provide the client with the appropriate products that the bank has developed based on its expertise. This *beige circle* covers a much larger surface than the client's circle.

3. **Intersection of circles:** Where the two circles intersect is where the encounter between banker and client takes place. Their heads are both connected in an attempt "to read the client's mind". The banker stands in front of a transparent wall through which the complicated machine can be seen.

4. **Relationship:** The banker should be able to read the client's needs and provide them with an appropriate response that caters to these needs. The skilful reading of the client would then result in providing an appropriate product. The expertise and knowledge derived from the "complicated machine" should feed into such a relationship. Confidence and trust should result from such a service encounter. The essential message of this construction is the bank's overall capacity to adequately serve the client's needs.

5. **Key characteristics of embodied metaphor:** The banker–client relationship seen as the need to match client needs and bank offerings; the focus is on responsiveness so as to read, interpret and respond to the client needs appropriately, and the bank's overall capacity to meet client needs. A machine metaphor of bank and its products is assumed.

FIGURE 7.2 *Example 1 of embodied metaphor "I know my banker" concept (Jacobs and Heracleous, 2006; used with permission).*

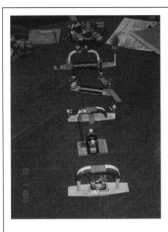

1. **Stage 1:** Client and banker face each other on the same level but are distanced. There is a huge gap between them. There seems to be no proximity, no mutual understanding. The ideas that the client has in mind are misread and misinterpreted by the banker.

2. **Stage 2:** The banker sits on a carousel and tries to get his/her "head around" the client's needs – with the ability of turning in all directions he/she attempts to pick up the "right"signals from the client. The goal of this endeavor is to find a means of understanding the client.

3. **Stage 3:** The physical connection between the two is already established. The bridge cannot be crossed easily, it is full of obstacles; but the huge initial gap has been literally "bridged".

4. **Stage 4:** The client and the banker resemble each other. They seem to have a similar perspective and they talk to each other face to face. They have a conversation around a wheel, having reached a stage where they can "turn the wheel together".

5. **Stage 5:** Client and banker are close to one another; they talk and understand each other under the protective roof of the bank. While the banker's figure has a tree on her head, the client's figure has a flag on his head. This highlights differences and potential misunderstandings between them. However, the client appears to smile and is happy that his initial idea is not only understood but also addressed by the banker.

6. **Key characteristics of embodied metaphor:** Focus on the development/growth of the relationship; orientation to reaching mutual understanding to cater to the client's needs.

FIGURE 7.3 *Example 2 of embodied metaphor "I know my banker" concept (Jacobs and Heracleous, 2006; used with permission).*

contradictions constructively by surfacing the differences, critically debating the consequences of each alternative perspective, and inviting a more informed conversation in terms of the potential to integrate certain perspectives or collectively privilege one over the other. The physical differences make the conceptual differences literally tangible and therefore facilitate such processes of inquiry. A skilled facilitator would attempt to point out structural similarities across constructions as well as systematic differences. Furthermore, the fact that each participant has by design the right for airtime in which to debrief his or her construction to peers implies a certain democratizing effect, because it invites some otherwise silent voices to the conversation. Finally, the process invites participants to practice listening as a central element in such conversations of development and change (Jacobs and Coghlan, 2005).

The occasion to collectively build three-dimensional, tangible models of a rather abstract strategic concept enabled participants to make collective sense of this concept. The nature of the customer–banker relationship could be made sense of, be "shown," and be visually presented and remembered, instead of only verbalized. Its fine features and details could be read and decoded by the groups from various angles. The recursive process of reading an analog while constructing it has facilitated a process of rendering visible differences and commonalities that were to be experienced physically, beyond a purely discursive or cognitive access to the concept. Metaphorical diagnosis of a specific, targeted issue that the client was facing was therefore made possible in the context of a collaborative, discursive, and embodied effort.

Contributions of embodied metaphors in organization development processes

Embodied metaphors represent a metaphorical approach to organization development that is quite different but complementary to traditional approaches. This approach draws on metaphorical reasoning not only as a cognitive–verbal exercise but also as a tactile, bodily experience that results in collectively constructed metaphors – metaphors in the flesh. This approach encourages OD practitioners to not only carefully identify metaphors in managerial discourse and reflect on what they reveal about the organization, but rather to actively induce embodied metaphors that encompass underlying assumptions and tap into bodily, prereflexive forms of knowledge in the process of construction. Embodied metaphors complement and extend traditional approaches to metaphor in OD in significant ways, as discussed earlier.

Reflecting on the process in view of Weick's (1995) generic categories of sensemaking, we saw the collective construction of six different embodied metaphors to represent the "I know my banker" concept. Each group drew on its past experience and learning in the bank and not only brought different physical manifestations of different perspectives to the surface, but allowed these differences to be examined through generative conversations. The exploration of the contentious "I Know My Banker" issue tapped into the ongoing conversation in the organization and brought so-far silent voices to the plenary. It furthermore facilitated exploration of the taken-for-granted notions of customers, competitors, and other agents in the environment. Finally, debriefing the six models in plenary engaged participants in a collective plausibility check of the constructions.

Sensemaking as a recursive process of interpretation and construction of embodied metaphors thus induces a shared expressive and linguistic repertoire constituted through shared meaning negotiation of concrete metaphors in use. Table 7.2 illustrates the use of embodied metaphors by drawing on the application of metaphors to the SwissBank case.

Being in the presence of physical models that are embodied metaphors, or metaphors in the flesh, can enable OD practitioners to pose

TABLE 7.2: *Embodied metaphors in OD: The SwissBank case*

Embodied metaphors in OD	Application to SwissBank case
Inducing embodied metaphors	Intervention process emphasized the construction of physical models of a strategic concept important to the client.
Builds on a developed base of diagnostic & intervention technologies	Antecedents included analogically mediated inquiry, cognitive sculpting and serious play technologies.
Metaphors arise from collaborative efforts	Metaphors collaboratively developed by participants rather than selected by the facilitator, formed the core of the intervention.
Metaphorical diagnosis through shared sensemaking	This process helped to surface conceptual differences within groups in the construction process, and across groups through differences in the resulting analogs.
Emphasis on targeted issue diagnosis and intervention	Cognitive divergences embedded in analogs formed the basis for probing questions by facilitator and further interpretation and collective sensemaking by participants.

(Jacobs and Heracleous, 2006; used with permission.)

probing questions triggered by the model and its detailed features. Why is there such a gap between customer and banker? Why does the banker sit much higher than the customer – although you told us they should be equals? Why is the circle of the "bank machine" much larger than the customer's needs circle? Within-model, intragroup interventions can help individuals or small groups in their local, collective construction processes, whereas cross-model, intergroup interventions can help to identify and explore differences and commonalities across models and within the whole participant cohort.

The role of the OD consultant and process facilitator is to probe the figurative meaning of literal constructions; invite peer projections on individual as well as collective models; pose probing questions at the superficial, metaphorical, and organizational levels; invite a critical yet appreciative inquiry into the constructions; and help in exploring similarities, differences, and blind spots. Whereas the facilitator should be clear on the structure and constraints of the process, they should exercise only a low level of directiveness in the construction and debrief sequences, because ownership of both construction and interpretation lies with the participants. Being aware of group-specific play dynamics, a skilled facilitator can ensure for example that the embodied metaphor that is created is a genuinely interactive and community-based product. A facilitator would help the group effectively debate the structures that are created and their implications in terms of organizational action by homing in and inviting critical debate on potentially insightful aspects of the construction.

Pondy (1983) suggests that metaphors could facilitate change by providing a bridge "from the familiar to the strange" (1983: 163). Embodied metaphors are particularly suited to serving as bridges between the old and the new, because they represent, or embody, existing organizational elements as perceived by participants, as illustrated by the two examples of embodied metaphors discussed earlier. From an intervention perspective, this can guide debate to precisely the aspects that matter to organizational actors (even if these were not the explicitly stated purpose of the workshop), and provide a nonintrusive and nonpersonalized way to address them.

Embodied metaphors are collective creations, and therefore from a political perspective, they can make it easier for contentious issues to be placed on the agenda for discussion. Individuals would be unlikely to bring such issues up on their own, but as part of a group such issues are easier to surface. In addition, embodied metaphors can bring to the agenda contentious issues because these issues are not overtly represented, but they have to be "decoded" with the help of the OD practitioner. Initially, participants may not be entirely clear as to why they built a certain structure, or what precisely it represents. Through the course of collaborative interpretation of the structure, new ideas and issues emerge. On a similar note, the process of constructing embodied metaphors enhances ownership and involvement. This is a fun and engaging way to address organizational issues, which makes it more likely that there will be active participation in this multimodal process of meaning-generation.

Directions for further research on embodied metaphors

One potential dimension for future research would be further exploration into the political implications of embodied metaphors, especially as metaphorical theorization has been criticized as failing to pay due attention to political issues (Morgan, 1996). Do embodied metaphors tend to "democratize" the process of organizational diagnosis and sensemaking regarding the issues that have to be addressed and the direction to follow? If so, what are the specific features of embodied metaphors and their construction process that allow this beyond that they are collective constructions based on a specific technology of elicitation?

From a creativity, generative perspective, embodied metaphors can help organizational members engage both in more conservative, experience-based "thought imagery" as well as in more unbounded, divergent, "imagination imagery" (Howe, 1989). In doing so, they can reinterpret and debate existing issues that their organization is facing, as was done in the SwissBank case discussed here, or more radically, imagine completely new possibilities, as can be done when participants are asked to construct analogs of how they see the future of their industry or organization. Such imagination imagery could thus fulfill the generative potential of metaphors not only in organizational theorizing but also in the applied domain of practitioners. One potential direction for future research therefore is the exploration of the relative generative potential of embodied metaphors as compared to other types of metaphorically based organization development interventions, and whether different construction processes would be more suited to either thought imagery or imagination imagery.

From a change efficacy perspective in addition, metaphorical thinking is inherent in episodes of organization development and change. Embodied metaphors extend the traditional semantic and cognitive dimensions of metaphors by tapping into pre-reflexive knowledge contained in human bodily experience and interpretations embodied in the constructed analogs. Embodied metaphors are exceptionally vivid and memorable; photographs of structures (or actual structures) can be taken back to the organization and can serve as constant reminders of the issues that need to be addressed and the changes that need to be made. Embodied metaphors can thus contribute to developing and sustaining a shared set of metaphorical repertoires as well as shared understanding, vital to the success of organization change and development efforts. Further research can therefore explore the process through which embodied metaphors can induce reframing of existing situations and the potential differences of this process from the way in which linguistic-based or map-based metaphors can induce reframing of perceptions or cognitive maps in the context of organization change processes.

Conclusion

For a process of constructing embodied metaphors to be effective, meaningful, and sustainable, sufficient time, appropriate workshop structure, flexibility to experiment, and mindful attitude of superiors are key resources in this respect. The process must be organized and resourced adequately, simultaneously allowing for enough "foolishness" to emerge within a frame that aims to explore and deliver insights on pressing strategic issues. Sufficient time must be set aside, because rushed sessions lose much of their effectiveness as functional and goal-constrained thinking tends to take over. If the CEO is involved, he or she should act as just one of the group, and be conscious of the potential of any defensive or dominating behavior by them leading to the construction of "politically correct" structures, where the process risks degenerating into a meaningless exercise. Furthermore, to facilitate the emergence of imaginative metaphors, and to sustain excitement, interventions should be designed and carried out with a maximum variety in construction materials.

Even if the insights gained through embodied metaphors might be uncomfortable, companies should be prepared to face and capitalize on them in a productive and developmental manner. An indication of the impact of embodied metaphors might be the extent to which an organization takes such sessions seriously, endeavors to capture insights from the session, debates them, and takes appropriate action. Often the colorful and evocative language inherent in the metaphors continues to inform strategic conversations long after the interventions have taken place. A vital element to sustain the intervention's effectiveness is to invite participants to take the actual constructions back to their organization or department and display them as an *aide-mémoire*, a reminder of the debate, issues arising, insights gained, and strategic directions decided on.

The next chapter will focus precisely on another specific domain of applying embodied metaphorical mapping, namely processes of strategy development. Strategy being about the long-term direction of an organization to cater for stakeholder needs is often subject to competing views and interpretations, and thus lends itself to an intervention technique that offers divergent, creative and synthetic thinking.

REFERENCES

Alderfer, C. P. 1977. Organization development. *Annual Review of Psychology*, 28: 197–223.

Armenakis, A. and Bedeian, A. 1992. The role of metaphors in organizational change. Change agent and change target perspectives. *Group & Organization Management*, 17: 242–9.

Barry, D. 1994. Making the invisible visible: Using analogically-based methods to surface unconscious organizational processes. *Organization Development Journal*, 21(4), 37–47.

Black, M. 1979. More about metaphor. In Ortony, A. (ed.), *Metaphor and thought*. Cambridge University Press, 19–43.

Broussine, M. and Vince, R. 1996. Working with metaphor towards organizational change. In C. Oswick and D. Grant (eds.), *Organisation development: Metaphorical explorations*. London: Pitman, 57–70.

Buergi, P., Jacobs, C., and Roos, J. 2005. From metaphor to practice in the crafting of strategy. *Journal of Management Inquiry*, 14: 78–94.

Buergi, P. and Roos, J. 2003. Images of Strategy. *European Management Journal*, 21, 69–78.

Burke, W. W. 1992. Metaphors to consult by. *Group & Organization Management*, 17: 255–9.

Clark, T. and Salaman, G. 1996. The use of metaphor in the client–consultant relationship: A study of management consultants. In Oswick, C. and Grant, D. (eds.), *Organisation development: Metaphorical explorations*. London: Pitman, 154–71.

Cleary, C. and Packard, T. 1992. The use of metaphors in organizational assessment and change. *Group & Organization Management*, 17: 229–41.

Doyle, J. R. and Sims, D. 2002. Enabling strategic metaphor in conversation: A technique of cognitive sculpting for explicating knowledge. In Huff, A. S. and Jenkins, M. (eds.), *Mapping strategic knowledge*. London: Sage, 63–85.

Friedlander, F. and Brown, D. L. 1974. Organization development. *Annual Review of Psychology*, 25: 313–41.

Grant, D. and Oswick, C. (eds.), 1996. *Metaphor and organizations*. London: Sage.

Heracleous, L. and Jacobs. C. 2008. Understanding organizations through embodied metaphors. *Organization Studies*, 29: 45–78.

Hirsch, P. M. 1986. From ambushes to golden parachutes: Corporate takeovers as an instance of cultural framing and institutional integration. *American Journal of Sociology*, 91: 800–37.

Howe, M. A. 1989. Using imagery to facilitate organizational development and change. *Group & Organization Studies*, 14: 70–82.

Huff, A. 2002. *Mapping strategic knowledge*. London: Sage.

Jacobs, C. and Coghlan, D. 2005. Sound from silence: On listening in organizational learning. *Human Relations*, 58: 115–38.

Jacobs, C. and Heracleous, L. 2006. Constructing shared understanding – the role of embodied metaphors in organization development. *Journal of Applied Behavioral Science*, 42: 207–26.

Keizer, J. A. and Post, G. J. J. 1996. The metaphoric gap as a catalyst for change. In Oswick, C. and Grant, D. (eds.), *Organisation development: Metaphorical explorations*. London: Pitman, 90–101.

Lakoff, G. and Johnson, M. 1980. *Metaphors we live by*. University of Chicago Press.

Marshak, R. 1993. Managing the metaphors of change. *Organizational Dynamics*, 22: 44–56.

Morgan, G. 1996. An afterword: Is there anything more to be said about metaphor? In Oswick, C. and Grant, D. (eds.), *Metaphor and organization*. London: Sage, 227–40.

Morgan, G. 1997. *Images of organization*. 2nd edn. Beverly Hills, CA: Sage.

Oswick, C. 1996. Insights into diagnosis: An exploration using visual metaphors. In Oswick, C. and Grant, D. (eds.), *Organisation development: Metaphorical explorations*. 137–51. London: Pitman.

Oswick, C., Keenoy, T. and Grant, D. 2002. Metaphorical and analogical reasoning in organization theory: Beyond orthodoxy. *Academy of Management Review*, 27, 243–303.

Palmer, I. and Dunford, R. 1996. Understanding organisations through metaphor. In Oswick, C. and Grant, D. (eds.), *Organisation development: Metaphorical explorations*. London: Pitman, 7–15.

Pondy, L. R. 1983. The role of metaphors and myths in organization and in the facilitation of change. In Pondy, L. R., Frost, P. J., Morgan, G., and Dandridge, T. C. (eds.), *Organizational symbolism*. Greenwich, CT: JAI, 157–66..

Porras, J. and Silvers, R. 1991. Organizational development and transformation. *Annual Review of Psychology*, 42: 51–78.

Sackmann, S. 1989. The role of metaphors in organization transformation. *Human Relations*, 42: 463–85.

Weick, K. E. 1990. Introduction: Cartographic myths in organizations. In A. S. Huff and M. Jenkins (eds.), *Mapping strategic thought* (pp. 1–10). Chichester, UK: Wiley.

Weick, K. 1995. *Sensemaking in organizations*. London: Sage.

Privatbank IHAG Zürich AG

Reviewing client relationship practices and team roles

Context

In October 2009, the head of a private banking team in Privatbank IHAG Zurich AG invited his four team members to a yearly one-day team workshop. Due to several retirements over the previous three years, the team membership had changed significantly and consisted mainly of recently hired staff. Thus, this year's workshop aimed at providing an opportunity for all team members to develop a shared understanding of how to best serve private banking clients as well as to critically reflect on the team's collaboration.

Strategic goal of intervention

Private banking, being a complicated and complex business, understanding the needs of wealthy clients is critical to success. While the team might share some professional commonalities, it seemed to differ in the underlying values of its members. Front-line staff in private banking not only require good sales skills but also equally, if not

Marco Sinkwitz (First Vice President, Privatbank IHAG Zurich AG) kindly provided his reflections on this workshop that he initiated and conducted.

more importantly, relationship management skills, as well as detailed content expertise. Thus and in view of increasing client needs and expectations, private banking requires a holistic approach to wealth management that combines competency, flexibility, and convenience to the client. Thus, the specific goal of the intervention was to raise the team's awareness of these current and future requirements and to prepare the team for impending changes.

Embodied metaphors

The picture at the top left of Figure E.1 shows the work identity of a recently promoted client manager who presents herself on the smaller podium on the left, while the client is located much higher on the right. The scattered bricks in front of her are intended to show her solution propositions to the client, while the client's issues and needs

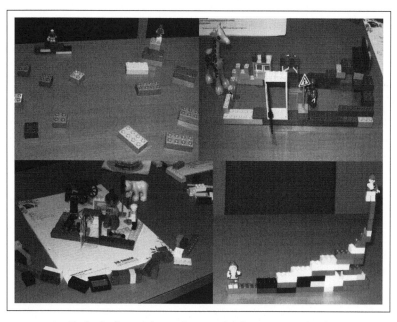

FIGURE E.1 *Embodied metaphors of private bankers at Privatbank IHAG Zürich.*

are much larger than her solutions. This model reminded the team manager to ensure that this team member would receive the necessary training to be content wise at the level of the client's needs.

The picture at the top right of Figure E.1 shows a recently recruited well-trained team member who views herself as challenging and as preferring to be challenged. The walls demarcate her field of activity that is always welcoming to the client (the giraffe), who can enter this field through door or window. This model symbolized this team member's ambitions and ability to set boundaries between her work identity, other team members and the clients.

The picture at the bottom left of Figure E.1 shows the work identity of a senior financial advisor who portrays his field of activities as clearly demarcated through a protective barrier to guard against impending threats (represented by policeman, canon and ice-bear). The chef figure is supposed to "prepare and create" the right solution for the client. Interestingly, a person figure or other model to represent the client is absent in this model.

The picture at the bottom right of Figure E.1 shows the work identity of a "wheeler dealer" who conceives of his job as primarily (high-risk) wealth creation – hence the exponentially growing curve model. The two risk types are represented by a bearded low-level person figure on the left and a young-ish person figure on the highest point of the curve – where a drop can be most painful. For the most part, this model is concerned with wealth creation and to a much lesser extend with actual client needs.

Insights gained: how was this session strategically consequential for the organization/the team?

The workshop revealed the different attitudes, values and beliefs of the team members in terms of their role as private bankers. The team manager realized during and after the session that his team had fundamentally different approaches to their work role identity as private bankers. Based on these insights, he was now in a position to train and develop his team members in a personalized fashion and in this way improve the coherence, and ultimately the performance, of his team. For instance, he initiated tailor-made training for each member to target what he considered to be the "blind spots" of his team, be it content expertise, client focus, or team-play. Lastly, he concluded that he would pay even more attention to the values and beliefs of new team members than he had in the past, since the workshop confirmed the relevance of this to the team's success.

CHAPTER EIGHT

Strategy as a crafting practice

Strategy has traditionally been thought of as an ideally rational, structured and objective process, and in this has led to a mainstream that has neglected understanding of the interpretive and discursive aspects of strategic praxis (what practitioners do) and practices (regularities and aggregations of strategic praxes) (Whittington, 2006). In spite of recent constructionist and discursive developments in the understanding of strategy (Barry and Elmes, 1997; Buergi, Jacobs, and Roos, 2005; Jacobs and Heracleous, 2005, 2006; Vaara, Tienari, and Santti, 2003), the role of metaphor, and particularly what we refer to as "embodied metaphors," remains largely unexplored by mainstream strategy theorizing. As previously discussed, the term "embodied metaphors" encompasses two interrelated ideas: first, the emergent and iterative construction of a simultaneously physical as well as metaphorical object directly involves the body in this process. Secondly, and importantly, however, the resulting physical metaphors have a body; they are metaphors in the flesh that can be touched, moved, and examined from various angles, and that can serve as engaging occasions for sensemaking.

This chapter is based on Heracleous and Jacobs (2008).

In this chapter we present an approach to strategizing through a process of crafting embodied metaphors. In this context we view strategy as a practice of crafting, where actors both metaphorically as well as literally construct their perceptions of strategic issues through and into embodied metaphors within facilitated workshops. We analyze an episode of a strategy team constructing an embodied metaphor of their ideal strategizing process, and suggest that embodied metaphors are an effective means of intervention that can help managers debate specific strategic challenges in a generative fashion. Secondly, we propose that the process of construction and interpretation of embodied metaphors can provide access to deeper understanding of organizational, divisional or task identities. Thirdly, we address other important benefits of the process, such as the potential for shifts in the mindsets of strategists and the ability to engage actors not ordinarily involved in strategizing. Finally, we offer some suggestions on how to foster a productive strategizing process of crafting embodied metaphors.

Discourses and strategic practices

At a fundamental level, the main premise of the "linguistic turn" (Deetz, 2003) in social science is that discourse is not just about functional communication but rather serves to construct ways of seeing and acting that over time become institutionalized into social norms and practices in recurrent cycles of institutionalization (Heracleous, 2004, 2006). If we accept this premise, the discourses of strategy then are crucial to how both researchers and practitioners view strategy and the actions they take. For example, strategy researchers schooled in the discourse of industrial economics might not allow for strategic intuition, mental maps, or creativity as important facets for understanding the beast of strategy. On the other hand, researchers schooled in interpretive approaches to strategy might not be terribly interested in empirically exploring a proposition such as the industrial organization assertion that "industry structure has a strong influence in defining the competitive rules of the game as well as the strategies potentially available to the firm," that subordinates managerial agency to the whims of the environment (Porter, 1975: 1).

Quite apart from the professional orientation implied by background and the concepts employed, however, metaphors are everpresent and unavoidable in strategic discourse of all persuasions. If we consider for example the influential Boston Consulting Group "growth-share matrix" (Stern and Stalk, 1998), intended to assist executives in portfolio planning decisions, the labels are in effect evocative metaphors that imply "appropriate" (but often mistaken) strategic actions (Hirsch, 1986) with regard to businesses denoted as "cash cows," "dogs," "stars," and "question marks." Further, the ubiquitous two-dimensional industry maps as well as two-by-two matrices are in effect spatial metaphors, where organizations are "positioned" in relation to their competitors and entities are allocated to their proper place according to the dimensions of the matrices.

When practitioners strategize (are engaged in activities they deem as strategic), the discourses and related processes or frameworks employed shape what can be on the agenda and what kinds of decisions can be taken. For example, a strategizing process of scenario planning would most likely lead to the construction of two or three possible futures and to the search for a strategy that is expected to be viable in these possible futures. A process of value chain and industry analysis would likely result in detailed prescriptions about desired organizational configurations, and lead to the search for strategies aimed to position the firm in a way that can mitigate the impact of trends in particular industry forces, or ideally in ways that can influence these forces.

Further, research has confirmed that discourse matters to strategic practices and praxis. At a fine-grained level of conversation analysis, for example, Samra-Fredericks has shown how strategy gets accomplished through everyday skilled relational–rhetorical exchanges among organizational actors (Samra-Fredericks, 2003, 2005). At a broader level, Vaara (2002) has shown how actors employ discursive strategies to frame success or failure of strategic processes such as post-merger integration in particular ways that legitimate one's actions and allocate responsibility in particular ways. Vaara, Tienari, and Santi (2003) showed how practitioners employed metaphor to construct the identities of the players involved in cross-border mergers and their perceived common future. Outlining the generative and diagnostic potential of different discursive repertoires, Jacobs and Heracleous (2005) have suggested that reflective dialogue can influence strategists' cognitive maps in ways that can foster strategic innovation. Thus, discourses are integral to strategizing, and in this chapter we explore the role of one discursive component, embodied metaphors within a strategizing episode.

Strategy as a practice of crafting

Strategy as practice has emerged as an approach that challenges conventional conceptions of strategy research that have primarily revolved around strategy content (Porter, 1980, 1985) and to a lesser extent around strategy process (Johnson, 1987; Pettigrew, 1987). The strategy as practice approach advances an inductive perspective on strategy that seeks to understand what strategists do: the praxes, practices, and practitioners of strategy (Balogun, Huff, and Johnson, 2003; Balogun and Johnson, 2004; Jarzabkowski, 2003; Johnson, Melin, and Whittington, 2003; Whittington, 2006).

In this chapter, we advance a notion of strategy as a practice of crafting, where strategy is both metaphorically and literally crafted through and into embodied metaphors by strategy practitioners in facilitated workshops, which can be viewed as strategizing episodes. Exploring the source domain of Mintzberg's (1987) initial metaphor of "strategy as craft" in more depth, Buergi, Jacobs, and Roos (2005) have conceptualized the literal, physical activity of crafting strategy as a form of bodily recursive enactment. Drawing on physiological, psychological and social aspects of enactment, this perspective emphasizes the relevance and potential of manual activities for processes of strategizing. At each level, crafting takes a form of recursive enactment – at the physiological level between hand and mind, at the psychological level between thought and action, and at the social level between interrelated speech acts and meaning-generation. Thus, here we conceive of crafting strategy as the integrative, inductive process of constructing embodied metaphors of strategically relevant domains.

Our approach builds on and extends the tradition in organization theory viewing metaphors as potent creative devices, whose creative potential increases especially where there is neither too much similarity nor too much difference between the source and target domains (Morgan, 1980). Gareth Morgan's work has been seminal in challenging dominant mechanistic and organic metaphors that had guided theorizing within a functionalist paradigm, through a conscious understanding and exploration of the impact of such taken-for-granted metaphors on organizational theorizing (Morgan, 1980, 1983). Morgan has gone so far as to suggest that trying to minimize or negate the influence of metaphors is not only counter-productive but also impossible, given their instrumental role in theorizing and sensemaking (Morgan, 1983, 1986).

Organizational identity as a strategic issue

Recent studies emphasize the strategic relevance of identity (Pratt and Rafaeli, 1997; Fiol, 2001). The concepts of identity and strategy are interlinked in a pragmatic, theoretical and methodological sense. In a pragmatic sense, an organization and its actors ideally need to have a sense of identity when deciding what the goals and direction of their organization should be, and often employ their sense of identity as a boundary-setting guide in making strategic choices (what the organization should or should not do). From a theoretical perspective, and in particular a social constructionist point of view, the identity of a collectivity such as an organization is seen as a discursive object that is (re-) produced in and through communicative interactions (Grant, Lawrence, and Hardy, 2005). A narrative view suggests that "organizations' identities are constituted by the identity-relevant narratives that their participants' author about them" (Brown, 2006: 734). If strategies are "the most prominent, influential, and costly stories told in organizations" (Barry and Elmes, 1997: 430) that to a large extent relate to what the organization wants to achieve or become in future, strategy can be seen as an identity-relevant narrative. Thus, identity and strategy are tightly connected through discourses that both constitute these domains, as well as mediate their recursive relationship.

Finally, in a methodological sense, when conceiving of identity as a collectively constructed set of meanings (Hatch and Schultz, 2002; Schultz and Hatch, 2004), the construction of embodied metaphors can facilitate conversations on collective identity. The methodology of crafting embodied metaphors can help researchers gain knowledge of how organizational actors perceive their identity, and also enable actors to externalize their assumptions on identity through what they construct. Since the participants in the context of this methodology are invited to construct their view of the organizational or task identities, their constructions are in effect metaphors for first-order perceived identities that can be explored both by themselves as well as by researchers involved in the process. The physical objects of the crafting activity, such as sculptures, models, or paintings, provide analogs that in turn allow strategists to surface, project and subsequently problematize and debate their individual and collective concepts of organizational, team, or task identity.

Conceptual basis of embodied metaphors

To contextualize what follows and link it to theoretical antecedents discussed previously, it is worth outlining some of the considerations presented in Chapter 2. We argued that views of strategy are associated with particular social science paradigms, and have a corresponding view of metaphor. We then noted that our embodied metaphors view of strategy is rooted in recent work in the sociology of knowledge placing our embodied nature at the core of how we perceive reality and acquire knowledge about it (Johnson, 1987; Lakoff, 1990; Lakoff and Johnson, 1999). In terms of ontology (the nature of things), embodied realism holds that reality neither possesses a fixed essence independent of perception, as positivism suggests, nor wholly depends on the institutionalization of interpretations and practices, as social constructionism suggests (Berger and Luckmann, 1966; Gergen, 1999). It holds, rather, that our bodily experience and ongoing patterns of interaction with the physical world are central to structuring our thoughts, interpretations and actions through the transfer of conceptual correspondences from embodied experience to more abstract domains (Lakoff, 1990; Lakoff and Johnson, 1999).

In terms of epistemology (what counts as valid knowledge), embodied realism views the rationalist–empiricist dichotomy as too simplistic and unhelpful, and as refuted by the empirical evidence gathered by neuroscience. This evidence shows for example that babies can learn even before they are born, during their stay in the womb; and therefore when they are born they have knowledge that is both innate (as rationalism suggests) as well as learned (as empiricism suggests) (Johnson and Lakoff, 2002). Embodied realism is proposed as an alternative that accepts both innate and learned aspects of conceptual systems, where our knowledge is based on our image schemas developed through our embodied experiences. Thus, the purpose of our study is to explore and illustrate the potential of an embodied metaphors approach as a practice of crafting strategy, whereby strategists construct embodied metaphors of strategic significance through a practice of metaphorical reasoning and praxis.

Crafting strategy through embodied metaphors

Further methodological considerations

As previously noted, we operationalized the concept of embodied metaphors in terms of these constructions that are embodied in two main ways: first, they are constructed through engagement of the body, involving a direct phenomenological relationship between the participants and the resulting constructions. Embodied engagement as our mode of being in the world (Johnson, 1987; Lakoff and Johnson, 1999) is actualized in the making of these constructions. Secondly, these constructions are not simply semantic or spatial metaphors, such as cognitive maps (Huff, 1990), but are tangible entities extending into three-dimensional space. They are metaphors in the flesh that are recursively and simultaneously constructed and interpreted. They embody the blending of source and target domains, and engender meanings both in the construction process and subsequent interpretations.

We discuss here some additional methodological considerations relating to the process of crafting embodied metaphors, beyond the discussion in Chapter 5. The use of any physical materials in such processes comes with both certain advantages as well as trade-offs. While some materials such as plasticine are more "neutral" in terms of any preconfigured meanings, others such as construction toy materials may be more effective in terms of connectivity and likelihood of swiftly inducing rich imagery. While the participants may be partly constrained by the nature of materials available, they are also enabled by these same materials in externalizing and debating their views. Methodologically speaking the constraints relating to preconfigured meanings inherent in the materials can be considered as limitations, but on the other hand participants are able to ascribe local meaning to their constructions through drawing from and combining these preconfigured meanings into broader metaphors and storylines, and therefore emergent, creative sensemaking is facilitated.

A further methodological consideration relates to the fact that the practice of embodied metaphors involves a double hermeneutic, the fact that facilitators/researchers interpret participants' own interpretations. Thus, reflexivity is important in this approach, as it is in interpretive research more broadly. The roles of facilitator and researcher, often played by the same individuals, are more prevalent at different points in time and with distinctively different motivations in interpreting the constructions built. While the facilitator needs to read (and help participants read for themselves) the metaphors in terms of their potential for critical exploration of strategic issues, a researcher engages in a systematic, a posteriori analysis that should ideally privilege participants' own interpretations.

The practice itself is a form of process consultation (Schein, 1999) whereby a practical reflexivity raises an awareness of discordant voices or the potential effects of the existing hegemony in the organization. The intervention however holds promise for – at least temporarily – a democratizing effect that is inherent in the method. Individual constructions for instance cannot be read prior to the participant's debriefing in plenary, which in turn creates an exclusive ownership of the interpretation; an attempt to overrule the owner's interpretation by a superior would violate the ethos of the intervention and has in our experience rarely, if ever, occurred.

Analysis of strategy team's embodied metaphors

We discuss here in more detail the embodied metaphors constructed by one of the three senior manager groups from CellCo, the strategy development team, initially discussed in Chapter 5. Our analysis proceeded in two stages. First, we reviewed the individual constructions of participants with regard to their respective target domains in order to get a sense of the context-specific metaphorical terminology employed when attributing meaning to the embodied metaphors produced. Being familiar with this emergent, situated vocabulary enabled us to iteratively sharpen our hermeneutic apparatus prior to interpreting the collective construction.

Secondly, we systematically analyzed both the collective construction (which we label the "grand metaphor") as well as its the primary constituent metaphors. We then analyzed metaphorical mappings in terms of the interactions between source domains and target domains, and the emergent meanings resulting from these interactions, drawing on participants' perspectives and discussions. Our analysis operated at what Gibbs (1999) referred to as the "interpretation" stage of metaphorical processing, where conscious reflection about the meaning of a metaphor takes place. These two stages are what we referred to in Chapter 5 as the first two analytical moments: the focus on the process of individual constructions, and within-case analysis of grand metaphors and constituent metaphors. In line with our interpretive, constructionist orientation, we have prioritized the participants' first-order concepts and interpretation of the three-dimensional objects and the meaning attributed to them.

Table 8.1 outlines our analysis of the source domains, target domains and the emergent meanings resulting from the interaction between these two domains, at the grand and constituent metaphor levels.[1]

The emergent vocabulary of the grand metaphor: individual-level metaphors

The first task of the participants was to portray the current status of the strategy process in CellCo. As an initial analytical moment, these individual constructions have enabled us to better understand the subsequent metaphorical terminology of the collective construction. One strategist portrayed the existing strategizing process as the journey of a small pig eager to travel. Having overcome several obstacles,

---

[1] In Chapter 5 we presented five constituent metaphors for this team, but here we examine in more detail the first four, which together make a tightly woven narrative.

TABLE 8.1: *Target domains, source domains and emergent meanings in the metaphors of the strategy development team*

	Emergent meaning	Target domain	Source domain
Grand metaphor	Strategy-making is a journey of confused individuals eventually reaching common ground (EMG).	Strategy development process (TG).	Journey of disoriented animals moving towards a common space (SG).
Constituent metaphors	Organizational members are an anonymous group of individuals seeking strategic guidance (EM1).	Organization members at beginning of strategy development (T1).	Troop of disoriented animals (S1).
	Strategy-making is a passionate, energetic transformation process (EM2).	Strategy-making as transforming force (T2).	Combustion engine, transforming fuel into kinesthetic energy (S2).
	Renewed, revitalized strategizing is essential to the journey (EM3).	Renewed strategy development process (T3).	Set of gearing wheels, transmitting energy between entities (S3).
	Strategic alignment provides a common framework while simultaneously allowing for degrees of freedom (EM4).	Relation of strategists and organization in renewed strategy process (T4).	Safari park as a fenced territory with degrees of freedom for different animals (S4).

(Heracleous and Jacobs [2008]; used with permission.)

it reaches the "promised land" where it learns that the short-term economic benefits, symbolized by apples, were much closer had it taken a different route. The participant explained, "We might be so hungry that we don't appreciate the journey and go straight to eat the apples first … We as a team do not seem to be sure whether to build a sustainable farm or whether we should go for the apples." Another participant portrayed current strategy-making as turning the wheel, where "a bunch of people standing in the middle of the wheel discuss strategy." With the new company now spread around the world, he noted, "We don't know any longer what the wheel consists of today." A third participant constructed a document that represented strategy as the corporate strategic plan, as well as the process of strategic alignment. While the "product" of strategy, i.e. corporate strategy plans was reasonably understood, there was more confusion in the strategic alignment process where "we don't know exactly what to do. Which process allows us to unlock the potential of our folks?" A fourth participant symbolized strategy as a house containing different kinds of animals. While cows – representing routine reporting and planning tools – were easy to lead, the motivational challenge was portrayed by a horse that "you can lead to water, but you can't make it drink." The hard task of strategy-making and implementation was represented by a set of cats where "strategy is like herding cats." The element providing access to the house of strategy was represented as a key that could only be found by making a difficult journey through the garden adjacent to the house. Finally, the fifth participant distinguished standard business planning and creative processes of strategy generation. The former was symbolized by a set of uniform people that "chunk around the wheels and go through the process. And numbers pop out in the end. And they start again." By contrast a more diverse, creative process of strategic conversations was portrayed as a set of multicolored, interrelated tubes that led to a small wheel – strategic thinking as an outcome of the conversation – that would have a "massive gearing effect" on the organization – portrayed as a much larger wheel.

Grand team metaphor: "Strategy as a journey"

The target domain of the strategy team's construction was their ideal, renewed strategy development process (target domain of grand metaphor, hereafter TG). Their strategy development process was portrayed as a troop of dispersed, disoriented animals (source domain of grand metaphor, hereafter SG) that undertook an energetic journey to reach safe and common ground in a safari park environment. The emergent meaning of the grand metaphor (EMG) arising from the combination of source and target domain was the aspiration of the team to design a dynamic strategy development process that – in contrast to conventional strategy-making – drew otherwise disinterested and confused organizational members into passionate strategic conversation that allowed for individual differences in outlook and identity while operating within the parameters of a collective framework

Each of these dimensions of strategy development as the target domain was further cognitively structured or given meaning by constituent metaphors, structured as stages of the strategic journey.

FIGURE 8.1 *Grand metaphor overview: strategy-making as a journey.* *(Heracleous and Jacobs [2008]; used with permission.)*

FIGURE 8.2 *Constituent metaphors 1 and 2: troop of disoriented animals and combustion engine. (Heracleous and Jacobs [2008]; used with permission.)*

Constituent metaphor one: "Strategists as confused animals searching for direction"

The first constituent metaphor, at the point of departure of the strategic journey, consisted of a "group of disoriented animals" (source domain of constituent metaphor S1, hereafter numbered accordingly) representing the confusion of organizational members at the beginning of the strategy development process (dimension of target domain of constituent metaphor T1). By combining source and target domain, participants conveyed the emergent meaning that organizational members were a somewhat depersonalized, confused group of individuals that were unclear about the needed processes and outcomes of strategy-making in CellCo and thus in need of some guidance (emergent meaning – EM1).

FIGURE 8.3 *Constituent metaphors 3 and 4: gearing wheels and safari park. (Heracleous and Jacobs [2008]; used with permission.)*

Constituent metaphor two: "Ideal strategy-making as transformative engine"

This stage of the journey led the traveller to a "chocolate bar and a shaken bottle of cola," symbolizing a dynamic, passionately desired strategy-making process. These were next to a "transformative engine" (S2) that contained at its entrance a large, monochrome block of bricks (S2) representing myopic, conventional strategic development (T2); but also the promise of an ideal strategizing process that would be passionate and energetic. In terms of emergent meaning, participants symbolized their belief that conventional strategy development had been perceived as myopic and lacking passion. Physically juxtaposing monochrome with multicolor elements illustrated this duality (EM2).

Constituent metaphor three: "Renewed strategizing as a set of wheels with massive gearing effect"

A set of person figures with extra sets of "eyes" at the center of the engine (S3) represented those strategists "with vision" (T3) that can lead strategy discussion groups, arriving at a multicolored set of bricks portraying new, creative perspectives of strategic thinking. Having gone through this engine, the strategic traveller reached an interconnected set of wheels (S3) that represented the "massive gearing effect" (EM3) such a renewed strategizing process (T3) could have for the organization. A set of interconnected, interoperable wheels suggested a combination of source and target domains that revitalized and illustrated the effects of an otherwise dead metaphor; the notion of a gearing effect (EM3).

Constituent metaphor four: "Strategic alignment as fenced territory with degrees of freedom"

The end-point of the journey was represented as a "safari park" (S4) symbolizing the outcome of the strategizing process, namely strategic alignment (T4) of organizational constituent functions, combined with specific degrees of freedom. The emergent meaning from the metaphorical mapping of this constituent metaphor was that the animals still differed in their shape and identity, but had now arrived in a fenced territory that provided them with different degrees of freedom, within certain parameters (EM4). Thus, initially disoriented animals, having traveled through a revitalized strategic development process, would in the end have a shared strategic framework: "They are still different, but they are in the same park." Participants "buried" a "blue book" (S4) in the grounds of the safari park, representing their corporate strategic framework (T4), seeing this as a necessary, yet less relevant or impactful outcome of the strategic journey (EM4).

Surrounding this "strategy as journey" embodied metaphor were further related representations. A group of conventional strategic business planners was portrayed as skeletons with black hats positioned in a repetitive cycle (S) of producing pointless and ineffectual (EM) corporate strategic documents (T). Skeletons and black hats suggested bloodless uniformity that produced somewhat meaningless outcomes (EM). Other representations included a hedged cage (S) symbolizing the strategy team's (T) safe environment (EM), protected by the head of strategy (T), a warrior person figure wearing a safety helmet and a sword (S), the protector (EM); keeping at bay the rest of the organization (T) represented by a dragon (S) (organization as a threatening creature, EM). Next to the strategy process was a tall tower in the colors of the national flag (S) of FixCo (T) overlooking the entire construction; on top of this tower sat a person figure holding a laser gun (S) representing the CEO of FixCo (T), indicating the perceived tight control and monitoring of CellCo by FixCo and its CEO (EM). Underneath the platform hosting the "transformative engine" was a large dungeon (S) containing key members of the formal hierarchy (T) such as the CEO of CellCo, the head of strategy of CellCo as well as the head of strategy of FixCo, indicating the importance of these actors in supporting a positive transformation of the strategy making process at CellCo (EM). Finally, a spider-shaped UFO (S) populated one corner of the overall model to represent unpredictable, unforeseeable threats and dangers (EM) in the competitive environment (T).

Discussion and implications

Embodied metaphors as a mode of intervention

The strategic episode of CellCo's strategy team demonstrates how by constructing embodied metaphors, this team engaged in surfacing and critically reflecting on their current mode of strategizing by means of this novel crafting practice. The use of embodied metaphors illustrates two aspects recently identified as emergent practices of strategizing, namely "workshopping" and "crafting symbolic artifacts" as emergent practices of strategizing (Whittington *et al.*, 2006). Organization development practitioners have long employed metaphor as an intervention device to facilitate a variety of organizational processes (Barrett and Cooperrider, 1990; Burke, 1992; Marshak, 1993). Such interventions have typically involved the application of metaphors selected by the organization development practitioner, based on a diagnosis of the organizational situation and on the desired organizational outcomes. While this top-down approach involves the application of a generic set of metaphors to organizational situations, an inductive approach such as the one outlined in this chapter operates on the assumption that organizational members can themselves generate and employ metaphors in view of their context and experience, that can be tapped on for the purposes of system diagnosis and change, emphasizing the emergent, local, and contextual nature of metaphors (Palmer and Dunford, 1996).

The embodied metaphors approach enables organizational members to construct and interpret these emergent metaphors in order to address specific, targeted issues (Heracleous and Jacobs, 2005); in our case, to design a revitalized strategy process, or to reflect on and develop shared understandings regarding the identity of participants' organization or division in the context of an unsettling acquisition. In terms of facilitating shared understandings, as one participant noted: "The long-term impact for me was that I had an image and understanding of the organization. I had just gone into that worldwide role and suddenly I got a knowledge that people accumulated over three years. I got their knowledge sharing within a day."

Participants in such interventions typically take photographs and even fragments of the actual constructions back to their organization to display as *aide-mémoires* of the issues debated, the insights gained, and the actions that should flow from them. As one participant recounted, "The photograph of the landscape of [CellCo] stood on my desk all the time. It was a prompt of the situation we were in." In terms of strategizing in practice, embodied metaphors can provide a means of surfacing taken-for-granted understandings and assumptions about the organization and its environment, and can consequently help participants debate what the appropriate strategic actions are, and offer a new shared vocabulary for doing so. As one participant noted: "Lots of strategy meetings are about people showing off about their intelligence. Somehow through this [exercise] this was eliminated ... It took out strange terminologies, the language became real. It wasn't full of corporate buff and hype ... So a quite grounded, down-to-earth approach to things that is quite helpful."

Constructing embodied metaphors can provide strategizing with a means to move beyond dry objectivist approaches to a more creative strategic thinking mode, and can at least temporarily reduce the impact of destructive politics. One participant, comparing the embodied metaphors process with a traditional strategy process suggested that "If all people talk about issues in a normal, traditional way it leads to a false consensus and orientation of the discussion. You can't find a new twist and vocabulary if you pursue that route ... a large part of the notorious politicking and power gaming did not entirely go away but it didn't influence the conversation as in other settings."

Embodied metaphors as windows to organizational,
divisional or task identities

Whereas organizational identity was initially conceptualized as those aspects of an organization that its members consider central, enduring, and distinctive, more recent work has advanced a more interpretive approach (Albert and Whetten, 1985; Gioia, Schultz, and Corley, 2000). In this approach, organizational identity emerges as a collective, shared understanding of an organization's characteristics, as a socially constructed set of meanings about the organization and its environment arising from inter-subjective meaning negotiations (Fiol, 2001; Pratt and Rafaeli, 1997). When reviewing the state of the art, Oliver and Roos observe that the increasing interest in the concept of organizational identity engenders the need for more empirical exploration and substantiation of the concept (Brickson, 2005; Dukerich, Golden, and Shortell, 2002; Foreman and Whetten, 2002; Oliver and Roos, 2007).

In our study, the target domain was integral to the identity of the key task of strategy development team, that is, the nature and context of the strategy development process. Collectively, the metaphors represent a rich source of empirical data for understanding actors' shared views of the identities they have literally constructed. The strategy team expressed core elements of its ideal identity when constructing the narrative of an overall journey that ends with a meaningful balance between individuality and alignment of organizational members; and when using a chocolate bar and a bottle of cola to symbolize the requisite dynamism and passion; and a multicolored set of bricks to portray the need for innovative, creative form of strategizing.

In terms of the other two CellCo senior manager groups, whose embodied metaphors we analyzed in Chapter 5, the business operations team portrayed its shared dismay by representing CellCo as a conquered castle, monitored and managed by the authoritarian CEO of FixCo. The brand, a previously central element of CellCo's identity, was positioned outside the castle, remote and detached. The empty seats in the merry-go-round symbolized a lost sense of fun. "Unbranded" insiders created unease for the more brand-conscious members; and the ghost of the founder placed in the midst of the operations staff indicated a lost sense of equality. The team's portrayal of CellCo's identity, previously seen as a solid fortress, appeared to weaken and disintegrate in terms of its ownership, detached brand, lack of fun and lost equality.

Further, the technical division's metaphor of its identity drew on a disconnected conglomerate of machines indicating a perceived lack of coherence within the division. Several black boxes in this representation indicated a lack of shared understanding of how things worked, and the dangerous but exciting jungle expedition indicated a risky expansion into uncharted 3G territory. The surgery operating theatre which included the mobile network as the guarded patient symbolized the centrality of the mobile network to the division's identity. The sinister black hats from FixCo represented malicious outsiders who would import unfettered business logic, threatening the current creative aspects of the identity through the forced imposition of order and uniformity.

An embodied metaphor approach thus provides a method that captures intangible and collective dimensions of organizational identity that cannot be as vividly or tangibly captured through the tools most commonly used in this field. The collectively built, shared constructions draw on a variety of source domains to represent the target domain of identity (organizational, team or, as evidenced in our study, task identity). This blending of domains produces rich, locally based meanings and narratives offering a perspective that cannot be easily gained through standardized questionnaires, document study, or interview-based research. Further, an embodied metaphors approach is inductive in nature, allowing key aspects of organizational identity to emerge in processes of analogically mediated inquiry, linked together in terms of meaningful narratives that offer a window to the group's innermost views and assumptions. Finally, an embodied metaphors approach allows for both current and aspirational aspects of identity to coexist in the same construction (as in the strategic journey, where the beginnings symbolize current identity and the conclusion symbolizes desired identity), in what Lakoff and Johnson (1980: 81) call an "experiential gestalt."

Benefits of the process of crafting embodied metaphors

Why should an organization engage in crafting embodied metaphors? Over time we have observed companies employing the method to address a variety of challenges. When reviewing its strategy after having been acquired by a main competitor for example, a mobile telephony company's strategy team was able to recognize thus-far neglected, impending competitive threats that in turn triggered an unanticipated, yet necessary critical reflection on the company's brand positioning. A senior management team of a food packaging firm were split on the strategic relevance of the company's after-sales activities.

After building representations of their company and its competitive environment, the team eventually appreciated after-sales activities as strategic and subsequently explored alternatives to raise its capabilities in this area. Finally, when the newly formed European management team of a global software provider engaged in crafting embodied metaphors to explore the team's identity and desired forms of collaboration across borders, they were able to start defining a shared identity and to create a platform for debating differences that, over time, would improve lateral collaboration.

As these examples illustrate, the process of crafting and decoding embodied metaphors can deliver insights and potential shifts in managers' mind-sets that would have been difficult to gain in more conventional, numbers-driven, board-meeting style sessions. Further, this process provides a context where senior teams can raise and debate contentious or critical management issues, presenting these issues in the form of embodied metaphors that are imbued with meaning and that can be debated from a variety of perspectives. The practice of crafting embodied metaphors in strategizing draws on rich imagery and stories, rather than dry statistics and figures, and thus helps to develop a memorable shared language that the group can draw on in future strategizing. Last but not least, the process fosters effective team-building, enabling an increased sense of involvement and ownership of the issues and decisions taken by participants, and thus facilitates more effective implementation of these decisions.

In addition to the novel perspectives on the strategizing process that emerged in the strategizing episode we analyzed, this recursive, co-creative potential of embodied metaphors holds promise for involving other organizational members than formal strategists. Since crafting embodied metaphors involves a practice of painting a three-dimensional map with a rough brush, even "lay" strategists can be invited to join the strategic conversation. Their thus-far neglected views could enable novel perspectives to emerge from what corporate strategists would consider the periphery of traditional strategy-making. Thus, embodied metaphors can provide a meaningful approach to include neglected, yet potentially relevant perspectives in such inductive strategy-making processes (Regnér, 2003). For example, members of other teams from CellCo, not ordinarily involved in strategizing processes, conducted similar workshops where interesting and challenging perspectives emerged on the CellCo brand, the wisdom of the organization's 3G investments, the management of its call centers, lack of intra-divisional integration, and the health of the mobile network infrastructure.

Crafting embodied metaphors can also raise issues of implementation and alignment at a very early stage of the process and can thus lead to revisions in strategy, the implementation plan, or even the need to garner political support before any initiatives. For instance, when an operations team in CellCo engaged in crafting embodied metaphors, they portrayed the acquiring company as a set of figures of "dubious, hostile gangsters;" an obvious indicator of potential roadblocks vis-à-vis any strategic initiatives from the new headquarters.

Fostering an effective process for crafting embodied metaphors

It is important to note that the approach does not substitute or supplant rational, conventional strategy-making, but rather complements it. Furthermore, it is certainly not the right choice for every stage of a strategizing process. Due to its exploratory, divergent and synthetic orientation, it might prove most valuable either in the early stages of strategy development where formal and highly structured processes can jeopardize generative strategic thinking, or in strategy review processes where looking at the big picture would be at least as important as detailed examination of deviations from plans.

The crafting of embodied metaphors needs to be organized and resourced adequately, while simultaneously allowing for enough playfulness to emerge, within a frame that aims to explore and deliver insights on real strategic issues. Sufficient time must be set aside, since rushed sessions lose much of their impact, as functional and goal-constrained thinking tends to take over. Further, if the CEO or senior managers are involved, they should be mindful of the potential of any defensive or dominating behavior by them leading to the construction of "politically correct" structures, where the process risks degenerating into a meaningless exercise. A skilled facilitator is useful in helping to bring about a healthy and productive generation, debate and integration of ideas. One pivotal aspect in the design of such processes is the choice of focus or strategic challenge that the group will construct as an embodied metaphor. It should be broad enough to be a meaningful issue with strategic relevance, but also specific enough so that it taps into participants' practical experience and can subsequently inform this experience. Furthermore, a skilled facilitator can ensure that the resulting embodied metaphor is a genuinely interactive and group-based product and can also help the group effectively debate the structures that were created and their implications in terms of organizational action, by homing in and inviting critical debate on potentially insightful aspects of the construction. Finally it is important to systematically capture the insights gained that can then be translated into a more conventional format of corporate communication that can provide crucial input to subsequent, more formal procedures of strategizing.

REFERENCES

Albert, S. and Whetten, D. 1985. Organizational identity, in Cummings, L. and Staw, B. (eds.), *Research in Organizational Behavior* (Vol. 7). Greenwich, CT: JAI Press, 263–95.

Balogun, J. and Johnson, G. 2004. Organizational restructuring and middle manager sensemaking. *Academy of Management Journal*, 47: 523–49.

Balogun, J., Huff, A. S., and Johnson, P. 2003. Three responses to the methodological challenges of studying strategizing. *Journal of Management Studies*, 40: 197–224.

Barrett, F. J. and Cooperrider, D. L. 1990. Generative metaphor intervention: A new behavioral approach for working with systems divided by conflict and caught in defensive perception. *Journal of Applied Behavioral Science*, 26: 219–39.

Barry, D. and Elmes, M. 1997. Strategy retold: toward a narrative view of strategic discourse, *Academy of Management Review*, 22: 429–52.

Berger, P. and Luckmann, T. 1966. *The social construction of reality*. London: Penguin.

Brickson, S. L. 2005. Organizational identity orientation: Forging a link between organizational identity and organizations' relations with stakeholders. *Administrative Science Quarterly*, 50: 576–609.

Brown, A. D. 2006. A narrative approach to collective identities. *Journal of Management Studies*, 43: 731–53.

Buergi, P. T., Jacobs, C. D., and Roos, J. 2005. From metaphor to practice in the crafting of strategy. *Journal of Management Inquiry*, 14: 78–94.

Burke, W. W. 1992. Metaphors to consult by. *Group & Organization Management*, 17: 225–59.

Deetz, S. 2003. Reclaiming the legacy of the linguistic turn. *Organization*, 10: 421–9.

Dukerich, J., Golden, B., and Shortell, S. 2002. Beauty is in the eye of the beholder: The impact of organizational identification, identity, and image on the cooperative behaviors of physicians. *Administrative Science Quarterly*, 47: 507–33.

Fiol, C. M. 2001. Revisiting an identity-based view of sustainable competitive advantage. *Journal of Management*, 27: 691–700.

Foreman, P. and Whetten, D. 2002. Members' identification with multiple-identity organizations. *Organization Science*, 13: 618–35.

Gergen, K. 1999. *An invitation to social construction*. Beverly Hills, CA: Sage.

Gibbs, R. W. 1999. Researching metaphor. In Cameron, L. and Low, G. (eds.), *Researching and applying metaphor*. Cambridge University Press, 28–47.

Gioia, D., Schultz, M., and Corley, K. 2000. Organizational identity, image and adaptive instability, *Academy of Management Review*, 25: 63–81.

Grant, D., Lawrence, T. B., and Hardy, C. 2005. Discourse and Collaboration. The role of conversations and collective identity. *Academy of Management Review*, 30: 58–77.

Hatch, M. J. and Schultz, M. 2002. The dynamics of organizational identity. *Human Relations*, 55: 989–1018.

Heracleous, L. 2004. Interpretivist approaches to organizational discourse. In Grant, D., Phillips, N., Hardy, C., Putnam, L., and Oswick, C. (eds.), *Handbook of organizational discourse*. Beverly Hills, CA: Sage, 175–92.

2006. *Discourse, interpretation, organization*. Cambridge University Press.

Heracleous, L. and Jacobs, C. D. 2005. The serious business of play. *MIT Sloan Management Review*, Fall, 19–20.

2008. Crafting strategy: The role of embodied metaphors. *Long Range Planning*, 41: 309–25.

Hirsch, P. M. 1986. From ambushes to golden parachutes: Corporate takeovers as an instance of cultural framing and institutional integration. *American Journal of Sociology*, 91: 800–37.

Huff, A. S. 1990. *Mapping strategic thought*. Chichester: Wiley.

Jacobs, C. D. and Heracleous, L. 2005. Answers for questions to come: Reflective dialogue as an enabler of strategic innovation. *Journal of Organization Change Management*, 18: 338–52.

2006. Constructing shared understanding – the role of embodied metaphors in organization development. *Journal of Applied Behavioral Science*, 42: 207–26.

Jarzabkowski, P. 2003. Strategy as practice: recursiveness, adaptation, and practices-in-use. *Organization Studies*. 25: 529–60.

Johnson, G. 1987. *Strategic change and the management process*. Oxford: Blackwell.

Johnson, G., Melin, L., and Whittington, R. 2003. Micro strategy and strategizing: Towards an activity-based view. *Journal of Management Studies*, 40: 3–22.

Johnson, M. 1987. *The body in the mind: the bodily basis of meaning, imagination, and reason*. University of Chicago Press.

Johnson, M. and Lakoff, G. 2002. Why cognitive linguistics requires embodied realism. *Cognitive Linguistics*, 13: 245–63.

Lakoff, G. 1990. The invariance hypothesis: Is abstract reason based on image schemas? *Cognitive Linguistics*, 1: 39–74.

Lakoff, G. and Johnson, M. 1980. *Metaphors we live by*. Chicago University Press.

1999. *Philosophy in the flesh*. New York: Basic Books.

Lawson, B. 2006. *How designers think – The design process demystified*, 4th edn. Oxford: Architectural Press.

Marshak, R. 1993. Managing the metaphors of change. *Organizational Dynamics*, 22(1): 44–56.

Mintzberg, H. 1987. Crafting strategy. *Harvard Business Review*, 65(4): 66–75.

Morgan, G. 1980. Paradigms, metaphor and puzzle solving in organization theory. *Administrative Science Quarterly*, 25: 660–71.

1983. More on metaphor: Why we cannot control tropes in administrative science. *Administrative Science Quarterly*, 28: 601–7.

1986. *Images of organization*, Beverly Hills, CA: Sage.

Oliver, D. and Roos, J. 2007. Beyond text: Studying organizational identity multi-modally. *British Journal of Management*, 18: 342–58.

Palmer, I. and Dunford, R. 1996. Understanding organisations through metaphor. In Oswick, C. and Grant, D. (eds.), *Organisation Development: Metaphorical Explorations*. London: Pitman, 7–15.

Pettigrew, A. M. 1987. Context and action in the transformation of the firm. *Journal of Management Studies*, 24: 649–70.

Piaget, J. 1971. *Biology and knowledge*. University of Chicago Press.

Porter, M. E. 1975. *Note on the structural analysis of industries*, Harvard Business School Note no. 9–376–054.

1980. *Competitive strategy: Techniques for analyzing industries and competitors*. New York: Free Press.

1985. *Competitive advantage: Creating and sustaining superior performance*, New York: Free Press.

Pratt, M. and Rafaeli, A. 1997. Organizational dress as a symbol of multilayered social identities. *Academy of Management Journal*, 40: 862–98.

Regnér, P. 2003. Strategy creation in the periphery: Inductive versus deductive strategy making. *Journal of Management Studies*, 40: 57–82.

Samra-Fredericks, D. 2003. Strategizing as lived experience and strategists' everyday efforts to shape strategic direction. *Journal of Management Studies*, 40: 141–74.

2005. Strategic practice, "discourse" and the everyday interactional constitution of power effects. *Organization*, 12: 803–41.

Schein, E. 1999. *Process consultation revisited*. New York: Wiley.

Schultz, M. and Hatch, M. J. (eds.), 2004. *Organizational identity – A reader*. Oxford University Press.

Stern C. W. and Stalk, G. 1998. *Perspectives on strategy*. New York: Wiley.

Vaara, E. 2002. On the discursive construction of success/failure in narratives of post-merger integration. *Organization Studies*, 23: 211–48.

Vaara, E., Tienari, J., and Santti, R. 2003. The international match: metaphors as vehicles of social identity-building in cross-border mergers. *Human Relations*, 56, 419–51.

Weick, K. E. 1987. Substitutes for strategy. In Teece, D. J. (ed.), *The competitive challenge: Strategies for industrial innovation and renewal*. Cambridge, MA: Ballinger, 221–33.

Whittington, R. 2006. Completing the practice turn in strategy research. *Organization Studies*, 27: 613–34.

Whittington, R., Molloy, E., Mayer, M., and Smith, A. 2006. Practices of strategising/organising: Broadening strategy work and skills. *Long Range Planning*, 39: 615–29.

World Vision New Zealand

Making Strategy in a Day

Context and goal

In February 2010, the newly appointed CEO of World Vision New Zealand – an international humanitarian relief and development agency – convened a one-day meeting of all 120 staff throughout New Zealand with the aim of "creating a strategic plan in a day." He had spent the month since joining the organization listening to staff and supporters, who repeatedly told him the organization lacked a strategic direction and focus. However, he had also become convinced that the staff and supporters shared a clear, compelling yet unarticulated strategic direction that required a forum and adequate form for its expression. He hoped that over the course of one day, through a range of activities including constructing embodied metaphors, play, storytelling, workshops, music and video, the vision and priorities would emerge and could then be structured into a new strategic plan. He was trusting that the momentum of the day, coupled with the "unorthodox" strategy development methods would enable the

Chris Clarke (CEO World Vision New Zealand) has kindly provided his reflections on this workshop that he initiated and conducted.

FIGURE F.1 *Embodied metaphors at World Vision New Zealand.*

collective generation of a vision as well as a broad staff consensus on priorities.

Embodied metaphors

The day started with three cross-organizational staff teams presenting their embodied metaphors for "Where the organization has come from." The teams, comprising seven to ten people in each, were drawn from across the organization and prior to the day commencing had met to develop their models.

Not surprisingly, the metaphors differed between the teams; however, there were common themes, reflecting the organisation's focus on vulnerable children, injustice, poverty and transformation. One team's portrayal (see Figure F.1) was of a river connecting the founding of the organisation in war-torn Korea to today's international agency active throughout the world, supporting sustainable farming, building and equipping schools, investing in infrastructure and healthcare. The river, which started as a stream, had broadened over time, reflecting the increasing size and complexity of the work. The river braided at one point before converging once again, reflecting a sense that the organization had lost its way at one point. The lifeboat symbolized rescue from disasters such as tsunami, floods, famine, and war, and also those who had lost their lives in these events. The lighthouse represented World Vision's Christian identity. A piece of string running through the image represented the connection between donors and the "field."

Another team used the metaphor of a dancer in a war-torn field to represent movement, dexterity and beauty amid ashes. The dancer was portrayed standing in a blackened field representing the devastation wrought by famine and crop failure. Green shoots starting to appear represented hope, while the dancer's raised and outstretched arms reflected the global reach of the organisation's work.

The third group created a children's playground, reflecting World Vision's work to help create a world fit for children to play in. Some of the children playing were missing limbs, others were heavily bandaged. The group explained that in some communities children with physical and mental disabilities are kept away from other children, but that World Vision stood for a world where all children were valued and could enjoy the freedom and pleasure of play.

Mode of interaction and role of leaders

Each team decided how they would create their metaphors. One team started by immediately creating the models without any explicit prior planning. The role of the leader became one of helping synthesize the various metaphors into one meta-narrative of the river connecting war-torn Korea with today's global movement. The second team deliberately chose as their leader someone outside the existing leadership structure, to ensure existing organizational hierarchies did not get in the way of free expression. This group, which developed the metaphor of a children's playground, was particularly effective as the leader also came from a cultural minority and a non-academic background. This helped in encouraging quieter and more reflective members to engage. The third group who created the dancer metaphor comprised a regional team some distance from the head office. This group quickly adopted familiar roles in part because they were so used to working with each other.

Following each presentation, the entire team was asked to reflect back on the overall process of crafting strategy through embodied metaphors. All commented on how much fun they had had, including new insights into colleagues. All agreed that the discussions leading to the creation of the metaphors had been the most important step in the process. One participant in particular commented that the process of play and the use of metaphor had emboldened her to voice thoughts that she would not have felt comfortable sharing in a more traditional discussion forum.

Insights gained: how this session was strategically consequential for the organization

The session worked at a number of levels and was thus strategically relevant for several reasons. First, it was a fun team-building exercise. Secondly, it enabled participants and those observing to celebrate and reflect critically on the past. Looking back on the session some six months later, the CEO observed that it also enabled some "closure" for staff – i.e. the opportunity to reflect on a proud tradition, to discuss those parts of their experience that had not been so positive, and then to move forward. One presenter explained that this particular use of embodied metaphors, usually associated with children and play, meant his group was able to express some quite critical thoughts, which might otherwise have caused offence.

Thirdly, the aim of creating a strategic direction in a day was achieved, since the three presentations and resulting discussions helped frame the balance of the day, with subsequent presenters drawing on the various metaphors in the models. The novelty value of play, coupled with the momentum generated through the day meant that participants were willing to "go with the flow," rather than getting bogged down in detail or unnecessary side discussions. By the end of the day a broad consensus around a strategic direction and key goals had emerged, which was subsequently structured, codified and eventually approved by the Board.

Fourthly, the embodied metaphors themselves, such as a children's playground embodying the ideal of a world fit for all children to play in, captured the imagination of participants. At one level it was a very simple, almost naive metaphor, yet at another level it conveyed a depth of aspiration, insight and understanding of development that would have been hard to convey through more traditional means. Six months later the metaphor of a playground is still in common usage by staff and is now used to help introduce new staff and visitors to the work of World Vision NZ.

Finally the session proved very effective in helping identify leaders outside the formal leadership structures, particularly among staff who otherwise would have been reticent to put themselves forward.

CHAPTER NINE

The process of strategizing through crafting embodied metaphors

This chapter aims at providing readers with some practical guidance to assess when it would be most appropriate to use embodied metaphors, as a synthetic, divergent intervention approach; and when other, more convergent or analytical intervention approaches would be most appropriate. Thus, we set out by discussing occasions within organizational life that lend themselves to be explored or supported by embodied metaphors more than others. Then, we describe the generic process of crafting embodied metaphors and provide some guiding principles based on our experience. We finally discuss the organizational context and enabling conditions for the most effective use of the approach, and outline what can meaningfully be expected from our approach, and what cannot.

When is it most appropriate to craft embodied metaphors?

Playing seriously may not always be the most appropriate choice in all stages of strategizing. Since this process helps to manifest

This chapter draws from Heracleous and Jacobs (2008), Jacobs and Heracleous (2007) and Heracleous and Jacobs (2005).

differences and creative tensions, both through the crafting process as well as through the various constructions, it lends itself
particularly well to stages in strategizing where novelty, difference
and ambiguity are appreciated and can indeed be productive – for
example, when agents need a way to help them see a strategic challenge in a different light and explore alternatives in an open-ended
way. We described such issues throughout the book; for example, a
strategy team whose strategy-making process has lost its vitality and
creativity wants to reassess what an ideal strategizing process might
involve; a top management team whose organization was acquired,
and wants to reassess the organization's role in the overall portfolio of the buyer; or a bank's top management team that has a new
marketing approach that is ambiguous and not well understood,
that wants to explore what this approach may mean in practice.
These are situations where a creative, divergent, synthetic mode of
thinking would help.

On the other hand, if the challenge involves strategy execution,
where a management team already knows what it wants to achieve and
what the strategy is, and there is already a good understanding of what
the strategy means, then other types of intervention that involve convergent, analytical, conventional thinking would be more appropriate. These include for example, creating balanced scorecards (Kaplan
and Norton, 1996), creating a detailed 7-S models (Waterman, Peters,
and Phillips, 1980) or working through an ESCO (Environment,
Strategy, Core Competencies and Organization) model (Heracleous,
Wirtz, and Pangarkar, 2009) to develop ways to achieve alignment
between these elements.

Both types of thinking are necessary and complementary, as
Figure 9.1 shows.

It follows from the above discussion, that one should be clear
about the kind of strategic challenge that is faced, and the goal of
such an intervention, so as to assess whether the qualities of the

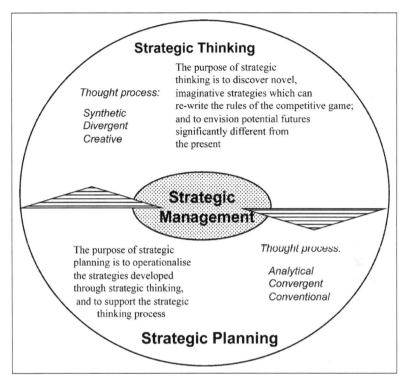

FIGURE 9.1 *Strategic thinking and strategic planning as complementary processes (Heracleous, 1998).*

process of crafting embodied metaphors fit with this purpose. If fostering divergent, synthetic, and creative thinking, or rendering visible differences of perspectives or viewpoints is at stake, then embodied metaphors might be an appropriate tool within the intervention repertoire.

In Table 9.1 we offer several illustrations (by no means exhaustive) which clarify which occasions might lend themselves better than others to the crafting process. We have clustered those in terms of strategy, organization and team related occasions and exemplify each with one of the cases included earlier in the book chapters.

TABLE 9.1: *Occasions and examples for using embodied metaphorical mapping*

	Case example	Goal of intervention	Main metaphors	Outcomes consequences
Strategy formation				
Examining competitive landscape	PackCo (Chapter 5)	Clarifying status of after-sales service offering.	PackCo as fortress; competitors as agile pirates.	Acknowledging strategic relevance of after-sales.
Reviewing strategy process	Orange UK Strategy Team (Chapter 6)	Reviewing and revitalizing strategy process.	Journey of a troop of disoriented animals traveling to the safari park.	Clarified focus and task of strategy team's role, core audience and ideal strategy process.
Identifying relevant challenges and an according strategic process	Hephata (Vignette D)	Identifying strategic challenges; defining a strategy process and initiatives.	Parallel towers of growing workload and shrinking staff base; old man carrying too much on his head.	Joint appreciation of competitive landscape and interrelationships among key actors – providing a solid ground for subsequent strategy development work.
Inclusive, large-scale strategy development	World Vision New Zealand (Vignette F)	Articulating a compelling, yet tacit consensus on a strategic vision; "Creating a strategic plan in a day."	Organization as river braided at one point – before converging – reflecting a sense that the organization had lost its way at some point.	A broad sense of a joint strategic direction provided a frame for subsequently specifying and codifying a strategic plan.
Organization				
Exploring organizational identity	Orange UK senior managers (Chapter 4)	Understanding Orange UK's new role within Orange Global.	Flotilla of ships traveling towards the lighthouse.	Reconsidering the role of the brand and appreciating the threat posed by an under-estimated competitor.

TABLE 9.1 (*cont.*)

	Case example	Goal of intervention	Main metaphors	Outcomes consequences
Designing organizational structure	UNICEF Germany (Vignette B)	Drafting a blueprint of a revised organizational structure.	Production line transforming child rights issues as the basis for successful fundraising.	Acknowledging the complexity of cross-functional interfaces and dependencies as well as structural inefficiencies.
Exploring a new go to market approach	SwissBank (Chapter 7)	Exploring and specifying a new go to market approach with first three management levels.	Set of two intersecting circles (of customer and bank); stages of developing mutual understanding.	Enabling participants to collectively make sense of this initially foreign concept; post-workshop debrief showed that concept required further explanation and discussion before launch.
Team				
Exploring team task identity	BASF PerForm (Vignette A)	Exploring consequences of a recent acquisition for the team's positioning in the division.	Platform of connection; clown face as enjoyment and commitment; absence of acquired firm in the model.	Realizing lack of transparency of offering; recognizing an overestimation of the readiness of acquired company for PerForm's offering at this stage.
Exploring interdisciplinary collaboration	Voltigo (Vignette C)	Exploring the status of a highly diverse, yet interdisciplinary collaborating team in terms of its cohesion, task and focus.	Six not yet connected person figures on a platform in a circle around a currently empty table.	Joint appreciation of lacking personal relationships; project focus and presence of all relevant professions – three key insights that prepared the ground for more focused development of this team.

TABLE 9.1 (*cont.*)

	Case example	Goal of intervention	Main metaphors	Outcomes consequences
Exploring client handling	Privatbank IHAG (Vignette E)	Raising awareness for responsiveness vis-à-vis clients and corresponding role expectations.	Protected zones of team competence with little interfaces to clients.	Acknowledging different approaches and values as the basis for individual development programs.

Crafting embodied metaphors – generic process steps and some guiding principles

Having clarified whether the issue in question lends itself to being explored through crafting embodied metaphors, the actual intervention process can then be designed. This is far from a standardized process, and it is most effective when designed to suit the context-specific needs of the participants. Crucial to the design is the specification of the goal of the construction process, which will form the core of the assignment that the group will jointly construct. Despite the customization needed for an effective intervention, there are some commonalities that in our experience proved useful and which should be taken into account when planning such sessions.

First step: warming-up to overcome concept resistance

In any group, some participants are initially skeptical about using material objects, let alone toy construction materials, for a serious purpose. They don't want to look ridiculous in front of their peers. These cognitive and emotional aspects need to be taken seriously and accounted for in the process. Thus, the process should not start directly with the "real" issue, but develop towards it by moving gradually from a playful start to the more serious issue. We typically start by warming-up individuals and the group with some playful exercises that aim at familiarizing them with the material and its expressive potential. Some of these exercises include:

1. Familiarizing participants with the material: asking them to individually build within two minutes the largest, widest or most stable structure possible.

2. Demonstrating the power of metaphorical mapping: Asking participants to build "just anything" and after approximately two to three minutes ask them how their model corresponds to, for example, their country's rail service, their worst flight experience, the United Nations or any other well-known source domain.

3. Demonstrating the power of narrative: asking participants to build their job or family, for example, and after approximately five minutes asking them to tell the story of their job to their colleagues.

At this stage, in our experience, individuals and the group will have "warmed-up" to the idea of exploring a serious issue by means of this technique. Skipping these exercises is tempting ("for the sake of time"), but risky: People tend to both overestimate their "building capabilities" and underestimate the extent of often silent concept resistance by some team members.

> Guiding principles: Do anticipate and take concept resistance seriously. And: Do not skip the warm-up exercises – they are critical to the success of the intervention.

Second step: build the real issue individually

At this stage, participants are asked to individually build the real, serious issue that is at stake in the workshop. One pivotal aspect in the design of such processes is the choice of focus or strategic challenge that the group will construct as an embodied metaphor. It should be broad enough to be a meaningful issue with strategic relevance, but also specific enough so that it taps into participants' practical experience and can subsequently inform this experience. This can range from rather generic assignments, such as "Build a model of your organization/department/team," to rather specific assignments such as "Build a model of the most pressing competitive challenge the organization is currently faced with." The most important consideration here is that the assignment is brief, precise and clear. People tend to interpret the assignment in various ways, and it is precisely the experience of these unexpected differences in perception that a supposedly unambiguous assignment can result in. The individual models should then be debriefed in detail and probed through the debriefing steps outlined below. Debriefing should ideally start at the artifactual level ("What do we see here – what are the key components of the physical construction?"), then proceed to the meaning level ("What does the model represent or mean?"). By initially distinguishing these two levels, participants are trained to "read" the models in these two distinct, yet interrelated ways.

Guiding principles: Do phrase the serious issue as briefly yet as precisely as you can. And: Debrief step by step: first the physical model, then its meaning.

Third step: build the real issue collectively

When the sessions are under way, sufficient time must be set aside, since rushed play sessions lose much of their effectiveness as functional and goal-constrained thinking takes over when participants feel compelled to achieve something by the deadline. Leaders should ideally be involved in such sessions, and if so, they should act as "serious team players," just members of the group, and be conscious of the potential that any defensive or dominating behavior by them would probably lead to the construction of "politically correct" structures, lacking insight, creativity, and challenge, whereby the process would risk degenerating into a meaningless exercise.

After the debrief of the individual models resulting from step two above, participants should be invited to explore the different models for commonalities and differences at the level of meaning. Despite differences at the artifactual level, which components are intended to mean similar things? Which elements are unique to an individual model? This exploration prepares participants to then engage in a collective process of creating a joint, single model of the serious issue the intervention aims to explore. It is here where the process is at its most serious stage. Subject to the micro-political stakes that the assignment in view of the group configuration involves, a most intense meaning negotiation is likely to occur. Which meaning is best represented through which artifact, where it should be placed vis-à-vis others, in which color and height, are all important details when participants strive for "getting it right." Encouraging participants thereby to make use of the three-dimensional qualities of the construction is crucial: what does the model look like from different angles? From above, north, east, south, west, at the height of the table? What new perspectives are gained, and which questions are triggered by changing perspective? Why is a certain component the highest thing on the table?

Again, it is important to debrief the model step by step, starting with artifact ("What do we see here?") then meaning ("What is this intended to mean?") and also the group's construction process ("How did you as a group go about constructing this model? What were the different roles/contributions here?"). For example, when we asked the St. Gallen Fulltime MBA Class of 2007 to build "a model of ideal team work," it was not only artifact and meaning that provided insights for participants, but also the fact that we debriefed how they worked as a team when working on this assignment. Equally, when we asked participants of the Oxford Strategic Leadership Program to build a "model of leadership," we also asked how leadership was enacted in the construction process.

Such questions help participants to engage in reflective thinking about group dynamics and their own contribution in these dynamics.

> Guiding principles: Debrief in three steps; from artifactual, via meaning, to collective construction process. Debrief the collective model in as much detail as possible: every artifactual detail can have meaning – even unintended. Check for a collective sense of having it "right" as the model takes shape. Check for things that are not on the table – why not? Check for relevance and appropriateness in terms of relative positioning, size, height, color or other features of (parts of) the model.

Fourth step: capture the insights gained

The technique can lead to facilitators getting overexcited with the intervention technique and neglecting or ignoring the challenge of capturing and translating back what workshop participants have experienced and concluded. Decoding an embodied metaphor requires a highly situational and subtle understanding of the symbols, meanings and images mobilized in creating a more or less coherent narrative. In other words, if you weren't there, you won't be able to read it in all its subtleties, if at all. A prerequisite to gain the most of the embodied metaphor approach is thus to make sure that you capture and document the process and outcomes in as much detail as possible. Arguably, the experience of the process is messy, which is part of its beauty and generative potential, but it is also a challenge. Thus, make sure someone takes detailed pictures of the models. But equally important, make sure someone captures important results and insights gained.

> Guiding principle: Plan for documenting the process and outcomes, at least in terms of pictures, and importantly in a mode (such as memoing or ideally a video recording) that allows capturing of the process and translation of the findings back to the organization.

A note on the materials

Over the years, we have experimented with a wide range of materials that can be used for crafting embodied metaphors. Most generally, materials without preconfigured meaning, such as wooden bricks or clay, have the benefit of a "white sheet" effect, that is, the meaning is mainly, if not exclusively, attributed by participants; though this means creation "from scratch" might be a bit more time-consuming. Materials with preconfigured meaning, on the other hand, such as toy construction materials, have the benefit of providing participants swiftly with rich images, but come at the expense of influencing participants' imagination. And yet, either types of material come with constraints that make certain types of constructions more likely than others. For instance, if you have a lump of white clay, it is possible but less likely that you will represent your competitor in terms of an alligator – which is more likely if you have an alligator figure in your material base. In turn however, white clay allows for more exploratory models, since no preconfigured meaning is attached to a lump of white clay. In the end, a combination of materials seems advisable. For instance, we have used in our interventions combinations of Lego, Tyco and Kazi toy construction materials, Mega Bloks, Play-Doh clay and generic wooden bricks. Doyle and Sims (2002) go as far as to suggest the use of just any mundane artifact, such as pen, paper or a bunch of keys to create what they call cognitive sculptures. Table 9.2 summarizes our guiding principles for each process step.

Context and conditions for crafting embodied metaphors

Crafting embodied metaphors cannot simply be spontaneous as far as organizational context is concerned. It must be organized and resourced adequately, simultaneously allowing for enough "foolishness" to emerge, within a frame that aims to explore and deliver insights on real strategic issues. This presupposes that the leaders of

TABLE 9.2: *Guiding principles for designing embodied metaphor interventions*

Generic steps	Guiding principles
First step: warming-up to overcome concept resistance	Do anticipate and take concept resistance seriously.
	Do not skip the warm-up exercises – they are critical to the success of the intervention.
Second step: building the real issue individually	Do phrase the serious issue as briefly and as precisely as you can.
	Debrief step by step: first the model, then what it is intended to mean.
Third step: building the real issue collectively	Debrief in three steps; from artifactual, via meaning, to the collective construction process.
	Debrief the collective model in as much detail as possible: every artifactual detail can have meaning – even unintended.
	Check for a collective sense of having it "right" as the model takes shape.
	Check for things that are not on the table – why not?
	Check for relevance and appropriateness in terms of relative positioning, size, height, color or other features of the model or its parts.
Fourth step: capturing the insights gained	Plan for documentation at least in terms of photos, and importantly in a mode (such as memoing or ideally a video recording) that allows capturing of the process and the translation of the findings back to the organization.

an organization have reflected on what the significant strategic challenges are, have committed to exploring them further through creative processes and provide an appropriate amount of resources for effective exploration.

Embodied metaphors are collective creations, and therefore from a political perspective, they can make it easier for contentious issues to be placed on the agenda for discussion. Any individuals would be unlikely to bring such issues up on their own, but as part of a group such issues are easier to surface.

A skilled facilitator is useful in helping to bring about a healthy and productive generation, debate and integration of ideas. Being aware of group-specific play dynamics, a facilitator can ensure for example that the embodied metaphor that is created is a genuinely interactive and group-based product. A capable facilitator would also help the group effectively debate the structures that were created, and their implications in terms of organizational action, by homing in and inviting critical debate on potentially insightful aspects of the construction, as well as to systematically capture the insights gained that can then be translated into a more conventional format of corporate communication that can form crucial input to subsequent, more formal procedures of strategizing. Leaders face a challenge here: they need to have the emotional maturity to accept objectively and gracefully the implied critique that arises from such constructions; for example, by the way they are portrayed or by the organizational shortcomings and strategic misalignments that may become apparent. If they are able to participate in the process in a collaborative, non-dominating and graceful way, then the benefits arising from the strategic conversations will be significant. Leaders can then anticipate that the gene pool of strategic ideas will be enlarged through a process that fosters out-of-the-box thinking, as well as involving managers in inter-disciplinary, inter-divisional teams that may not conventionally have access to the strategy process. Leaders might also enhance ownership, acceptance and commitment to their strategy by participating in the play process in the same manner as all other participants. It follows that the organization should take play seriously; it must endeavor to capture insights from the session, and act on them. Often participants take back to their organization and display the actual constructions, as a reminder of the debate, issues arising, insights gained, and strategic directions decided upon. Even if such insights and directions are uncomfortable, organizations should be prepared to face and capitalize on them in a productive and developmental manner.

Expected outcomes – or is the process the outcome?

What type of outcomes can be expected from the use of embodied metaphors? Not surprisingly, it neither produces a detailed quantitative analysis of the competition, nor a detailed budget spreadsheet, nor a fully fledged chart. But it can provide crucial input when developing each of these. Crafting embodied metaphors helps to clarify differences in mental maps, political fence lines, topical misunderstanding and so forth. It also helps to paint the world with a rough brush, so that people can develop a shared understanding of what the map looks like, and then are more likely to agree on the right way forward when being in the actual territory.

Even though we are highly sympathetic to organization development and process-oriented interventions, we'd like to point to two of the biggest misunderstandings with this kind of intervention. First, OD purists/optimists risk misreading the effectiveness of the intervention in replacing an entire strategy or development process. Even though the technique can play a crucial role in delivering insights to pressing strategic issues, and even new strategic directions, it may not offer a fully fledged strategy complete with implementation actions (something that would need more analytical modes of thinking), and cannot replace longer-term OD interventions. Secondly, OD purists/optimists risk misreading the group *process* for the main, if not exclusive, *outcome*. However, in organizations, non-participants would like to see the outcomes of the strategy retreat of their top management team, or whoever participated. We'd like to emphasize that, yes indeed, outcomes matter. The process quality is one outcome, but is not the only one. So it is important to capture insights and outcomes and reflect on how they can be mobilized further in organization and strategy development processes.

Some outcomes that are highly relevant to executives, managers, strategists and organization development practitioners include:

- *Shifting mental models*: The process of crafting and decoding embodied metaphors can deliver insights and potential shifts in managers' mind-sets that would have been difficult to gain in more conventional, numbers-driven, board-meeting style sessions.
- *Make strategy tangible*: It provides a context where senior teams can surface and debate contentious or critical management issues, by formulating these issues as embodied metaphors that are imbued with meaning and that can be debated from a variety of perspectives.
- *Tapping into more creative and less analytical domains and developing a shared language*: The practice of crafting embodied metaphors in strategizing draws on rich imagery and stories, rather than dry statistics and figures, and thus helps to develop a memorable shared language that the group can draw on in future strategizing.
- *Team cohesion*: The process fosters effective team-building, enables an increased sense of involvement and ownership of the issues and decisions taken by participants, and thus facilitates more effective implementation of these decisions.
- *Democratizing effect*: The recursive, co-creative potential of the process of crafting embodied metaphors enables the involvement of other organizational members than formal strategists, and those who do not tend to participate in other types of group conversations.
- *Lowering the entry level for strategic conversation*: Since crafting embodied metaphors involves a practice of painting a three-dimensional map with a rough brush, even "lay" strategists can be invited to join the strategic conversation.
- *Anticipating road blocks for implementation*: Crafting embodied metaphors can also raise issues of implementation and alignment

at a very early stage of the process and can thus lead to revisions in strategy, the implementation plan, or even the need to garner political support before any initiatives are undertaken.

We started this book with two main aims. The first was to provide a sound conceptual basis for strategic thinking through crafting embodied metaphors, which has been a significant gap in the strategic management literature. The second was to provide applied illustrations and guidelines for putting the crafting of embodied metaphors into practice, through not only several vignettes, but also in-depth analysis of workshops where this process has been employed, discussion of how it was employed, and distillation of the principles involved. We hope we have succeeded in both these aims, and that our discussions will inform and inspire other scholars to continue along the path of understanding the other side of strategizing; the creative, divergent and synthetic side that has not to date received the attention it deserves.

REFERENCES

Heracleous, L. 1998. Strategic thinking or strategic planning? *Long Range Planning* 31: 481–7.

Heracleous, L. and Jacobs, C. 2005. The serious business of play. *MIT Sloan Management Review.* 47(1): 19–20.

2008. Developing strategy: The serious business of play. In Gallos, J. (ed.) 2008. *Business leadership,* 2nd edn. San Francisco, CA: Jossey Bass, Chapter 25: 324–35.

Heracleous, L., Wirtz, J., and Pangarkar, N. 2009. *Flying high in a competitive industry: Secrets of the world's leading airline.* Singapore: McGraw-Hill.

Jacobs, C. and Heracleous, L. 2007. Strategizing through playful design. *Journal of Business Strategy.* 28(4): 75–80.

Kaplan, R. S. and Norton, D. P. 1996. *Translating strategy into action: The balanced scorecard.* Cambridge, MA: Harvard Business School Press.

Waterman, R. H., Peters, T. J., and Phillips, J. R. 1980. Structure is not organization. *Business Horizons,* June: 14–26.

Glossary

This glossary provides definitions of useful terms relating to crafting strategy and embodied metaphors.

Ambiguity Ambiguity and uncertainty are fundamental occasions for sensemaking. While one aspect of uncertainty refers to a situation where future consequences of present action cannot precisely be estimated, ambiguity is characterized by a situation where too many interpretations exist. Uncertainty can be reduced (but not eliminated) with access to more relevant information. In contrast, ambiguity as confusion refers to a situation in which several different interpretations at the same time emerge and persist so that additional information cannot resolve the confusion. Multiple interpretations and meanings that create confusion call for social construction and invention of meaning, and developing shared understandings in conducive conversational modes and settings. Metaphorial reasoning is often involved in ambiguity handling, as Karl Weick (1995) proposed.

Analogical reasoning Cognitive process of applying knowledge from a relatively familiar domain (the source) to another less familiar domain (the target), aiming to improve understanding or gain further insights with respect to the target. It involves two forms of analogy, namely superficial similarity recognizing correspondences between the features of the objects in the source and target domains; and structural similarity recognizing a semblance of the deep structures within the source and target domains. Main proponent in organization studies has been Haridimos Tsoukas (1993).

Craftsmanship Skillful manual work, often associated with practical knowledge in the making of unique, singular objects. US sociologist Richard Sennett refers to craftsmanship more generally as the skill of making things well and considers craftsmanship as an enduring, basic human impulse, the desire to do a job well for its own sake. Such impulse is not limited to traditional manual workers but similarly applies to artists, doctors, laboratory technicians or computer programmers. In this book, following Mintzberg's classic article on crafting strategy, we extend and apply the concept to craftsmanship to strategy process, specifically crafting of embodied metaphors within facilitated strategy workshops.

Design thinking and process Lacking a universal definition, design can be both a noun and a verb, and in this way refer to a product as well as a process. Different professions scope it differently: design as a systematic, quasi-scientific sequence of steps whereby the requirements and desired specifications of the end product are known (e.g. structural engineering), design as a fluid, open-ended, inspirational practice (e.g. fashion design), design as systematic yet imaginative process (e.g. architecture). As discussed in Chapter 1 of this book, Lawson (2006) suggested an integrated design process model involving six broad stages.

Formulating: effectively identifying, stating, understanding, exploring, and providing structure to ill-structured design problems.

Representing: externalizing ideas and thoughts through models, sketches or prototypes.

Moving: creating solution ideas, or moves, thereby distinguishing between lateral design moves (the extension of an existing idea or its application to a new setting), and vertical design moves (the development of a novel idea).

Bringing problems and solutions together: since in design practice, problem and solution rarely follow a clear, linear sequence, maintaining a sense of ambiguity and fluidity and not getting too concerned about the one single right answer or silver bullet during the process is crucial to good design.

Evaluating: integrating objective/technical as well as subjective/aesthetic judgments in making choices among competing designs – while temporarily suspending judgment so as to maintain the creative flow.

Reflecting: reflecting in action as well as on action – on how designers go about the design process itself, on the design philosophy and guiding principles they follow.

Dialogue Reflective mode of communication; in contrast to competitive, zero-sum modes of advocating one's viewpoint such as adversarial debate. Dialogue facilitates mutual understanding and critical self-reflection; combines diagnostic with generative elements. Proponents in organization studies include Edgar Schein (1993) and William Isaacs (1999).

Discourse In its most basic form, a discourse is a collection of texts. Discourse theory has a variety of antecedents ranging from social theory, to linguistics, to hermeneutics and rhetoric. In critical theory discourses as collections of texts construct subject positions and identities and reflect dominant power arrangements. From a structurational perspective, discourses are a duality of communicative actions, both verbal and textual, that are patterned and underlied by certain structural features, and that are constructive of social and organizational reality (Heracleous and Barrett, 2001).

Discourse analysis A set of approaches in social science that focus on analysis of textual data; exploring these in terms of such aspects as how they construct meaning, how they link to social practices and their intertextual relationships. Organizational discourse analyses often aim to reconstruct (or deconstruct) objects and concepts as they appear in discourse, such as organizational culture, identity, or collaboration, and tend to be underpinned by a social constructionist ontology. Proponents in organization studies include Nelson Phillips and Cynthia Hardy (2002).

Embodied metaphors Metaphors that are created through our body and that have a body, a physical existence in three-dimensional space. Embodied engagement as our mode of being in the world is actualized in the making of these constructions; they are metaphors in the flesh that are recursively and simultaneously constructed and interpreted; they embody the blending of source and target domains, and engender meanings both in the construction process and subsequent interpretations. They are material exemplars of metaphorical image-schemas, since they draw from particular source domains to represent target domains such as organizational or divisional identity or group task, as perceived by organizational actors. The process of constructing these metaphorical structures through the engagement of the corporeal body actualizes the experiential perspective on embodiment and results in these constructions as unique artifacts, metaphors-in-the-flesh providing access to agents' thoughts and interpretations.

Embodied realism A position in philosophy and cognitive science assuming that we perceive and understand physical and social reality through the way our body shapes our experiences and perceptions through ongoing patterns of interactions with the world; from this perspective there is no ultimate separation of mind and body. Furthermore, it posits that we perceive social reality via our image schemas, themselves both metaphorical as well as with a neurological basis, and arising from the way we exist, experience and interact with the world in and through our bodies. Research from an embodied realist perspective operates ideographically and seeks to gain understanding through focus on the embodied nature of interpretation, the constructive role of metaphors, and aspects such as space and inter-relationships. Main proponents include George Lakoff and Mark Johnson (1999).

Embodiment Process of cognition and being in the world based on and shaped by our bodily experience. Rohrer (2007) distinguished four modes of usage: first, a metatheoretical mode that sees embodiment as inherent to cognition and which stands against a Cartesian philosophy that views knowledge and thought as distinctly and ideally separate from any bodily involvement or perspective. Secondly, a perspective on embodiment as broadly an experiential phenomenon, relating for example to how socio-cultural aspects such as child-rearing practices can influence cognition and language, to the phenomenology of the lived experience of our bodies and its influence on our self-identities, or to our bodies as enablers of particular, subjective vantage points. Thirdly, embodiment as the physical substrate of experience, as for example in studies of the unconscious neurophysiological processing that enables routine cognitive activities. Fourthly, embodiment has a temporal dimension in that organisms go through developmental changes over time that relate to their ability to acquire certain cognitive skills, and in the context of longer time frames and as whole species, through evolutionary developments such as humans' acquired ability to use language.

Hermeneutics Hermeneutics is the art of interpreting texts, initially religious texts but gradually being extended to all kinds of texts including action or artifacts viewed as text. Whereas hermeneutics traditionally had epistemological concerns, it is more recently concerned with the theory of understanding and interpretation itself, and the nature of being, moving to the ontological arena. The three main meanings associated with the term hermeneutics in ancient Greek usage are first saying or expressing something, secondly explaining or clarifying something drawing on context and pre-understanding, and thirdly translating, or mediating between two different worlds (Palmer, 1969).

Image schemata Patterns of bodily experience that enable the structuring of bodily interactions with the world at more abstract levels. Image schemata – figurative, analogical and non-propositional in nature – emerge primarily from spatial relations, and more particularly from perceptual interactions with the manipulation of objects. Human thought is organized through metaphorical elaborations of image schemata that form and structure experience and understanding. Thus, meaning is firmly rooted in, and emerges from bodily experiences. In this respect, metaphors become constitutive for structuring bodily experience and also emerge from this experience. Metaphors are often based on characteristics found in the physical world, as illustrated by the three generic image schemata of up/down, container, and link or connection. Main proponents include George Lakoff and Mark Johnson (1980, 1987, 1990).

Interpretivism A social science paradigm inspired by the German idealist tradition, beginning with Kant's emphasis on the importance of a priori knowledge of mind as logically and ontologically preceding efforts to grasp empirical experience. This tradition challenged the dominant paradigm of sociological positivism on the grounds that science was not, and could not be value-free and able to offer objective, unmediated access to universal truth as assumed; and secondly, that the nomothetic methods employed in the natural sciences aiming to identify general laws and causal explanation were unsuitable for the "cultural sciences," whose domain was human life, its processes and outcomes (Burrell and Morgan, 1979). From an interpretive perspective, social life is not a predetermined, independent universe of objects that are there to be discovered and their stable interactions analyzed, but is instead an ongoing, skilled, contingent accomplishment constituted by active and reflexive agents. Agency is seen as intentional but constrained, as historically located and both bounded and enabled by broader structures.

Linguistic turn A movement in Western philosophy beginning in the twentieth Ccentury that recognizes and engages with the fundamental role of language as constructive and constitutive of social reality rather than merely representative and functional. Associated with Ludwig Wittenstein's later thinking in *Philosophical Investigations* (1967) as well as with the philosopher Richard Rorty (1967).

Mental model Cognitive structure through which individuals make sense of current stimuli in the context of longer-term perceptive repertoires. Highly local and contextual and developed primarily in the context of social and cultural practices; they shape arguments, interpretation and ultimately action.

Metaphorical mapping Typically a linguistic, in our case here also a physical, process of mapping a source onto a target domain; thereby not only existing meaning is transferred from source to target domain; rather the interaction of source and target domain often generate new meaning.

Metaphor Viewing A (target domain) in terms of B (source domain). On the surface, a figure of speech, but more substantively a fundamental process of perception where a less known domain is conceptualized in terms of with a more familiar domain. Also the archetype for a broader set of tropes such as metonymy, synecdoche, simile and analogy.

Phenomenology A position in philosophy that highlights the embodied nature of human experience and reasoning. In a radical rejection of the Cartesian dichotomy, the body is seen as mediating human perception and experience of the world: "I am my body" (Merleau-Ponty, 1962: 159). Human embodied existence is experienced and expressed prior to conscious processes of thinking; thus phenomena are not only purely cognitive but enacted in and through the body.

Play Basic human activity typically mostly occurring in childhood. It involves exploratory, experimental dialogue with materials and rules; is associated with development of cognitive skills, the capacity to understand meaning in context as well as the development of social institutions and forms of cultural identity. There are two forms of play, namely competitive games, whereby ex ante rules structure the play process to determine a winner; and exploratory play, whereby the material, its usage and the rules are continuously and often simultaneously being written and rewritten.

Positivism A paradigm in philosophy and social science that operates from the assumption of essentialist realism, that reality is rule-governed, external, fixed, and independent of observers' perception and experience. In terms of gaining knowledge, it posits a rationalist perspective, namely that knowledge derives from pure reason and can be expressed and analysed in terms of formal logic or other symbolic systems. Research from a positivist perspective seeks to uncover universal regularities and causal laws of a rule-governed reality via survey instruments and statistical analysis so that valid predictions can be made. A proponent of positivism in organization studies is Lex Donaldson (1996).

Practice turn A position in philosophy and the social sciences that emphasizes the relevance of actual, everyday, mundane activities (praxis) and institutionalized routines guiding these (practices) for our understanding of social behavior. Schatzki (2001) defines practices as embodied, materially mediated arrays of human activity centrally organized around a shared practical understanding, and identifies three common themes of a practice perspective. First, a practice view foregrounds actual human activities, and thereby highlights the potential relevance of even the most mundane ones. Then, any such praxis is considered to be situated in a field of practices that in turn provides the necessary communal resources for sensemaking and action. Finally, a practice view emphasizes the role of human actors, their skills and resources in carrying out their activities. Proponents of the practice turn include Pierre Bourdieu (1990) and Michel de Certeau (1984).

Sensemaking Process by which we give meaning to experience. In organization studies, Karl Weick (1995) suggested that sensemaking involves the following seven properties: it is grounded in the construction of individual and organizational identity; retrospective in nature; based on enacting "sensable" environments to deal with; fundamentally a social, not an individual process; ongoing; focused on cues in the environment; and driven by the plausibility of possible interpretations.

Serious play Educational approach fostering ethical behaviour. Suggested initially by Plato, combines playful interaction with serious intent; one of the conceptual cornerstones of Lego Serious Play, a structured, trademarked intervention technique owned by Lego company – recently gone open source.

Social constructionism A position in philosophy and social science that operates from an ideationist perspective, namely that social (and for some authors even material) reality is context-dependent, shifting, based on perspective, values and interests of observer. There are no fixed essences but only ephemeral social constructions. Embracing an early philosophical empiricism, it assumes that we can only know reality through our sense perceptions or mental constructs, rather than a priori. Research from a social constructionist perspective operates ideographically, namely it seeks to gain understanding of unique life-worlds through in-depth immersion and direct, empathetic engagement. Reflexivity is essential in this endeavor. Main proponents include Peter Berger and Thomans Luckmann (1967), and Kenneth Gergen (1999).

Strategy-as-practice A perspective in organization studies that aims to mobilize the broader practice turn in social sciences in the field of strategic management. Rather than conceiving of strategy as a position that a firm has, the practice-based view of strategy views strategy as an activity, something that organizations and their members actually do. Strategy is conceptualized as a situated, socially accomplished activity that is consequential for the organization. A practice-based view of strategy aims to understand the messy realities of doing strategy as a lived experience and how people go about the process of making strategy. It is one of the fastest growing research communities with presence at the Academy of Management (Special Interest Group) and the European Group of Organizational Studies (Standing Working Group).

Technology of foolishness Practice or method that – in contrast to technologies of reason – assumes an emergent and transitional nature of purpose, encourages ambiguity and fluidity of action, and accepts a relaxation of functionally rational imperatives. The basic human activity of play would qualify as a technology of foolishness. Term was initially introduced by James March (1979).

Technology of reason Practice or method that tends to presuppose a pre-existing purpose for action; insists on the necessity of consistency among actions, and rests on the primacy of functional rationality. Rational forms of planning in organization are one example for a technology of reason. Term was initially introduced by James March (1979).

REFERENCES

Berger, P. and Luckmann, T. 1967. *The social construction of reality*. London: Penguin.

Bourdieu, P. 1990. *The logic of practice*. Cambridge Polity.

Burrell, G. and Morgan, G. 1979. *Sociological paradigms and organizational analysis*. Andover: Gower.

de Certeau, M. 1984. *The practice of everyday life*. Berkeley, CA: University of California Press.

Donaldson, L. 1996. *For positivist organization theory*. London: Sage.

Gergen, K. 1999. *An invitation to social construction*. Beverley Hills, CA: Sage.

Heracleous, L. and Barrett, M. 2001. Organizational change as discourse: Communicative actions and deep structures in the context of IT Implementation. *Academy of Management Journal*, 44: 755–78.

Heracleous, L. and Jacobs, C. 2008. Understanding organizations through embodied metaphors. *Organization Studies*, 29(1): 45–78.

Jacobs, C. and Heracleous, L. 2006. Constructing shared understanding – the role of embodied metaphors in organization development. *Journal of Applied Behavioral Science*, 42(2): 207–26.

Isaacs, W. 1999. *Dialogue and the art of thinking together*. New York: Doubleday.

Johnson, M. 1987. *The body in the mind: The bodily basis of meaning, imagination, and reason*. University of Chicago Press.

Lakoff, G. 1990. The invariance hypothesis: Is abstract reason based on image schemas? *Cognitive Linguistics*, 1: 39–74.

Lakoff, G. and Johnson, M. 1980. *Metaphors we live by*. University of Chicago Press.

Lakoff, G. and M. Johnson. 1999. *Philosophy in the flesh*. New York: Basic Books.

Lawson, B. 2006. *How designers think – The design process demystified*, 4th edn. Oxford: Architectural Press.

March, J. G. 1979. The technology of foolishness. In March, J. G. and Olsen, J. P. (eds.), *Ambiguity and choice in organizations*. Bergen: Universitetsforlaget, 69–81.

Merleau-Ponty, M. 1962. *Phenomenology of perception*. London: Routledge.

Palmer, R. E. 1969. *Hermeneutics*. Evanston, IL: Northwestern University Press.

Phillips, N. and Hardy, C. 2002. *Discourse analysis: Investigating processes of social construction*. London: Sage.

Rohrer, T. 2007. The body in space: Embodiment, experientialism and linguistic conceptualization. In Ziemke, T., Zlatev, J. and Frank, R. (eds.), *Body, language and mind*, Vol. 1. Berlin: Mouton de Gruyter.

Rorty, R. 1967. *The linguistic turn: Recent essays in philosophical method*. University of Chicago Press.

Schatzki, T.R. 2001. Introduction: practice theory. In Schatzki, T. R., Knorr Cetina, K. and von Savigny, E. (eds.), *The Practice Turn in Contemporary Theory*. New York: Routledge, 1–14.

Schein, E.H. 1993. On dialogue, culture, and organizational learning. *Organizational Dynamics*, 22(2): 40–51.

Tsoukas, H. 1993. Analogical reasoning and knowledge generation in organization theory. *Organization Studies*, 14: 323–46.

Weick, K. 1995. *Sensemaking in organizations*. Beverly Hills, CA: Sage.

Wittgenstein, L. 1967. *Philosophical investigations*, 3rd edn. Oxford: Blackwell.

Index

Abell, D. F., 6
Albert, S., 195
Alderfer, C. P., 158
Alvesson, M., 22
ambiguity, 9, 24, 26, 30, 93, 94, 210.
    See also sensemaking
American Psychological Association, 151
analogical reasoning, 28–33, 97–9.
    See also recursive embodied
    enactment. *See also* domain
    (source and target)
analogically mediated inquiry, 30–2, 123,
    197
Ansoff, H. I., 5
Argyris, C., 9
Aristotle, 23
Armenakis, A., 25, 157
Ast, F., 51, 54
Astley, W. G., 34, 44

Baden Fuller, C., 6, 102
Balogun, J., 180
Barrett, F. J., 22, 23, 97, 104, 194
Barrett, M., 22, 47, 49
Barry, D., 22, 30, 123, 177, 182
Barthes, R., 54
BASF, 1–3
Bedeian, A., 25, 157
Berger, P., 34, 183
Bittner, E., 43

Black, M., 22, 23, 32, 157
body, 28–9, 177. *See also* hand
Bougon, M. G., 27
Bourdieu, P., 76, 80
Bourgeois, V. W., 22, 24
Brickson, S. L., 195
Broussine, M., 123, 158
Brown, D. L., 158
Brown, J. L., 54
Brown, J. S., 76, 103
Brown, S. M., 27
Buergi, P., 14, 32, 123, 125, 177, 180
Burke, W. W., 25, 157, 194
Burrell, G., 43

CAD (computer assisted design), 69–70
Calori, R., 27
cheirotechnon, 68
Choi, D., 102
Clark, T., 158
Clarke, I., 27
Cleary, C., 25, 26, 159
Coghlan, D., 107, 164
cognitive sculpting, 31–2. *See also*
    thinking
Cole, M., 94
competitive advantage, 5–6, 91
Cooperrider, D. L., 23, 97, 194
Corley, K., 195
Cornelissen, J., 35

craftsmanship. *See also* recursive embodied
  enactment. *See also* play. *See also*
  hand
  and CAD, 69–70
  as strategic practice, 76–8
  community-based, 67–9
  defined, 65–6
  in Enlightenment era, 70
  organization of, 199–200, 219–24
  tools in, 72–3

de Certeau, M., 76
decisionmaking, 6, 8–12, 179
Declerck, R. P., 5
deductive strategy, 25, 157
Deetz, S., 178
demioergos, 68
Denzin, N., 46
design
  process, 8–12
  thinking, 7
dialogue, 103–11, 151–4
Dijk, T. A. V., 22
Dilthey, W., 43, 44, 45, 46, 50, 52, 54, 150
discourse, 33, 180–1
domain (source and target), 8, 22–4, 33,
  54–5, 78, 135–42, 180–6. *See also*
  analogical reasoning
Donaldson, L., 153
double hermeneutics, 46, 49–50, 185
Doyle, J. R., 31, 123, 219
Duguid, P., 76, 103
Dukerich, J., 195
Dunford, R., 24, 25, 158, 194

Eco, U., 46
Eden, C., 27
Elliott, R., 32
Elmes, M., 22, 177, 182
embodied metaphors. *See also* sensemaking.
  See also play. *See also* hermeneutics
  analysis, 135–48
  benefits of, 197–9
  future research in, 168–9
  interpretation, 48–50, 167–8
  materials in, 219
  occasions for use, 209–11
  process steps in, 214–18
embodied realism, 34–8, 151–4, 182–3
Enlightenment era, 70
Eysenck, M. W., 38

facilitator, 159–65, 185, 199–200, 221
Fiol, C. M., 181, 195
Fish, S. E., 103
foolishness. *See* play
Forbus, K. D., 97
Forceville, C., 124
Ford, J. D., 22, 104
Ford, L. W., 22, 104
Foreman, P., 195
Frery, 5
Fribourg. *See* VOLTIGO
Friedlander, F., 158

Gadamer, H. G., 51, 52, 53, 56, 94
Gardner, H., 32
Geertz, C., 74, 94
Gentner, D., 97
Gergen, K. J., 22, 80, 104, 183
Gergen, M. M., 104
Gherardi, S., 76, 80
Gibbs, R. W., 81, 125, 128, 186
Giddens, A., 43, 46, 49, 50, 54, 76, 80
Gioia, D., 195
Golden, B., 195
Grant, D., 24, 32
guiding principles (of embodied metaphors),
  214–18

Hadar, U., 79
hand, 71–2, 78–9. *See also* craftsmanship.
  See also body
Harel, I., 80
Harrington, A., 45
Hatch, M. J., 182
Hayes, R. L., 5
Heath, C., 126, 128
Heidegger, M., 51, 52
Hendry, J., 77
Hephata, 115–20
Heracleous, L., 5, 6, 7, 14, 22, 25, 44, 47, 48,
  49, 53, 58, 103, 125, 157, 177, 178, 180,
  194, 210
Heritage, J., 126
hermeneutics. *See also* embodied metaphors
  double, 46, 49–50, 185
  meaning, 42–4, 50–4, 135
  validity of, 54–5
Hindmarsh, J., 126, 128
Hirsch, P. M., 25, 157, 179
Hocevar, S. P., 22
Hodgkinson, G. P., 27

Holyoak, K. J., 97
Hopwood, A. G., 76
Howe, M. A., 159, 168
Huff, A. S., 27, 124, 180, 184
Huizinga, J., 13, 94
Huxham, C., 27

identity, 83. *See also* strategy
    organizational, 181–2, 195–7
    work, 174–5
image schemata, 32–3, 34
imagination, 67, 73, 168–9
Imagination Lab Foundation,
inductive strategy, 25, 26, 47, 157, 180–1,
    194
Inhelder, B., 12, 94
innovation, 6, 7, 29, 94, 103, 117, 180
Inns, D., 26
inquiry
    analogically mediated, 30–2, 197
    and language, 105–6
interpretation. *See* sensemaking. *See also*
    hermeneutics
interpretivism. *See verstehen*
Isaacs, W., 104, 105–6, 107

Jacobs, C., 6, 14, 25, 48, 58, 95, 107, 123, 125,
    157, 164, 177, 180, 194
Jarzabkowski, P., 65, 76, 77, 180
Joas, H., 28
Johnson, G., 27, 76, 77, 180, 184
Johnson, M., 22, 23, 27, 28, 31, 33, 34, 35,
    81, 123, 124, 142, 152, 153, 157, 183,
    184, 197
Johnson, P., 180
Johnson-Laird, P. N., 103

Kant, I., 43, 71
Kaplan, R. S., 210
Karreman, D., 22
Kearney, R., 54
Keenoy, T., 24, 32, 123
Keizer, J. A., 158
Kets de Vries, M. F. R., 53
Kim, D. H., 104
Kokinov, B. N., 97
Krauss, R., 79
Kuhn. T., 104

Lakoff, G., 22, 23, 27, 31, 33, 34, 35, 81, 123,
    124, 142, 152, 153, 157, 183, 184, 197

Langley, A., 76
Law, K., 97
Lawson, B., 7–8
linguistic turn, 178–9
Linux, 68–9
Luckmann, T., 34, 183

MacIntosh, R., 92
Mackaness, W., 27
MacLean, D., 92
Makkreel, R. A., 46, 52
March, J. G., 6, 92
Markides, C., 5, 6, 103
Markman, A. B., 97
Marshak, R., 22, 25, 26, 47, 157, 158, 159, 194
Marzke, M., 71
Mayer, M. Smith, 193
McKinsey & Company, 6
McNamee, S., 104
Melin, L., 76, 180
mental model, 6, 103–11
Merleau-Ponty, M., 28, 34
metaphor. *See* embodied metaphors
metaphorical mapping, 26–7, 135–48,
    156–9
metaphorical organizational development,
    156–9
metaphorical reasoning, 26, 32, 165
Miller, D., 53
Miller, P., 76
Minsky, M. I., 103
Mintzberg, H., 5, 78, 81, 92, 180
model
    BASF, 1–3
    CellCo, 128–48, 185–95
    construction materials, 219
    Hephata, 115–20
    Orange, 82–7
    PackCo, 99–102
    Privatbank, 173–6
    Swiss Bank, 159–65
    UNICEF, 17–20
    virtual, 69–70
    VOLTIGO, 61–4
    World Vision New Zealand, 204–8
moderatum generalizations, 47
Molloy, E., 77, 193
Montgomery, J., 26
Moore, K., 32
Morgan, G., 23, 24, 25, 29, 43, 153, 158, 168,
    181

Norton, D. P., 210

Oliver, D., 195
Orange, 82–7
organization theory, 25, 35–8, 43–4, 181
Orlikowski, W. J., 76
Ortony, A., 97
Oswick, C., 22, 24, 26, 32, 123, 158

Packard, T., 25, 26, 159
Palmer, I., 24, 25, 158, 194
Palmer, R. E., 50
Pangarkar, N., 210
Papert, S., 80, 103
Petchenik, B. B., 27
Peters, T. J., 210
Pettigrew, A. M., 180
phenomenology, 28, 33–8
Phillips, J. R., 210
Phillips, N., 54
Piaget, J., 12, 79, 94
Piano, R., 69
Pinder, C. C., 22, 24
play, 73–4, 91–6. *See also* strategy.
    See also embodied metaphors.
    See also craftsmanship
Pondy, L. R., 26, 167
Porras, J., 158
Porter, M. E., 179, 180
positivism, 151–4, 183
Post, G. J. J., 158
practice turn, 76–8
Prasad, A., 53
Pratt, M., 181, 195
prejudices (in interpretation), 56
IHAG Privatbank, 173–6
Putnam, L., 123

Rafaeli, A., 181, 195
Rakova, M., 153
Randell, R
reasoning
    analogical, 28–33, 97–9
    metaphorical, 26, 32, 165
recursive embodied enactment, 81.
    See also craftsmanship. *See also*
    analogical reasoning
Regnér, P, 199
Ricoeur, P., 45, 53, 54, 55
Robinson, A. H., 27

Rohrer, T., 33, 124
Roos, J., 14, 32, 123, 125, 177, 180, 195

Sackmann, S., 25, 159
Salaman, G., 158
Samra-Fredericks, D., 180
Sandberg, J., 50
Santi, R., 177, 180
Sarnin, P., 27
Schatzki, T. R., 76
Schein, E. H., 56, 104, 105, 106–7, 108,
    185
Schiltz, M., 182
Schmidt, D. J., 52
Schon, D., 23
Schutz, M., 43
Schultz, M., 195
Seidl, D., 77
Sennett, R., 65, 66–7, 68–70, 71–2, 73–4
sensemaking, 12, 22–3, 32–3, 97–9, 135,
    157–9. *See also* embodied metaphors.
    See also ambiguity
serious play. *See* play
Shortell, S., 195
Silverman, D., 43
Silvers, R., 158
Sims, D., 31, 123, 219
social constructionism, 157, 183
Soroker, N., 79
source domain. *See* domain (source and
    target)
Stake, R. E., 122
Stalk, G., 179
Statler, M., 90, 93, 95, 98, 101–2, 125
steps
    design process, 8–12
    embodied metaphor process, 214–18
Stern, C., 179
Stopford, J. M., 6, 102
strategy. *See also* play. *See also* identity
    conventional, 4, 5, 7
    crafting, 65–81, 180–1, 184
    cultural-materialist approach, 66–7
    deductive, 25, 157
    inductive, 25, 26, 47, 157, 180–1, 194
    substitutes, 87
Sutton-Smith, B., 13, 94

target domain. *See* domain (source and
    target)

Tattersall, I., 79
Thachankary, T., 53
Thagard, P., 97
Thatchenkery, T. J., 22
thinking. *See also* cognitive sculpting
   and role of the body, 28–9
   design, 7
Thomas, G. F., 22
Tienari, J., 177, 180
Tsoukas, H., 22, 24, 97, 98

uncertainty. *See* ambiguity
UNICEF, 17–20

Vaara, E., 177, 180
Valikangas, L., 102
Van de Ven, A. H., 44
Vedder, B., 52
verstehen, 42, 44–5, 47–8, 150
Vince, R., 123, 158
virtual model, 69–70
VOLTIGO, 61–4

Vosniadou, S., 97
Vygotsky, L. S., 94

Waterman, R. H., 210
Weber, M., 43, 44, 45, 46, 150
Weick, K. E., 13, 27, 29–30, 81, 87, 94, 157,
   165
Wenger, E., 103
Wenkert-Olenik, D., 79
Whetten, D., 195
Whittington, R., 65, 76, 77, 177, 180, 193
Wikipedia, 68–9
Williams, M., 47
Wilson, F., 79
Winnicott, D. W., 94
Wirtz, J., 210
Wittgenstein, L., 22, 51
World Vision New Zealand, 204–8
Worren, N., 32
Wright Mills, C., 68

Yin, R., 47, 122